This book is a quantitative study into the influence of the process of industrialization on the nature and strength of family relationships in a Dutch community between 1850 and 1920. There are two main sets of theoretical focal points. The first one is structural-functionalist theory assuming an inevitable causality between the more loosely knit nuclear family system and industrial society. The second set consists of historical assumptions about the resilience and tenacity of family relationships. The study makes use of the unique and unusually rich source of Dutch population registers, so that successive cohorts of the families can be tracked down from the formation of the family household until its dissolution. Family aspects such as extended kin co-residence, family care for the elderly and the pattern by which children break away from their parents are examined in the light of the transformation of the local society. The study closely relates aspects of family and household with the social processes characteristic of an industrializing society, such as increasing rates of social and geographical mobility and the shift of production from the home into the factory. Results reveal a striking continuity in the strength of nineteenth-century family relations despite the gradual but profound process of social change surrounding these families. Changes in behavioural patterns did occur, however, under the influence of changes in demographic rates, regional geographical mobility systems and local developments in the housing market. Nevertheless, these changes cannot be taken as a weakening of family relationships.

Family and social change

*Cambridge Studies in Population, Economy and
Society in Past Time 21*

Series Editors

PETER LASLETT, ROGER SCHOFIELD and E.A. WRIGLEY
ESRC Cambridge Group for the History of Population and Social Structure

and DANIEL SCOTT SMITH
University of Illinois at Chicago

Recent work in social, economic and demographic history has revealed much that was previously obscure about societal stability and change in the past. It has also suggested that crossing the conventional boundaries between these branches of history can be very rewarding.

This series will exemplify the value of interdisciplinary work of this kind, and will include books on topics such as family, kinship and neighbourhood; welfare provision and social control; work and leisure; migration; urban growth; and legal structures and procedures, as well as more familiar matters. It will demonstrate that, for example, anthropology and economics have become as close intellectual neighbours to history as have political philosophy or biography.

For a full list of titles in the series, please see end of book

Family and social change

The household as a process in an industrializing community

ANGÉLIQUE JANSSENS

Nijmegen University

CAMBRIDGE
UNIVERSITY PRESS

Published by the Press Syndicate of the University of Cambridge
The Pitt Building, Trumpington Street, Cambridge CB2 1RP
40 West 20th Street, New York, NY 10011–4211, USA
10 Stamford Road, Oakleigh, Melbourne 3166, Australia

First published 1993

Printed in Great Britain at the University Press, Cambridge

A catalogue record for this book is available from the British Library

Library of Congress cataloguing in publication data

Janssens, Angelique.
Family and social change:
the household as a process in an industrializing community/
Angelique Janssens.
p.   cm. – (Cambridge studies in population, economy, and society in past time ; 21)
Includes bibliographcal references.
ISBN 0 521 41611 6
1. Family – Netherlands – Tilburg – History – 19th century.
2. Industry – Social aspects – Netherlands – Tilburg. 3. Tilburg (Netherlands) – History
– 19th century. 4. Tilburg (Netherlands – Social conditions. I. Title. II. Series.
HQ635.15.T52J36   1993
306.85'09492'45 – dc20 92-37612 CIP

ISBN 0 521 41611 6 hardback

To my parents Henk and Annie Janssens

Contents

Figures

Tables

Appendices

Preface

Until recently, the field of family history was heavily dominated by work on the British, French or American family. In the last few years other countries, for instance in the south or east of Europe or even Asia, are speedily catching up with the pioneers. The Netherlands, however, appear to be suffering from a persistent time lag in the study of the family and the household. This is regrettable when we consider its regional variety in social, economic and cultural development combined with the exceptional richness of its sources. In particular, the population registers, which were in use in The Netherlands from 1849 onwards, are of great value to the historian of the family. These registers allow us to observe households and families, even those belonging to the poorest section of the population, on a day-to-day basis over long time spans. They therefore allow the historian to meet the widely proclaimed requirement of a longitudinal perspective on family and household. However, the registers not only provide vital demographic information but when combined with additional sources they also yield a wealth of social and economic data on individuals and families.

This study is a first attempt to analyze the structure and composition of the household during industrialization in the Netherlands from the population registers. It attempts to provide an insight into the effect of macro-level changes on micro-level processes involving the family. Or, stated differently, it seeks to assess the strength of the bonds between families and their extended kin as well as those linking parents and children in times of turbulent social and economic change. To borrow a phrase from Charles Tilly, I have tried to answer the question which in a more general form is basic to social history: how did these families live through the big changes of their time? I hope to have made clear in this book that families and individuals are not just cast and moulded by the great forces of history, or ruled by economic principles of behaviour as social scientists sometimes seem to think. They bring something to it of their own. Hopefully this study will produce some enthusiasm among historians for the use of this type of data so that in retrospect it will only prove to be the first in a long line of longitudinal family studies based on the Dutch population registers.

This book is a revised version of my PhD thesis which I completed at the Department of Social and Economic History of Nijmegen University. Dissertation projects are usually rather solitary enterprises and the present one is no exception to that rule. Nevertheless, it owes a great deal to several people for its successful completion. I would like to thank the Netherlands Organisation for Scientific Research (NWO) for the grant that enabled me to carry out this project; thanks are also due to Piet van Slooten who has been a valuable source of practical help and advice over the years. However, it is no exaggeration to say that without the encouragement of Professor Paul Klep I would not even have begun this work. During the course of this project I have benefited considerably from his advice in pointing out the various pitfalls in my reasoning. Onno Boonstra at various stages offered essential help: he advised me on data-file structure and wrote some of the more complex programs I used to analyze the data. The staff of the Netherlands Textile Museum in Tilburg have been generous with their facilities. Jan Esman, P.J.M. van Gorp and Ton Wagemakers all played an essential role in my efforts to unravel the various mysteries of the Tilburg weavers' books. The Tilburg Municipal Archive generously offered facilities and hospitality for many a day in the past few years; my thanks in particular go to Frans van Zutphen for his continuing advice and assistance. Ali de Regt, Theo Engelen, Chris Gordon and Peter Laslett read parts of the manuscript and provided me with many wise and helpful criticisms. Chris Wilson read the entire manuscript conscienciously, improving it greatly in matters of style and language. Richard Wall played an essential role. He not only provided me with helpful comments on my text, but also persuaded me to offer the manuscript to the editors of this series for publication.

One of my greatest debts, however, is to my parents without whose family history all this would not have been possible. Thanks are due not only for their continued trust and support, but also for their active involvement. My father painstakingly carried out a check of the population registers for missing births in almost 200 family histories and my mother helped me to master the hundreds of copies of the population register with which I returned from the archive.

Nijmegen, January 1992

1

Family and industrialization

Industrialization is widely seen as the most important social and economic change of the last 200 years; it is frequently credited with the power to modify or destroy any pre-existing social arrangement that stands in its way. In particular, there is often assumed to be an adversarial relationship between the traditional extended family and the process of industrialization. In this chapter I examine this long-held belief, focusing on the origins of this idea and the contributions to it by the great theorist of structural-functionalism, the American sociologist Talcott Parsons. I shall then try to trace the formulation of new hypotheses resulting from empirical historical research concerning the relation of family to industrial society. After that I proceed to the formulation of the questions that have guided the present research.

1.1 Traditional family theory

Until the later 1960s virtually all historians and sociologists subscribed to the popular tradition of the large preindustrial extended family.[1] Before industrialization and urbanization, it was believed, people lived together in large households with great numbers of relatives and servants. The world we lost as a result of industrialization con-

---

[1] Unless stated otherwise, the terms 'family' and 'household' are used alternately in this text to refer to the same phenomenon: a co-residential group sharing in a number of important activities (e.g. production and consumption) and consisting for the most or the entire part of people related by blood. By 'nuclear family' or 'nuclear family household' is meant a household consisting of one or two parents with or without their unmarried offspring. 'Extended family' or 'extended family household' refers to those households that in addition to nuclear family members contain any other kin. Both types of household may be augmented by live-in servants or other unrelated individuals.

1

sisted of households engaged in a wide range of functions of which
the economic function was most important. The household was the
locus of many productive activities in which all household members
participated. Individual aspirations in the traditional household were
made subject to the stability and the material interests of the family
group. Industrialization, it was asserted, resulted in the disintegration of the family group into smaller units of nuclear families consisting of parents and their unmarried children. The family was robbed
of all of its productive economic functions to become a unit of consumption. Romantic love replaced economic calculation between
husband and wife. The ideology of individualism replaced patriarchy;
thus greatly affecting the relationship between generations.

All serious discussion of the demise of the preindustrial extended
family in Europe ultimately is shaped by the ideas put forward by
Frédéric Le Play, one of the founding fathers of modern empirical
social science.[2] Writing in the second half of the nineteenth century
he described three ideal family types showing differing degrees of
stability. The patriarchal family type, which was found according to
Le Play among nomadic communities in the East, encompassed all
male descendants of the family head and their associated depen-
dents. They all lived and worked together as a unit under the
absolute authority of the father who represented the interests of the
family as a whole. The patriarchal family, laying great emphasis on
authority and lineage, was dominated by a spirit of tradition which
stifled change. The second family type elaborated by Le Play was the
stem family, which he considered typical of *some* European peasant
communities. It consisted of the parents, the unmarried children and
the family of one married son, the heir, chosen by the father to
continue the family property after his death. The heir's siblings had
the right to stay on in the household of their brother as long as they
remained unmarried. Alternatively, they could leave and strike out
on their own. In this way a balance existed between paternal authority and the freedom of the children, between stability and mobility.

Le Play painted a nostalgic picture of the stem family in which
harmony ruled and all members worked together in a shared sense of
solidarity and self-sufficiency within the family. However, Le Play
saw industrialization and commercialization as destroying the stem

---

[2] Le Play, *L'Organisation*, see pp. 3–28; for further information on Le Play, as well as
translations of some of his work, see: Bodard Silver, *Frédéric Le Play*, pp. 76–80 and
259–80; Anderson, *Approaches*, pp. 22–3; Kloek, *Gezinshistorici*, pp. 21–2. Le Play was
not the only writer on these subjects at the time. Similar notions were found in
Riehl, *Die Naturgeschichte*, see vol. 3, pp. 145–65.

family because its economic basis, the family property, had been removed. Family life disintegrated because children were no longer prepared to stay on in the parental household and left at early ages leaving ageing parents to fend for themselves. This was further aggravated by the abolition of impartible inheritance, leading to the splintering of the family property which had to be parcelled out equally among all children. These developments created the unstable family type which was centered around the marital couple: it was created at their marriage and dissolved again upon their death. Children left the household when they married or possibly earlier. The bonds between generations were lost, thereby threatening the stability of the entire social order.

Although Le Play nowhere actually stated that the stem family was the predominant family form in preindustrial Europe, his writings gave rise to the idea that the history of the family in Europe involved a linear development from large extended family households towards a small nuclear family unit isolated from kin and community. Most social scientists cited urbanization and industrialization as principal factors to account for this development of 'progressive nuclearization'.[3] This development created a sharp dichotomy between the preindustrial or agrarian family on the one hand and the industrial or modern family on the other.

In the 1950s influential structural-functionalist theories were formulated on the basis of these traditional convictions within family history and sociology.[4] These theories tried to explain the historical development of the family in terms of a process of structural differentiation. A society undergoing modern economic change will necessarily differentiate its kinship-based social structure. Non-kinship structures like the state, the church, schools, factories and labour unions will take over functions that were traditionally maintained by the kinship system.[5]

The family system, itself part of the process of functional specializa-

[3] Berkner, 'Recent research', see especially p. 401.
[4] Morgan, *Social theory*, contains a chapter on the varieties of functionalism. Most of the following is based on the writings of Talcott Parsons: Parsons, *The social system*; Parsons and Bales, *The family*; Parsons, 'The kinship system'. A short summary on the nature of the modern family and its relation to the social structure can be found in Parsons, 'The social structure'. For a short discussion of Parsons' family theory see: Rodman, 'Talcott Parsons' view'.
[5] Parsons and Bales, *The family*, p. 9. The process of change of the social system conforms to the principle of structural differentiation. Change in the social system initiates changes in social subsystems such as the family. All of those processes of change take the formal shape of a process of structural differentiation. For a historical application of this theory see: Smelser, *Social change*.

tion, develops towards a system of small nuclear family units. This modern type of family is considered to be structurally isolated from kin and neighbours, to have an intensive, 'hot-house' type of family life, and to observe a strict role segregation between husband and wife. Only two functions have been left to the modern family.[6] First, the family is the main socializing agent of new members of society. The seclusion of the nuclear family guarantees a slow, step-by-step socialization process through which the child is prepared to cope with a complex, functional and fragmented type of society. The family's second function is to regulate the emotional stability of its adult members by offering a safe harbour from the hostile world outside. This has become necessary because of the breakdown of extended kinship relations and the tensions which result from functioning in a complex world.

For structural-functionalists like Talcott Parsons the family's main characteristic was to be found in its structurally isolated position in relation to more extended kin.[7] All rules of modern industrial society provide for the formation of nuclear families only. People may actually want to form all sorts of extended family groups, but they get no help from the rules governing the social system. Moreover, Parsons states that the most stringent kinship obligations are restricted to the nuclear family, thus isolating it in a relative sense from wider kinship units.[8] In other words, kinship obligations to the nuclear family take precedence over obligations to kin outside it.

Crucial to structural-functionalist thinking is the supposed 'structural fit' between the nuclear family and industrial society. By virtue of its particular characteristics the modern family is thought to be functionally adapted to the demands posed by the industrial system. Or to put it more succinctly, the modern economic system necessitates the isolated nuclear family.

Why is this so? One of the most important characteristics of modern industrial society is its need for relatively high rates of social and geographical mobility of individuals. The adult male worker must be free to move at the behest of the economic system. While on the one hand individual social and geographical mobility is hampered by extensive family solidarity, it is also believed that extensive family ties will be weakened or destroyed with the social and geographical mobility of individual family members.[9]

---

[6] Parsons and Bales, *The family*, pp. 16–22.
[7] Ibid., pp. 10–11.
[8] Parsons, *The social system*, p. 186.
[9] Parsons, 'The social structure', pp. 192–3.

In traditional societies the family group coordinates a number of shared economic and productive activities which tie the individual to his family group through mutual occupational, property and status interests. Thus, in order to make possible the mobility of the individual it was necessary not only to limit kinship obligations to nuclear family members, but also to strip the family group of its economic functions. Only after production had been taken away from the household could the segregation of the modern family from the economic system be achieved. Parsons counted the farmers among one of the notable exceptions in post-war America to his ideal family type precisely because they had not yet fully realized the segregation between the family and the occupational sphere.[10]

This segregation of the modern family from the economy is related to the existence of opposing value systems in both. The successful growth of the industrial system was made possible by the adoption of values which Parsonian theory calls 'universalism' and 'achievement'.[11] Achievement refers to the belief that people should not be categorized on the basis of qualities inherent to them or on the basis of their relationship to a particular person. Rather, people should be differentiated between in terms of their achieved qualities. Universalism tells us to treat all members of a particular social, occupational or any other category in a similar way, irrespective of their relationship to us. For instance, taxi drivers should not distinguish between passengers who are kin and those who are not in the fares they charge.

It is evident that within the family system other values prevail. A father treats his own daughter differently from all other daughters, which means that the father acts upon 'particularistic' values instead of universalistic ones. Also his behaviour towards his daughter is solely dependent upon her inherent quality of being his daughter, and should not turn on achieved qualities such as her education or on the social position she has achieved. Which means that he is behaving on the basis of 'ascriptive' values.

The 'conflict of values' which would ensue between the family system and the occupational system is solved in the Parsonian system by means of the double segregation of the nuclear family.[12] First of all, the nuclear family is segregated from the wider extended kin group, and, second, within the family there is the role segregation between the husband-worker and the wife fulfilling the family oriented role. Interference between the two conflicting value systems is avoided by

[10] Parsons, 'The kinship system', p. 185.
[11] Parsons, *The social system*, pp. 182–91.
[12] Ibid., p. 186.

limiting family solidarity to the nuclear family in which only one
person, the husband, is supposed to assume roles in both the economic and the family system. In this way family values do not interfere
with the world of work while economic values cannot intrude into
family life. By differentiating sharply between the world of work and
the world of family life Parsonian theory contributed strongly to what
is now believed to be 'the myth of separate worlds'.[13]

All this renders the nuclear family functionally adapted to industrial society, or in other words there exists a 'structural fit' between
the family and the economic system. Families organized on structural-functionalist terms are best fitted to meet the requirements of
the industrial system. Consequently, these families will do better,
career-wise, than extended family groups. Individuals and families
most mobile and successful in social and economic respects will form
the nuclear type of household. Moreover, those individuals living in
nuclear family units will be best equipped to reach the higher placed
positions in life. A functionally adapted family system will also
permit individuals to be mobile in a geographical sense. Hence,
geographical mobility and extended family groups are considered to
be mutually exclusive. Geographically mobile indivduals will not,
and cannot, live in extended family households while those living in
nuclear family households will be free to move to where the economic
system needs them.[14]

Clearly, structural-functionalist theory considers the functional
adaptation of the family system to industrial society as being a positive one. Functional family adaptation has made possible industrial
development, which leads necessarily to the conclusion that residential extended family groups would slow down or perhaps even
prevent modern economic change.[15] Although today few adherents
of the traditional point of view in family history remain, the influence
of Parsonian ideas continues to be strong.[16]

[13] Pleck, 'Two worlds'.
[14] These ideas soon reached Dutch empirical sociology. In his article on 'The extended
family in transition', P. Taietz examines the frequency of social visits to their parents
of farmers' sons who were socially and/or geographically mobile as opposed to those
who were not. Taietz's research was carried out in 1958 in the eastern part of the
Netherlands, which at that time was still strongly characterized by kin co-residence
among agrarian households. Results indicated that social mobility as a determining
factor was only relevant for sons living in the village, while geographical mobility in
all instances reduced the frequency of social contacts between parents and sons.
[15] Parsons, 'The social structure', p. 192.
[16] See e.g. Degler, *At odds*. See also T.K. Hareven's review of this book in *Journal of
Social History*, 17 (1983–4), pp. 339–44; Kertzer, Schiaffino, 'Industrialization', pp.
371–2.

Structural-functionalist family theory has been heavily criticized from various angles.[17] Of direct interest to the present research is the opposition concerning the structural isolation of the nuclear family in modern society. Post-war sociological research among American and British families discovered elaborate patterns of aid and assistance between the respective nuclear families of parents and their married offspring.[18] Moreover, it was not possible to establish a clear negative influence of social or geographical mobility, although the latter did appear to lessen the frequency of social contacts between parents and children. Structurally speaking, the modern family conforms to the nuclear type, but when focusing on family relations the kinship system allows for elaborate or intensive extended family networks. Litwak coined the term 'modified extended family' to describe the family patterns he had found.[19]

However, this type of criticism only involved minor adjustments to Parsons' theory. The 'classical extended family', which refers to the traditional residential extended family, was still thought of as being irreconcilable with the industrial system. Parsons never saw any immediate cause in these criticisms to change his theoretical views. In his answer to his critics he stressed that the help patterns they found between parents and the families of their children were not contradictory to his proposition of the relative structural isolation of the nuclear family.[20] Most cases, Parsons indicated, concerned financial aid from parents to children which remained strictly limited to the private sphere. Hence, the segregation between the economic system and the family system remained.

It would seem to follow logically from Parsonian theory that those social classes or groups which are best adapted to the industrial system should reflect most closely the ideal of the nuclear family.[21] Obviously, in the modern industrial system the middle and upper classes are by definition more successful; they dominate the system and direct its future. However, the structural-functionalist sociologist William J. Goode had already pointed out that in most societies family behaviour among the higher social classes is less close to the ideal

---

[17] For a discussion of the various issues see: Harris, *The family*; and Morgan, *Social theory*, pp. 39–48.

[18] Litwak, 'Occupational mobility'; Litwak, 'Geographic mobility'; Sussman, 'The isolated nuclear family'; Sussman and Burchinal, 'The kin family network'; Young and Willmott, *Family*.

[19] Used by Litwak, 'Occupational mobility', p. 10.

[20] Parsons, 'Reply'.

[21] On deviant cases in different social groups see: Parsons, 'The social structure', pp. 180–1.

than among the lower social classes.[22] Higher social classes maintain the most elaborate extended kin network, they exercise most control over the career and marriage choices of their children and are most likely to give and to receive aid and assistance from relatives. The lower-class family pattern is that of the nuclear family. They are the least encumbered with extended family relations, enjoy least family stability and family-based economic and material security. Goode compares their freedom from kin to their 'freedom' to sell their labour in the market. They are not hampered by the weight of extended kin relations because there are no kin who will interest themselves suffi-ciently in their actions. The higher social classes, on the other hand, have the most to lose; they are backed by resourceful kin networks and will therefore resist the system's undermining pressures. It is precisely these networks that enable them to make the most of the opportunities offered by industrialization. Consequently, they will let go of their family ties more slowly, so that changes in upper-class family patterns will occur in a later phase of the industrialization process.

Parsons himself considered the modern nuclear family to be most conspicuously developed among the urban middle classes of post-war America. This particular social group in his view was the clearest representative of that modern and mobile industrial society with which the nuclear family was in such close structural harmony. Among the exceptions Parsons listed agricultural families in which, as we have seen, the segregation between the family and the occupa-tional system was still incomplete. Some lower-class families, charac-terized by unstable marriages and a mother-centered family structure, constituted a second type of deviance from the main pat-tern. Finally, Parsons considered some elite groups to form the third exception to his rule. In these aristocratic-like families the importance of ancestry and lineage, and the ancestral home, were thought to promote continuity of intergenerational kinship solidarity.[23]

The idea that the history of the family can be adequately described in terms of a unilinear development from large extended family households towards the small household of the nuclear family is also found among historians. One of the earliest and most prominent of them was Philippe Ariès in his famous and influential history of childhood.[24] In this work he also applied the idea of differentiation or specialization of the family, albeit implicitly. Ariès depicted an idyllic

---

[22] See chapter 1 of Goode, *World revolution*; Goode, 'Industrialization'.
[23] Parsons, 'The kinship system', pp. 185–6.
[24] Ariès, *L'Enfant*; English edition: *Centuries*.

image of the traditional household in which no distinctions were made between family members or kin, visitors or servants. These traditional households were busy centres of a rich social life in which people of different social standing could meet and which formed an ideal place in which to socialize children.

Ariès saw the rise of the modern nuclear family concurrent with the emergence of a prolonged childhood and the institutionalization of education. The modern family was 'closed-off' from society so that an isolated and intensive family life could come into existence. However, from Ariès' point of view the modern family deprives the child of the possibility of taking part in grown-up life from an early start. The child is denied a wealth of life experience necessary to function optimally in the adult world. This makes the nuclear family less fit to function as a place of socialization. Through Ariès' eyes we witness a process of disintegration taking place rather than one of positive adaptation. Like most historians of the school Ariès belonged to, termed the 'sentiments approach' by Michael Anderson, he placed this development first among the higher social classes after which it slowly trickled down to the working classes.[25]

It is clear that Ariès' position is diametrically opposed to the Parsonian when it comes to the functionality of the modern family. Its virtues to Parsons are vices to Ariès. The family's specialization and separation from the outside world, which for Parsons are a necessary condition to realize a step-by-step socialization of children, are seen by Ariès as imposing serious limitations on human possibilities.

Inspired by the conflicting opinions of Parsons and Ariès, the American sociologist Richard Sennett investigated a number of middle-class families in Chicago in the second half of the nineteenth century.[26] These families all lived in one particular neighbourhood of Chicago in a period of great industrial and urban expansion. Sennett examined their family life and the social and economic circumstances with which they had to cope. It is his contention that the rapid process of transformation the city was undergoing at the time promoted an intensive, 'hot-house' type of family life within the group of nuclear families. Family members fled into the safe harbour of their own family life from fear of the rapidly changing and competitive world outside. Sennett argues that the smaller nuclear family type offered a better breeding ground for this defensive reaction against the city than the larger extended families. The latter were charac-

---

[25] Anderson, *Approaches*, pp. 39–64. Major works in this area besides Ariès' *Centuries of childhood* are: Shorter, *The making*; Stone, *The Family*; Flandrin, *Families*.
[26] Sennett, *Families*.

terized by a more 'open', competitive character: most of them had more working adults present, which made it difficult to prevent outside values from penetrating the family. The nuclear family however made it possible for the husband-breadwinner, as the sole person with connections to the occupational world outside, to retreat from the competitive sphere of work and submerge himself in the warm bosom of the family, in which he could negate the necessity to compete and strive upwards.

Thus, the nuclear family became a defence mechanism against the city with severe consequences for those involved. The heads of nuclear families were not able to maintain or improve their social and economic position because they had virtually retreated from what they considered to be the frightening and hostile world outside. This made them unable to fulfil a role model for their children. The children in these closed, introverted families were raised in a climate whose values were antithetical to the rest of society. Non-competitive, ascriptive values were characteristic of the family while 'outside' competition and universal values were dominant. This situation made them ill-prepared for adult life. In their turn the children experienced difficulties in getting ahead in life. The non-competitive, 'hot-house' family life of the nuclear family was responsible for its inadequate operation in society. On these grounds Sennett dismissed the functional relation between the nuclear family and industrial society.[27]

1.2   Historical revisionism

A few years before Sennett published his Chicago research another myth in family history had been exposed. In 1972 Peter Laslett and his colleagues from the Cambridge Group published their *Household and Family in Past Time*.[28] On the basis of English census-like listings from the period 1574 to 1821 these scholars asserted that the nuclear family had been the dominant family type long before any industrial development. Laslett and his colleagues reacted against generations of social scientists who, on the basis of the writings of Le Play, had presumed that the stem family was the predominant type of family form for centuries before the onset of industrialization.[29] The scholars

---

[27] In a review of this study (by R. Lubove in *Journal of Social History* 5 (1972), pp. 388–91) Sennett was criticized for not having substantiated in any way the objective basis for the fear against the city. In other words, Sennett was relying too heavily on unproven psychological assumptions in trying to make his case against the nuclear family.

[28] Laslett and Wall (eds.), *Household*.

[29] See P. Laslett's introduction in *Household*, specifically pp. 1–23.

of the Cambridge Group insisted on a small European family of simple structure from the Middle Ages onwards. Consequently, major shifts in the past centuries such as industrialization and urbanization were thought to have had little or no effect whatsoever on the structure of the family and the household. The old hypothesis of the unilinear development from preindustrial extended family households to industrial family nuclearization was replaced by a new one stressing continuity in family form and structure over many centuries. In doing so they created a new paradigm, which some scholars saw as showing, at the very least, 'an imbalanced emphasis'.[30]

The Cambridge Group research was the take-off for a long line of studies further undermining all previously accepted tenets concerning the preindustrial European family. One of these studies by Van der Woude indicated that as early as the seventeenth century the family in the Western provinces of the Dutch republic had been extremely small and simple in composition. While Laslett had found coresiding kin in about 10% of the English households, this was the case for only 3.6% of the households in the Noorderkwartier. The mean household size in the province of Holland was found to have been 3.7 compared to 4.7 for England.[31] Van der Woude related the small numbers of extended families he found to the fact that livestock farming, the predominant economic activity, in contrast to arable farming was labour-extensive and favoured an individualistic spirit. The overwhelming evidence for the long history of the nuclear family contained in these and other studies led some researchers to proclaim the nuclear family to be one of the necessary preconditions for modernization or industrialization.[32] This line of reasoning implicitly finds its roots in structural-functionalist notions concerning the relation between family and industrial society. Here again the nuclear family is associated with the dynamics and the mobility of the industrial system.

The work of Laslett and his colleagues has provoked a considerable amount of criticism.[33] To begin with, this focused on methodological aspects.[34] Laslett's concept of the household relegated it to a static phenomenon. His critics pointed out that the developmental cycle of

[30] Levine, 'Industrialization', especially p. 169.

[31] van der Woude, 'Variations', pp. 309–13.

[32] Greenfield, 'Industrialization'. This idea can also be found in the work of Dutch historians. See for instance: Peeters, Dresen-Coenders and Brandenbarg (eds.), *Vijf eeuwen gezinsleven*, especially p. 14.

[33] Critical reviews may be found by R.T. Vann in *Journal of Social History*, 8 (1974–5), pp. 105–18 and T.K. Hareven in *History and Theory*, 14 (1975), pp. 242–51. See especially Berkner, 'The use and misuse'; and Anderson, 'Some problems'. A useful critique of methodology can also be found in the appendix of Kertzer, *Family life*, pp. 199–210.

[34] Methodological problems will be discussed in greater detail in chapter 3.

this household had to be taken into account as this played a crucial role in determining a household's structure. Moreover, Laslett had given scant attention to the influence of demographic factors, such as the structurally high level of mortality in preindustrial Europe. A mean life expectancy of forty combined with first marriage at the mean age of twenty would severely reduce the chance of finding extended family households. Furthermore, social and economic factors had been disregarded. A household's social standing, the head's profession, the specific social and economic context in which families operate were thought to have far-reaching effects on family structure.

More importantly even, Laslett and colleagues appeared to some to lose themselves in technological innovations and empirical matters of great detail without considering theoretical criticism. They went ahead with great zest to undermine empirically all previous theoretical frameworks of traditional family historians and sociologists, but had nothing with which to replace them. Is it really plausible to believe that the family remained unchanged from the Middle Ages until the twentieth century? That all major social and economic changes of the past centuries left the family untouched? Could it be possible that the family played a structural role in the bringing about of these changes? Hans Medick perhaps best voiced these concerns when he wrote that Laslett convincingly refuted the old hypothesis of the preindustrial extended family, but that this:

did not lead him to the construction of a substantial theory which would have allowed a more precise location of household and family as functional elements and social-structural factors in the genesis of industrial capitalism.[35]

The work of the Cambridge Group in its turn prompted numerous studies showing that the European peasant family experience was not as uniform as Laslett had originally suggested. Family forms in eastern Europe were widely different from those found in the northwest, whilst even within what is considered to be western Europe a great deal of regional variation existed.[36] Even within so small a country as the Netherlands regional variation in family forms was extensive, lasting until after World War II.[37] As Kertzer has shown, family practices in a number of regions in southern Europe are different again from those found elsewhere. His book on the Italian family provides an effective challenge to Laslett's thesis that western

---

[35] Medick, 'The proto-industrial family economy ', pp. 292–3.
[36] See e.g. the contributions in Netting, Wilk and Arnould (eds.), *Households*; or Czap, 'The perennial multiple household', on household structure in Russia.
[37] Klep, 'Het huishouden'; van der Woude, 'Variations'; Hofstee and Kooy, 'Traditional household'; Ishwaran, *Family life*, p. 39.

Europe has been characterized everywhere by small and simple households.[38] In southern Europe too, family forms did not follow uniform patterns.[39] In fact, the diversity in household forms in different areas and periods of European history has proved to be so great that no single law or mechanism governing family behaviour can be detected.

In 1983, in a new collection of articles on the historical household Peter Laslett and colleagues acknowledged most points of criticism and sought to adapt their approach accordingly.[40] For instance, much more attention is given to the influence of occupation on household structure and to the variations in the European social structure of past times. In addition, many contributors to this volume attempted to incorporate a dynamic perspective in one way or another in their work. As Sieder and Mitterauer argue, the 'importance of the developmental approach to the history of family life and to the changing structure of the individual family during its life cycle would now appear to be undisputed'.[41] However, they also show that the dynamic perspective is not without its problems. I will return more extensively to these and other methodological issues in chapter 3.

Important new insights concerning the role of the family during industrialization, an important problem already indicated by Medick, emerged from Michael Anderson's study of family structure in nineteenth-century Preston, Lancashire.[42] This study originated from criticism of those structural-functionalist and modernization theories that connected the formation of nuclear family structures to the process of industrialization. Anderson felt this to be contradictory to the finding that large sections of the modern British labouring class maintained an elaborate and intensive family network.[43] His case study, chiefly based on census material, shows that industrialization can actually lead to an increase in the incidence of extended families.

Anderson found that interdependency between kin members as well as the possibility of living with kin increased during industrialization and urbanization. In contrast to the rural situation people were more dependent on kin in order to overcome a number

---

[38] Kertzer, *Family life*.
[39] See the articles on the Iberian family in the first number of vol. 13 of *Journal of Family History*.
[40] Wall, Robin and Laslett, *Family forms*; criticism remained, see: Kertzer, 'Future directions'.
[41] Sieder and Mitterauer, 'The reconstruction', p. 309.
[42] Anderson, *Family structure*; review by Katz: *Journal of Social History* 7 (1973–4), pp. 86–92.
[43] Young and Willmott, *Family*; Bott, *Family*.

of 'critical life situations'. Among these were the obvious problems associated with urban industrial life: illness, old age, and death, lack of employment or housing. Moreover, young mothers working long hours in the Preston textile factories had to rely on kin for child-care services during working hours. These and other industrial hardships promoted the formation of extended family households, especially among young couples and the elderly.

In his book Anderson makes use of exchange theory. This specific theoretical orientation 'postulates that people engage in a kind of mental bookkeeping before they enter into relations'.[44] In Preston kin relations were taken up and maintained because it was felt to be beneficial to all parties involved. Indeed, nineteenth-century Preston offered no alternative to kin relations in helping to adapt to the tremendous impact of the process of social change. Kin relations actually appeared to be highly functional. Young migrants to the city making use of kin relations found steady jobs more quickly than migrants who did not. In Anderson's account of family and industrialization the extended family features as a positive and functional adaptation to industrial life instead of being a dysfunctional, deviant case.

Anderson's claim that the rise of the extended family in the nineteenth century was related to the hardships of industrial city life has recently been challenged by Steven Ruggles.[45] In his book *Prolonged Connections* he argues that extended family living arrangements in the nineteenth century were strongly related to a higher social and economic position. We must therefore consider the formation of extended family households to be a luxury affair. His conclusion is based on a statistical analysis of five samples taken from American and English census manuscripts at different points in time during the nineteenth century. Next, on the basis of computer simulations Ruggles demonstrates the decisive impact of demographic factors on the increase in the number of extended family households during the nineteenth century. Declining mortality and an earlier age at marriage provided the necessary demographic conditions which, combined with a rise in the standard of living, enabled people to form extended family households more frequently than before. Moreover, on the basis of a demographic micro-simulation model, he also suggests that the relative absence of extended family households in eighteenth-century England must be attributed to demographic constraints. High

---

[44] Katz, 'Essay review', in: *Journal of Social History*, 7 (1973–4), pp. 86–92.
[45] Ruggles, *Prolonged connections*. See the critical review by: J.E. Smith, 'Method and confusion in the study of the household', *Historical Methods*, 22 (1989), pp. 57–60.

levels of mortality prevented the formation of household structures other than the nuclear family. By taking this stand Ruggles challenges the results of the advanced statistical study by Wachter and others which had indicated that whatever residency rules were adopted in past societies they cannot in any way have been crucially dependent on demographic constraints.[46] While Ruggles' ideas are stimulating, others have seen his simulation model as containing some potentially serious flaws.[47]

Ruggles' analysis might at first glance suggest that from the eighteenth to the nineteenth century residential preferences had not changed. After all, in both periods people preferred living in extended family households; but the eighteenth-century demographic regime made this impossible or difficult to realize. However, this is not the case. Residential preferences probably did change,[48] according to Ruggles, in the sense that the incentive to form extended family households in the nineteenth century was different from the preindustrial period. Preindustrial extended families were formed to ensure the preservation of the family property and a steady supply of labour to work the farm. However, the shift of employment away from agriculture towards industrial wage labour not only removed the economic incentives towards extended family formation. It also diminished earlier economic constraints: the low level of real incomes. The shift in employment patterns and the resulting higher real incomes enabled people to afford the luxury of extended family households.

As Ruggles himself rightly remarks, this does not tell the whole story. His analysis provides information on structural changes creating the conditions that made extended families possible. But we do not know *why* nineteenth-century families formed extended households once they could afford to do so. The answer to this question, Ruggles asserts, cannot be found in explanations based on demography or economy. Instead we must look for traces of a process of cultural change to explain the rise in extended families. Whether in his opinion this process of cultural change is autonomous or in some way related to processes of economic or social change is not stated

[46] Wachter, Hammel and Laslett, *Statistical studies.*
[47] See the review of Ruggles' study cited in note 45 above.
[48] The phrase 'residential preferences' is rather confusing here. Ruggles does not refer to an individual's personal preference for a certain residential arrangement. Residential preferences relates to all influences, cultural, economic, social, political or psychological, on residential arrangements with the sole exception of demographic determinants.

explicitly; but he does not appear to think so. On the whole, Ruggles has a clear dislike of economic explanations because of their function-alist character.

The work of Tamara Hareven on migrant families in the textile community of Manchester, USA, during the first three decades of this century has strong similarities with Anderson's Preston study.[49] Hareven also set out to disprove structural-functionalist notions of family and industrialization. She encountered the existence of large and intensive family networks among the French-Canadian migrants to the city. In Canada a system of extended family households had remained alive, and many of its features survived after relocation to Manchester. These migrants used their kin relations as an important tool in the battle of daily life. They helped each other out with jobs, child-care, illness and death. The family network also functioned as a migration agency, providing stepping stones for new arrivals from Quebec. Family and factory were in constant interaction with each other. The kin group was the main organizational unit in the factory. The extended family functioned to allocate jobs, to socialize new workers and to mediate in case of any grievances between workers and company. The retarded unionization of the mill Hareven investi-gated confirms the effectiveness of the family system in these matters.

Hareven's work was severely criticized.[50] Almost without excep-tion this criticism concerned the romantic image she evoked of family and factory life. Many found the relationship between the two too harmonious to be convincing. This flaw in her work resulted mainly from a rather uncritical use of the technique of oral history. Another critical note made by Smelser and Halpern is of direct interest to the present research.[51] They pointed out that the French-Canadian extended family system could only survive because the factory offered no opportunity for occupational or social mobility. In this Smelser and Halpern conform to the Parsonian axioms that the extended family system is disrupted in the face of social mobility.[52]

---

[49] Hareven, *Family time*.

[50] See reviews in: *Journal of Family History*, 10 (1985), pp. 196–205; *Journal of Economic History*, 43 (1983), pp. 337–8; *Journal of Social History*, 17 (1983–4), pp. 513–15.

[51] Smelser and Halpern, 'The historical triangulation', p. 292. In this they responded to an earlier publication by Tamara Hareven on Manchester which was published in the same volume: 'The dynamics of kin'.

[52] Smelser in general adheres to the traditional structural-functionalist points of view although he also acknowledges the fact that the decline of the extended family system is a complex one. He agrees that traditional family structures may survive industrialization for a long time. See: Smelser, 'The modernization', p. 124.

Hareven's position on the matter of family change and social change may be summarized as follows. Preindustrial values stressed the importance of family life and family solidarity. The process of industrialization and urbanization does not destroy these central values, rather, people use them in a very active way to adapt to the economic and social changes. This means that they may recruit kin members as new workers in the industrial system, provide domestic services for those family members working in the factories, in the process of which they may form extended family households, or that the familial organization of work is carried over into the factory. Traditional familial values thus continue to operate under quite different structural circumstances.

This same notion has been stressed by other scholars. In his oral history of family and work among East European immigrants in Pennsylvania, USA, John Bodnar makes it clear that these concepts are closely integrated in daily life.[53] Strong family commitments dominated all social, economic and personal activities. The collective needs of the family determined where and when the individual was launched onto the labour market. Conversely, the kinship system was used to facilitate the process of migration and to acquire stable jobs. The mutual influence between the private and the economic sphere is also observed among Italian immigrants into the USA.[54] Despite the confrontation with the modern economic system of the United States these rural migrants successfully maintained their extended kinship system.[55]

The fact that industrialization does not necessarily entail the breakdown of complex coresidential family arrangements has also been supported by research on contemporary industrializing populations in various parts of the world. The 'joint family' in India continues to coexist with modern urban-industrial structures. The traditional Japanese *ie* preserved many of its features during the rapid process of social change in post-war Japan. Although sons no longer follow the traditional course of marrying into their parental household, a great majority of the parents are received into their sons' households upon ageing. Likewise, in Latin America the extended family system is

---

[53] Bodnar, *Workers' world*.
[54] Yans-McLaughlin, 'Patterns of work'.
[55] Even at a higher level of aggregation figures indicate a coexistence of extended family living and industrial economic structures in nineteenth-century USA: Seward, *The American family*, pp. 130–1. The most industrialized areas in the northeast appeared to have the highest percentages of extended family households.

used in the process of adaptation to new social and economic circumstances.[56]

Before proceeding it may be useful to sum up this discussion of the relevant literature in this field of study. I could begin by stating that the research initiated and conducted by the Cambridge Group successfully demonstrated the untenability of the close association between the extended family household and preindustrial Europe. Centuries before the coming of industrial society large segments of the population were living in relatively small households of simple composition. However, we should not go from one extreme to another by declaring the nuclear family to have been the universal norm in preindustrial Europe with extended family households virtually non-existent. Preindustrial European family life was infinitely more varied over time, space and social group. This also indicates that families and households are moved and moulded by many other forces apart from industrialization or urbanization. As for the nineteenth-century experience, research demonstrates that extended family households may perhaps have risen in frequency under the pressures which accompanied the process of industrialization. In addition, researchers suggest that extended households came to be a feasible option in the nineteenth century because of rising incomes and declining death rates. Finally, there is some evidence which suggests that 'traditional' extended family ties are activated in order to adapt to processes of change. Research in this direction seems to be indicating that extended family networks, and perhaps even the residential extended family, instead of being marginalized in industrial society, were highly functional to the individuals concerned.

1.3   Towards a historical model of social change

The way traditional values operate in new environments has been given a new theoretical perspective by Joan Scott and Louise Tilly in their studies of women workers in nineteenth-century Europe. They have advanced the hypothesis that the increasing participation of women in the labour market was strongly related to the traditional values of the 'family economy'. The preindustrial family economy expected all its members, including women, to work in the interest of the family. As most economic activities went on within households

---

[56] Conklin, 'The household'; Conklin, 'Family modernization'; Kumagai, 'Modernization'; Cancian, Goodman and Smith, 'Capitalism, industrialization'; Deere, 'The differentiation'; Hareven, 'Postscript'.

men and women worked together in a familial setting. When structural changes created new opportunities, daughters were sent by their families to work for wages outside the household. These families responded to new opportunities in accordance with values prevailing in the preindustrial setting. The growing participation in the labour market of young unmarried women in the nineteenth century, Scott and Tilly point out, does not therefore reflect a shift away from family values towards increased individualistic patterns of behaviour on the part of these young women. Rather daughters continued to work in the interests of the family group.

Continuity of traditional values is apparent in the strong familial orientation of young women workers, sometimes living and working far away from home. Despite their new economic roles they continued to define themselves as members of the family enterprise. According to Scott and Tilly, it did not bring them economic independence leading to increased sexual activity, as Shorter has proposed. Most working daughters handed over most or all of their earnings to their families. In addition, job allocation and timing of entry into the labour market were familial affairs.

Scott and Tilly react in this to William Goode's contention that the relatively high labour participation of women in the Western world should be attributed to the individualistic Protestant ideology of equality. In Goode's view the Protestant ethic undermined traditional views about women's place in the home. However, Scott and Tilly not only oppose Goode's analysis, they also challenge his model of social change. Goode directly links structural, ideological and behavioural changes. In conformity to his structural-functionalist background he assumes changes in one field to lead directly and necessarily to changes in another field.

Under Scott and Tilly's analysis behaviour is less the product of new ideas than of the effects of old ideas operating in new or changing contexts. Social structural change does not result in immediate changes in attitudinal and behavioural patterns. Rather, as Scott and Tilly note: 'Old values coexist with and are used by people to adapt to extensive structural changes. This assumes that people perceive and act on the changes they experience in terms of ideas and attitudes they already hold.'[57] Scott and Tilly demonstrated an elaboration of their model in their much cited *Women, Work, and Family*. In this book they distinguished three types of domestic organization. Each type of family organization was related to different modes of production.

[57] Scott and Tilly, 'Women's work', p. 42.

Thus, the family organization of the 'family economy' corresponded
to the domestic organization of production. When economic activities
still largely went on within the context of the household, family
organization and family relationships were determined by the household's labour needs and subsistence requirements. The industrial
mode of production created the 'family wage economy'. Families no
longer needed to organize a productive process; instead, all family
members had to enter the labour market for waged work. The family
now had to balance those family members engaged in waged work
with those that were not. Continuity in familial values existed in that
both the family economy and the family wage economy expected all
its members to work in the interest of the family under penalty of
disintegration or pauperization of the household.

In processes of change old values and attitudes will be transformed
slowly and gradually before finally disappearing altogether. In other
words, a 'time lag' exists between the processes of social and economic change and changes in behaviour and mentality. In the development of their theoretical model Scott and Tilly were inspired by the
sociologist Bert F. Hoselitz who pointed out the role of traditional
behaviour in times of social change. Although, according to Hoselitz,
traditional behaviour will retard economic change, 'the persistence of
traditions in social behaviour may be an important factor mitigating
the many dislocations and disorganizations which tend to accompany
rapid industrialization and technical change'.[58]

Most authors seem to stress first of all that the preservation of
traditional behaviour is used as a positive tool in processes of adaptation to changing circumstances.[59] The retention of traditional
behaviour however may also thwart development and adaptation of
specific social groups and thereby social and economic development
in general. Hoselitz is not the only writer with second thoughts on
the merits of traditional behaviour. Paul Klep has also suggested that
the persistent adherence to the traditional system of familial production among small rural producers in eighteenth and early nineteenth-
century Belgian Brabant turned out to be a trap leading to extreme
processes of exploitation of the households concerned while seriously
retarding the transition to more advanced centralized means of production.[60] Proto-industrial and mixed agrarian households simply
refused to be driven to the factories as long as they could squeeze
meagre incomes out of their familial production unit. In order to

[58] Hoselitz and Moore, *Industrialization*, p. 15.
[59] Yans-McLaughlin, *Family*, p. 22.
[60] Klep, *Bevolking*, pp. 299–308.

preserve the traditional organization of work and family they were prepared to pay high rents and work long hours in exchange for continually declining piece rates.

A comparable approach to that applied by Scott and Tilly was taken by Virginia Yans-McLaughlin in her study of family forms among nineteenth-century Italian immigrants to the USA. She has based her research strategy on the writings of a number of anthropologists who have concerned themselves with the historical transition from tradi-tional to modern societies. Following their example Yans-McLaughlin argues that social change 'does not necessarily imply the dissolution of traditional family forms or a systematic fit of institutions'.[61] She continues by stating that the relationship between the old and the new is dialectical in nature.

The dialectical nature of the time lag is also apparent through its resemblance to the Marxist notion of *gleichzeitige Ungleichzeitigkeit* or 'synchronous anachronism'. This concept specifically marks out household and family as bearers of residual traditional structures in relation to the large processes of social and economic transformation. To Medick this is the only theoretical context in which 'the structural function of household and family in the transition from traditional agrarian society to industrial capitalism can adequately be assessed'.[62] His proto-industrial family economy thus formed 'part of the long post-history of peasant society to the same extent that it formed a part of the pre-history of industrial capitalism'.[63]

The model of social change offered by the concept of time lag certainly appears to be more attractive to historians than the one proposed by structural-functionalism. Functionalist theory assumes a direct, one-to-one causal relationship between different subsystems and the social system, and among the subsystems themselves. All parts of the social system are mutually, and in relation to the whole, functionally adapted. The social system will constantly try to main-tain this state of functional equilibrium. Therefore, if changes occur in one part of the social system, all other parts will have to adapt them-selves, as all functional relations between them necessarily have to be in harmony for the social system to function successfully.

Thus, Parsons expects family and kinship to adapt to changes in the economic or occupational system. The family as a social sub-system will have to change, and in addition subsystems within the family, in particular the role segregation between husband and wife.

[61] Yans-McLaughlin, *Family*, p. 22.
[62] Medick, 'The proto-industrial family economy', p. 293.
[63] Ibid., p. 310.

According to Parsons: 'from the perspective of the institutionalization of a universalistic achievement value system the kinship structure and the patterning of sex roles should be considered primarily as adaptive structures'.[64] If these adaptations do not take place modern economic change, or in Parsons terminology 'the institutionalization of a universalistic achievement value system', may not be possible. For he continues: 'There is . . . every indication that they are of such crucial significance to the motivational economy of the occupational system itself that their institutionalization is of high strategic importance.'[65] Functionalism thus presents us with a rather static and ahistorical explanatory model because Parsons leaves no room for contradictions and discrepancies between various components of the social system.[66] This results from a total exclusion of the time factor. Parsons simply compares the features of the nuclear family with the requirements of the social system and argues that they fit. He is unable to show how the family was affected in different stages of the industrialization process. Parsonian theory is also static because it ignores human 'potentiality for change', as D.H. Morgan has put it.[67] After all, in Parsons' view family and kinship patterns in modern society will and must inevitably be of the type he describes. Such an approach not only strongly legitimizes the existing family and economic system, it is also unable to explain the vast amount of empirical variation in family patterns. Furthermore, historical studies have made us aware of the fact that the family must be considered as a process. Parsons' use of the concept of the family however is a static one. He never poses the question whether a family's needs and functions may differ from one phase of its cycle to another, while its relation to the social system is viewed as a constant.

Historians will regard the above considerations as serious disqualifications. Family historians, however, will most likely come up with at least one other point of criticism. From the above quotations the family emerges as a passive 'agent of change' which unresistingly responds to the great forces of macro-economic change. Recently, inspired by 'historical revisionism', family historians have begun to question the causal relationship formerly posed between family and economic change.[68] These researchers would rather look upon the family as a 'mediating unit' between the individual worker and the economic

[64] Parsons, *The social system*, p. 187.
[65] Ibid.
[66] For partly opposing views on this see: Harris, *The family*, pp. 60–2; and Morgan, *Social theory*, pp. 42–3.
[67] Morgan, *Social theory*, p. 43.
[68] The phrase 'historical revisionism' is used by David Kertzer and Andrea Schiaffino to indicate those studies that have questioned the traditional view of the impact of

system.[69] Decisions about the reproduction of labour were made in the context of the household. In this decision-making process families brought with them their own traditions, values and interests. A good illustration of this perspective may be found in Laura Strumingher's work on artisan's families in Lyon. When confronted by the pressures of economic and political change these families reacted 'largely through the filter of family life, which provided the basis for the strategies they adopted to deal with those changes'.[70]

The Scott–Tilly model, which could best be termed the 'time lag model', enables us to consider family and household as relatively autonomous phenomena. After all, those 'ill-adapted' households that continue to react to vast economic changes on the basis of traditional values appear to have their own rationality. They resist the pressures exercised by the process of change and in their turn may influence its course. Such an approach may explain variations in household formation between areas, classes, occupational or ethnic groups since it relates family patterns to pre-existing values and attitudes guiding the family behaviour in each group.

The Parsonian model therefore disqualifies itself for the historical study of the family. The approach is much too formalistic and reduces the historical development of the family to a set number of separate stages. It fails to explain how and why the family evolved under specific historical conditions of the process of industrialization. It is not concerned with explaining variation in family forms between different times, places or social groups. In contrast, the time lag model provides a much more complex and historical way to look at families. The idea that family forms and behaviour do not just give way to the pressures of changing social and economic structures, but are rather used as tools of adaptation, may explain specific historical developments in family forms and the vast amount of historical variation that is found. Materialist explanations of family patterns are not excluded by this approach. There may even be a close relationship between social and economic change and family organization. However, family patterns did not change quickly or easily. Different social groups adopted different and complex strategies in an attempt to preserve customary practices. In this way the dangers of simple reductionism may be successfully avoided.

industrialization on household and family patterns: Kertzer and Schiaffino, 'Industrialization'.
[69] Tilly, 'Occupational structure', p. 110. See also: Hareven, 'Family time', especially p. 188.
[70] Strumingher, 'The artisan family', especially p. 211.

1.4   Objectives and organization of research

In this research I shall confront the structural-functionalist view concerning family and industrialization with the model of social change
formulated by Scott and Tilly. In the process of this confrontation
crucial elements in Parsonian theory concerning the relationship
between the family and industrial society will be discussed. Taking a
dynamic view of family and household I shall examine changes in
family life-cycle patterns occurring under the influence of the early
stages of the industrialization process. The essential question is as
follows. Did households develop by means of a 'process of adaptation' from a traditional family system characterized by cohesive
kinship ties into the more loosely structured system of nuclear family
units qualified by individualism and independency between generations? And, if they did, to what extent did this happen and among
which social or occupational groups?

Of course, Parsonian theory relates the nuclear family to a kind of
industrial society characterized by high levels of social and geographical mobility, high levels of job differentiation and a high degree of
skill required. In other words, it concerns a fully developed industrial
system. However, consensus on this issue appears to be lacking. One
of Parsons' major critics stated that: 'Parsons' hypothesis tends to be
valid only during periods of emerging industrialization.'[71] Nevertheless, it is not the purpose of this study to relate family patterns to
advanced processes of industrialization. Rather, it is my contention
that in order to understand fully the relationship between the nuclear
family and industrial society proper, we should begin by trying to
understand what happened to family and household during the early
phases of the process. However, for this to be possible we need to be
aware of what the changes at that stage precisely entail. What we are
interested in here is the way in which family behaviour was affected
during an ongoing process of transition from a mixed urban economy
of artisanal and proto-industrial workers towards a more centralized
and mechanized system of production, in what we could call an
industrializing context. This transitional phase was characterized by
structural shifts in the economy, involving a process of proletarianization and the introduction of the family wage economy as well as by
accompanying processes of increases in the population density and
decreases in the level of mortality. This study seeks not only to describe family patterns during a specific and unique historical process of

[71] Litwak, 'Occupational mobility', p. 9.

change but it also aims at advancing our theoretical understanding of the relationship between family change and social change.

We can only hope to gain an insight into the complex relationship between the family and social change on the basis of micro-level studies in which a careful selection of geographical area, and social or occupational groups has been made.[72] Geographically, this research focuses on the textile town of Tilburg in the south of the Netherlands during the period 1840–1920. The town was selected because it could meet the theoretical requirements for this research. In the latter part of the period the town underwent an extensive process of industrialization, thereby decisively transforming its traditional social and economic structure. At the same time, the southern part of the Netherlands is supposed to have been characterized until recently by strong normative kinship ties and more generally by a collectivist outlook on life.

This study is designed to make a contribution to the study of the family in the field of methodology. As was outlined above the household must be considered as a process. In trying to adapt to the demands of a dynamic approach historians have met with problems not only concerning empirical data but also concerning analytical requirements. In this study I will make use of the Dutch population registers which provide us with longitudinal data on individuals and households. These registers make possible a fully dynamic view of the household. This will enable us for one thing to answer the question of what it may mean when in a given population at a specific point in time 10% of the households are found to be extended. Does this indicate the marginal significance of the phenomenon or could it still be that a large majority of the households are undergoing at least once a stage in which kin form part of the household? As yet few studies have employed longitudinal data of this type while pursuing similar research goals. This implies that analytical tools were hardly available and had to be devised through a time-consuming process of trial-and-error during the course of this research project.

Having established our analytical agenda, we now need to consider which research strategies are best suited to the task in hand. In the following pages four strategies are elaborated, each leading us to the identification of certain key questions. First of all, changes in family and household patterns over time need to be considered. Parsonian theory assumed industrialization to cause a positive adaptation of the family system to the economic system. The process of structural dif-

---

[72] Medick, 'The proto-industrial family economy', pp. 293–4.

ferentiation mirrored itself in the specialization process of the kinship system. As a consequence the extended family system broke down into smaller units of nuclear families. From the work of the Cambridge Group we know that the preindustrial family was far from being universally large and extended. Empirical evidence, however, indicates that in some areas of agricultural Europe and within certain social groups extended family living was the dominant cultural norm during certain stages in the development of the household. In addition we also have evidence showing that industrialization in some instances favoured extended family coresidence.

The first strategy therefore must involve the question of whether the industrialization process in Tilburg during the nineteenth century led to any significant change in family patterns. To what extent do we find differences in the structural evolution of the households of successive generations during the second half of the nineteenth century? If family patterns changed, what was the direction of this change? Were nineteenth-century Tilburg families loosening their kinship ties or did they perhaps activate their extended kin network in the face of industrial turmoil? In short, was industrialization accompanied by a development from a less to a more intensive extended kinship system, or should we rather think of it the other way around? Changes in the degree of kin cohesion will be examined by looking for changes in the frequency with which households were taking in extended kin members. Another important indicator of the strength of family ties we will be looking at is the relationship between parents and children. Did this change over time towards more or perhaps less autonomy and independence?

In addition, we shall want to know the nature of the causal relationship between industrialization and family change. If family change occurred what was the reason for it? Did the Tilburg families respond to the changes surrounding them in a direct way, as structural-functionalism would have us believe? Were they indeed merely 'adaptive structures' or were they on the contrary pursuing their own traditions and goals in life, and hindered in doing so, to a lesser or greater degree, by the process of change surrounding them? In other words, to what extent did a time lag exist between family change and social change, and to what extent should we speak of a one-way relationship between them? In order to shed more light on these questions we shall need to make careful distinctions in family patterns between different social, economic or occupational groups. This dimension of the research is pursued by way of the remaining three strategies.

The second strategy I wish to pursue takes as its target the very heart of Parsonian family theory, namely its proposition of the 'structural fit' between the nuclear family and industrial society. The nuclear family is considered to be best adapted to industrial society and to be most functional to its members because it enables a high degree of social and geographic mobility. The middle and upper social classes in industrial society therefore should approach most closely the ideal family type. In this context family patterns of different social classes will be analysed over time. I shall examine the extent to which the process of adaptation of family patterns followed different courses for different social classes. Do some social groups adapt more quickly while others experience a time lag? What is the precise relationship between family and social class, and does this relationship change under the influence of the process of social change? Does a given family structure at one point in the development of the family have the same meaning and function for both higher and lower-class families? Even more important is the issue of social mobility which is the central element in the concept of the structural fit between the nuclear family and industrial society. Do nuclear families enable individual members to achieve a higher degree of social mobility when compared with extended families? To what extent, conversely, do socially mobile individuals dispose of their most inconvenient extended kinship ties?

In empirical research the relationship between family and class in an urban-industrial context has proved to be a complex one. Most of the scholars adhering to the thesis of an increase in extended family arrangements during industrialization, such as Anderson and Hareven, have stressed that the extended family arose out of and was functional in 'critical life situations'. As a result the nineteenth-century extended family came to be associated with the working classes and their attempts to cope with poverty and other industrial misfortunes. The working-class extended family thus 'primarily functioned as a private institution to redistribute the poverty of the nuclear family by way of the kinship system'.[73] This would appear to confirm the functionalist association of the extended family with the unsuccessful margin of industrial society.

We have already seen, on the other hand, that William Goode believes the middle and upper classes to maintain the most extensive kinship relations. There is some empirical historical evidence sustaining this view. Here the family seems to have functioned as a means to continue control over economic resources and to uphold the family's

---

[73] Ibid., p. 295.

social status by providing care for less fortunate kin members.[74] Recently, Steven Ruggles reasserted this idea when he proclaimed the nineteenth-century extended family household to be a luxury affair.

The third strategy concentrates on migrant households. The process of industrialization in Tilburg was accompanied by intermittent heavy in-migration from the surrounding countryside. Following structural-functionalist reasoning we would expect migrant families to display less family cohesion and form extended families to a lesser degree than non-migrants. Geographical mobility and extended family living would be two mutually exclusive elements.

The key to an understanding of this issue is a comparative analysis of the structural evolution of migrant and non-migrant households. The following questions are central to this part of the analysis. Did migration indeed loosen the bonds between extended kin members? Did migrant families as a result more often display a tendency towards nuclearization of the household? From other studies we have seen that in some circumstances migrants managed to keep their extended kin network alive and adapt it to the exigencies of a new social and economic context. In empirical historical research, however, it has not always been possible to establish a positive relationship between migration and extended family networks.

Most of the Tilburg migrants moved into the town from the surrounding countryside while the latter was still dominated by a traditional peasant culture. If we ought to look upon households as resilient bearers of traditional structures, instead of responsive and adaptive agents of change, these Tilburg migrant families would have to be characterized by traditional elements. Did a time lag in adaptation occur in the case of the migrant families? In the analysis of the relationship between migration and family structure I shall keep in close touch with the aspect of social class. Social class may well have acted as a mediating factor between the two, resulting in different family patterns for lower and upper-class migrant families or specific occupational groups.

The final strategy employed in this analysis concerns an aspect of the relationship between family and social change to which most social theorists, not only structural-functionalists, attach great importance – the impact of the loss of the household's economic functions. According to Parsons, the nuclear family could only emerge after the segregation between the family system and the econ-

---

[74] Kocka, 'Familie'; Griffen and Griffen, 'Family'; Crozier, 'Kinship'.

omic system had been successfully realized. This segregation depended upon the removal of the economic functions from the household. Most historians would agree with the idea that the loss of economic functions constitutes a breaking point in the history of the family. The productive unit of the household provided an incentive for strong kinship ties; family members were held together in shared productive and propertied interests. Nuclearization and the weakening of extended kin relations occurred once the family had to rely on wage labour for a living. The most recent historical contribution stressing the importance of the productive functions of the household has come from Tilly and Scott.[75]

The last part of the analysis is therefore devoted to a structural comparison of the households of proto-industrial domestic weavers with those of industrial wage workers. Those Tilburg domestic weavers who were still active in the second half of the nineteenth century were the last and in some respects the most tenacious representatives of a preindustrial domestic mode of production. What did the structural evolution of these households look like when compared with the households of industrial wage workers? To what extent did the involvement with industrial wage labour alter the life cycle of the household? The introduction of (industrial) wage labour is believed to have affected generational links; it increased the autonomy of children who were no longer dependent upon their parents for economic opportunities. Can we find any evidence of this in the household histories of the industrial workers in Tilburg and their children? If not, this would support the work of Scott and Tilly which suggests a continuation of familial values and a prolongation of filial attachment to the interests of the family as a result of a time lag.

The analysis involves for the most part the use of two large samples of households consisting of almost 400 households each. For both groups complete household life histories are reconstructed with the help of the town's population registers. The first group covers the period 1849–1890, the second one covers 1880–1920. The first three strategies, as explained above, will be employed using these two samples of households. Chapter 4 contains the results of the comparative analysis of family structure over time. Chapter 5 examines the issue of social class and social mobility in relation to family structure, while the matter of geographical mobility and family structure is raised in chapter 6. Finally, chapter 7 contains the comparative analysis of the structural development of the households of domestic

[75] Tilly and Scott, *Women.*

weavers and industrial wage workers. For this part of the study two further samples of about ninety households each were collected with the help of wage registers from a number of textile factories, the population registers and the civil registration records. The nature and the quality of sources and data used in this study are extensively discussed in chapter 3, which also deals with a number of relevant methodological issues in the field of quantitative family history. Chapter 2 is reserved for a short excursion into the history of nineteenth-century Tilburg, covering the main features of its economic, demographic and social development.

2

*The industrializing context: continuity
and change in nineteenth-century Tilburg*

The geographical focus of this study into the relationship between
social change and the family is the town of Tilburg, situated in the
southern Dutch province of Noord-Brabant. In the course of the
nineteenth century the town developed, at times rapidly, from a rural
community of several dispersed hamlets engaged in farming and the
domestic production of woollen cloth to a medium-sized town with
an industrial character of a very typical blend. This chapter outlines
the major features of the town's social, economic and demographic
development in that period. It will be clear that a comprehensive
survey is not offered here; rather, I intend to touch upon those
aspects which are most relevant to the purposes pursued in this study
and which most clearly highlight the town's specific characteristics.

2.1 Population

When Tilburg was awarded formal city status in 1809 this was not on
account of impressive size or the density of its population. At that
moment the town counted only 9400 inhabitants scattered over
twelve little hamlets. These hamlets, at a mutual distance of a fifteen-
minute walk, were connected to each other by sandy tracks along
which in the course of the period ribbon building took place. In the
middle of the century the result of this very particular 'urban'
development occasioned surprise among visitors. The town was still
described in 1851 as being 'a collection of dispersed hamlets, of
unconnected groups of buildings which were thrown onto the earth
crosswise and at oblique angles'.[1] Even in the seventies after a period

---

[1] Boeren, *Het hart*, p. 71.

of intensive growth the town gave the impression of an 'American city' because of its spacious character.[2]

During the first half of the nineteenth century the population of Tilburg grew slowly but steadily, mostly as a result of an excess of births over deaths rather than as a result of migration. The high level of infant mortality during the twenties and thirties was the main factor contributing to the slow rate of growth during this period.[3] The steady pace of growth was however interrupted by a period of stagnation in the decade following 1840 during which the Tilburg population in some years actually declined in total numbers. This stagnation, which made itself felt throughout the country, was a consequence of the economic crisis of the forties leading to the postponement of many marriages,[4] a fall in the number of births as well as an increase in the level of mortality and a negative migration balance. In the next decade the growth rate recovered again to return to its previous level.

The 1860s mark a clear break in the town's population development; from that decade onwards the flight out of the town was stopped and the birth surplus rose to a higher level, which was maintained throughout the next six decades. Most conspicuous however is the high level of migration during the sixties which to a lesser extent continued into the seventies. From 1865 onwards until the beginning of the next decade in-migration peaked at amazing levels because of the large numbers of young families flooding into the town. This heavy in-migration resulted from expanding economic opportunities in the local textile industry which affected the entire Tilburg economy. As a consequence of the American Civil War shortages in cotton supplies had increased and prices had soared which greatly pushed up demand for woollen textiles.[5] After the 1870s in-migration declined to more modest levels leaving the natural increase once again as the main factor in the town's rate of growth. In the final decade of the period covered by this study, the 1910s, in-migration again increased due to the rising demand for labour during the World War I boom in woollen textiles.

Compared with both national and provincial levels, the capacity for natural growth was high in Tilburg in the second half of the century, due to both the low level of mortality and the high birth rate.[6] In

---

[2] Sassen, 'Een blik', p. 234.
[3] van de Put, *Volksleven*, p. 146; Simons, 'De armoede', p. 193.
[4] Frinking and van Poppel, *Nuptialiteit*, pp. 29–30, 34–5.
[5] Peters, 'De migratie'.
[6] Derks, 'De bevolkingsontwikkeling', p. 142.

Table 2.1 *Population development, Tilburg, 1811–1919*

Period	Total inhabitants	Total growth %	Birth surplus %	Migration surplus %
1811–1819	9416–10,297	9.4	9.8	−0.4
1820–1829	10,297–11,726	13.9	14.0	−0.1
1830–1839	11,726–13,348	13.8	12.3	1.6
1840–1849	13,348–14,373	7.7	10.4	−2.7
1850–1859	14,373–15,854	10.3	8.4	1.9
1860–1869	15,854–21,523	35.8	18.4	17.5
1870–1879	21,523–28,390	31.9	21.6	10.3
1880–1889	28,390–33,905	19.4	17.9	1.6
1890–1899	33,905–40,628	19.8	19.1	0.8
1900–1909	40,628–50,405	24.1	22.9	1.2
1910–1919	50,405–61,557	22.1	18.5	3.6

comparison with mortality in the province of Noord-Brabant as a whole, figures for Tilburg continued to remain relatively low throughout the nineteenth century up to 1920. This is generally related to the rural character of the town; the relative dispersal of the population lowered the risk of infectious diseases spreading quickly. However, around the turn of the century Tilburg started to lag behind in the substantial decreases in the national death rate caused by the lowering of infant mortality. Improvements in child care and medical facilities had brought down the level of infant mortality in other urban areas in the country. In Tilburg, however, rates continued to be high and had even increased compared to the middle decades of the century. The rural mentality of the Tilburgers, as expressed by a generally reluctant attitude towards innovations, prevented improvements in hygienic conditions of infant care and the integration of the modern medical sector into society.[7] Nevertheless, the average age at death in Tilburg, infant mortality excluded, increased between 1865 and 1915 from 38 to 50.[8]

Little is known about the marital pattern of the Tilburg population but it is clear that the province of Noord-Brabant, in which Tilburg is situated, had the lowest proportion of married men and women in the age category of 40–44 throughout the entire nineteenth century. In 1849 only about three-quarters of the men and women in the 40–44 age group were or had been married, and in 1909 figures were only

[7] van de Put, *Volksleven*, pp. 146–7.
[8] Ibid., p. 267.

little higher.[9] It is hardly likely that marriage was as infrequent in the Brabantine towns as in the surrounding countryside, but there is no reason to expect that marriage frequency in Tilburg was as high as in the urban areas in the north and the west of the country. The ages at which the men and women of Tilburg married were rather low compared to those in rural areas of the province. In the following chapter we will see that the median age at first marriage in Tilburg remained remarkably stable during the century: 26 for men and 25 for women. In Breda, one of the few other towns in the province, the timing of marriage of both men and women corresponded exactly to the pattern found in Tilburg.[10] In the rural communities in the area marriage was quite late, often around the age of 31 or 32 for men and 27 to 29 for women.[11]

2.2   Economy

Throughout the period of this study the local economy remained heavily dominated by the woollen textile industry. Traditionally, as far back as the Middle Ages, the people of the province of Noord-Brabant had combined small-scale peasant farming with domestic industrial activities such as spinning and weaving. Until the eighteenth century the Brabantine domestic textile industry produced primarily for entrepreneurs in the west of the country, operating from textile cities such as Haarlem and Leiden. Due to the economic decline of the textile cities in the west the agents and entrepreneurs started to transfer the entire textile production to the province of Noord-Brabant, the process being stimulated by the low wage level in the province.[12] Tilburg benefited most from this geographic shift in economic activities despite its rather unfavourable transport and communications system. In the course of the nineteenth century Tilburg managed to develop into the country's principal wool-producing centre.[13]

Already at the beginning of the nineteenth century the textile industry had become the town's primary means of subsistence. In 1810, 4650 workers were employed in the production of woollen cloth

---

[9] Hofstee, *Korte demografische geschiedenis*, pp. 128–9.
[10] Engelen and Hillebrand, 'Vruchtbaarheid', p. 258.
[11] Meurkens, *Bevolking*, p. 189; van Lieshout and Rikken, 'Geen lusten', p. 38; van der Heijden, 'Gezin', p. 139.
[12] Harkx, *De Helmondse textielnijverheid*, pp. 61–4.
[13] At the beginning of the twentieth century 75% of the Dutch woollen industry was situated in Tilburg. See: van den Eerenbeemt, *Ontwikkelingslijnen*, p. 136.

out of a total population of 9676.[14] In the previous year the town had
counted 30 independently operating woollen cloth factories, another
75 which were producing on commission for other manufacturers and
in addition to these there were 300 small independent weaving
shops. In the same year mechanical spinning was first introduced in
the factory of Van Dooren en Dams, and in subsequent years it
rapidly superseded home-spinning. Apart from spinning, the woollen and worsted factories in the first half of the century mainly concentrated within the factory walls activities such as fulling and
dyeing. Weaving, in particular, continued to be concentrated within
the domestic family economy until the very end of the century. Steam
power began to be used from 1827 onwards but for a long time it
remained supplemented by horse power.

During the first half of the nineteenth century the woollen industry
expanded and mechanized only slowly. For its welfare the industry
relied heavily on its ability to acquire Dutch military orders in the
absence of a stable set of national and international markets. Stagnation in this period resulted from the heavy British competition which
made itself felt soon after French domination had ended, but also
from the loss of the Belgian market in the 1830s and the general
economic crisis of the 1840s. In 1845, fifty-two woollen and worsted
mills were in operation of which only thirteen were using steam
power.[15] Home-spinning had almost completely disappeared by that
time, but in 1853 as many as 2100 workers were still reported to be
employed in domestic weaving and burling.[16]

The 1850s marked a period of growth under the influence of a
modest relaxation of protective policies stimulating textile manufacturers towards substantial improvements and innovations in the production process. By 1857 the number of woollen factories had
increased to eighty-eight, of which twenty-seven were driven by
steam power. Also in 1856 the first power looms were introduced, by
the company of Diepen. During the later 1860s and early 1870s the
Tilburg textile industry experienced a boom resulting from the crisis
in cotton, already discussed above, and the large military orders at
the time of the Franco-Prussian War. The number of woollen textile
mills continued to expand until it reached its height in the middle of
the 1870s with about 142 mills, 55 driven by steam. Demand for
labour increased enormously in this period because manufacturers,

[14] Keune, 'De industriële ontwikkeling', p. 11; Derks, 'De bevolkingsontwikkeling', p.
130.
[15] Keune, 'De industriële ontwikkeling', p. 37.
[16] Ibid., p. 41.

rather than investing in labour-saving technology, were inclined to apply more of the same. The boom of the 1860s and 1870s was to a great extent also made possible by the connection on to the national railroad network, which finally brought the town out of its isolation.

In the 1880s expansion came to an end as a result of the protectionist policies implemented by the French and the German governments. Production further broke down as a result of decreasing opportunities on the internal market for heavy cloths, in which the Tilburg industry had come to specialize, because of the agricultural crisis and a shift in demand towards the more refined qualities and cotton.[17] The stagnation of the 1880s finally forced the larger mills to modernize thoroughly their weaving departments.[18] In this period they were still employing surprisingly large numbers of domestic weavers. It is estimated that in 1887 between 2200 and 3000 workers were employed within the domestic weaving economy.[19] The smaller companies being unable to make the necessary investments did not survive: in 1889 the number of textile factories had already gone down to 116. After 1895 economic fortunes began to look brighter, the agricultural crisis had passed and export opportunities increased again. But it was mainly the larger manufacturers who were able to benefit from the economic revival which was to continue until the 1930s. Not even World War I turned out to have negative effects; on the contrary, large orders for military cloth created a boom in the woollen industry and shortages on the Tilburg labour market. By that time the textile trade had finally become fully mechanized and concentrated within the factory walls. Thus, from the middle of the nineteenth century onwards Tilburg had become one of the few major industrial centres in a country which was otherwise only slowly embarking upon the path of industrialization.[20] Tilburg differed however in important respects from most industrial cities in the country, or abroad for that matter. Industrial growth in Tilburg had above all expressed itself in a growing number of factories being erected rather than in increases in scale of existing companies; factories employing hundreds of workers at the same time were non-existent. The prolonged existence of domestic textile activities was another typical element of Tilburg's industrialization. Indicative of both aspects are the figures relating to male workers of the Brouwers, Van Dooren en Dams, and Diepen mills. These three companies,

---

[17] de Jonge, *De industrialisatie*, p. 91; Keune, 'De industriële ontwikkeling', pp. 51–3.
[18] van den Eerenbeemt, *Ontwikkelingslijnen*, p. 135.
[19] Wagemakers, 'Over buitenwevers', p. 118.
[20] See de Jonge, 'Industrial growth'.

some of whose weavers we will be examining in chapter 7, were employing in total 150 male adult workers within the factory walls in 1887, but they were also reported to have had another 248 at work in the domestic industry.[21] These latter workers can hardly have been engaged in anything else but domestic weaving.

The remarkably slow decline of the domestic textile economy in Tilburg comes out in the following figures also. At the beginning of the century about 4400 domestic workers were engaged in both spinning and weaving. For 1855 the number of domestic weavers (spinning was by then exclusively concentrated in the mills), is estimated at about 2000. This declined to about 1500 in the late 1880s.[22] As late as 1890 a total number of 1355 hand-looms were reported to be in operation in the homes of domestic weavers.[23] Then, between 1890 and 1910, the total collapse of domestic weaving took place: from 1500 in 1890 to 350 in 1910. Most of the few remaining weavers in 1910 were middle-aged or elderly.[24] By contrast, in the cotton towns in the east of the country, where power-loom weaving had been introduced in the late 1850s, domestic weaving was completely superseded by 1870, within the space of ten years.[25]

As has already been made clear, the local economy was heavily dependent upon the textile sector throughout the entire period of study. In 1815, 47% of the young men who were called up for military examination reported themselves to be employed in the textile trade. This had decreased to 32% in 1870. In the latter year, however, we should probably have to add those described as factory workers, which was another 23%.[26] Of the total working population in 1899 29% were employed in textiles.[27] Some of the other industries were highly dependent on the textile sector, such as the wool washeries and dyers, the engineering works and the wool card factory. Of those that were not, we might mention the tanneries of which there were ten in 1816 and thirty-five in 1870. They were small-scale enterprises however; together, the twenty-seven tanneries in 1857 employed only about a hundred workers. In addition, we must not forget that

[21] In addition the three mills were employing 18 women, 26 boys and only 4 girls between the ages of 12–18 within the factory walls, and another 112 women, 40 boys and 12 girls who were all working at home. de Jong, 'Enige sociale aspecten', pp. 186–7.

[22] Klep, 'Over de achteruitgang', p. 36.

[23] van den Eerenbeemt, *Ontwikkelingslijnen*, p. 58.

[24] *Onderzoekingen*, III, pp. 23–35.

[25] de Jonge, *De industrialisatie*, pp. 100, 106.

[26] In 1815 none of the 20-year-olds was listed as factory worker which category only started to appear from the late forties onwards, see: van Doremalen, *Arbeid*, p. 35.

[27] Rossen, *Het gemeentelijk volkshuisvestingsbeleid*, p. 152.

as late as 1870 about 6% of all household heads in Tilburg were said still to be engaged in agriculture.[28] The opening of the national railroad construction yard in 1869 marked an important addition to the local economy. In its initial years it employed about 450 workers, a total which was to rise to 700 or 800 towards the end of the century.[29] In 1909 the national railroad employed as much as 8% of the Tilburg working population.[30] Also opening in the later 1880s and 1890s were two shoe factories as well as two cigar factories.

2.3   Social conditions

In spite of this limited diversity in employment we may still say that the larger part of the Tilburg population remained dependent on the textile trade for its welfare. Sharp declines in textiles would, therefore, plunge the entire town into unemployment and misery. In 1840, for instance, 2000 people were out of work while in 1838 not one had been registered as such. The rather unstable demand for woollen cloth probably constituted one of the main factors inducing the manufacturers to continue to put out major parts of their weaving to the domestic economy. But even in relatively favourable times the textile workers would have found it difficult to make ends meet. Wages paid in the textile industry were considerably lower than in other sectors of the economy.[31] In the middle of the century incomes earned in some of the major textile occupations came lowest in rank, together with day labourers and unskilled workers, in a list of thirty of the most frequently cited trades and occupations.[32]

Textile wages, especially those in the domestic economy, it was argued at the time, could be low on account of the fact that most of the workers cultivated small plots of land providing the family with potatoes and some vegetables. In addition the family would sometimes keep a goat and a pig.[33] This low wage level is likely to have played a part in the initial attractiveness of the town in the eighteenth and early nineteenth centuries for the textile manufacturers of the west. However, in the final decades of the nineteenth century the Tilburg manufacturers started to pay higher wages in factory weaving in an effort to entice some of the domestic weavers

---

[28] van Doremalen, *Arbeid*, p. 145.
[29] Keune, 'De industriële ontwikkeling', p. 48.
[30] Rossen, *Het gemeentelijk volkshuisvestingsbeleid*, p. 153.
[31] Sassen, 'Een blik', pp. 235–6.
[32] van Doremalen, *Arbeid*, p. 34.
[33] de Jong, 'Enige sociale aspecten', p. 176.

into factory labour. It appears to have been difficult to discipline the domestic weavers to the rigours of industrial labour. The overseer of one of the Tilburg textile factories explained in 1887 that 'most [of the domestic weavers] do not like to go to the mill. They say: freedom comes first and it is better than being locked up in the mill, where one goes in at seven in the morning in order to leave again in the evening. Many are put off; that is why people in the mill have to be better paid.'[34] The combination of low wages, frequent crises in production and the truck system which was still widespread was responsible for much poverty and misery among the domestic weavers.[35]

The town may be said, however, to have escaped some of the more extreme miseries generally associated with industrial towns in that period such as the relentless exploitation of child and female labour in the mills. To be sure, labour of very young children was an integral part of the domestic economy throughout the entire nineteenth century. Moreover, the increased mechanization and the gradual disappearance of the domestic industry from the middle of the century onwards indeed only served to increase the number of children at work within the textile industry. However, contemporaries liked to state that the children working in the mills were almost all above the age of 11 or 12. That this was not completely true was revealed by an inquiry into child labour held in 1867 which indicated that 35% of the 200 male factory workers, at the time aged 20 or over, had started work before the age of 12. However, 76% of the male workers under the age of 20 had begun their work in the mill at the age of 11 or 12, so that it seemed as if conditions had recently started to improve. Girls in general appear to have been admitted to the mills at considerably older ages: 80% of the female labourers in 1867 were said to have started work after their fourteenth birthday.[36] That a growing number of children were involved in the textile industry in the entire province is also indicated by their increased share in the working population in the sector: in 1819 children had made up 16% of all textile workers and by 1871 this had risen to 37%.[37]

In 1874 the national government issued a child labour law prohibiting child labour under the age of 12. Thirteen years later in 1887 a State Inquiry was undertaken into the extent to which the child labour law was being evaded as well as into the possibility of extending the working of the law in the future to children under the age of

---

[34] *Enquete*, Tilburg, question 11529.
[35] Boeren, *Het hart*, p. 90; Simons, 'De armoede', p. 203.
[36] de Jong, 'Enige sociale aspecten', p. 193.
[37] Ibid., p. 195.

15 or 16. Tilburg was one of the places visited by the inquiry committee. The interviewees, all representatives of the industrial and
administrative middle and upper classes in Tilburg, maintained that
child labour under the age of 12 had completely disappeared.[38] It was
claimed that the local clergy had played a major role in the early
renouncement of child labour even before 1874.

Untroubled by the absence of conclusive evidence and the biased
composition of its group of witnesses the committee concluded that
child labour under the age of 12 had disappeared entirely both in the
mills and in the domestic industry. There is every reason to doubt the
correctness of the committee's conclusion. In 1885 as many as 142
boys and another 142 girls were reported as not attending school,
figures which were substantially higher than in non-textile towns of
comparable size in the area.[39] As late as 1896 the provincial authorities
reported that school attendance in Tilburg was problematic in particular because of the involvement of children under the age of 12 in the
domestic textile industry.[40] We may therefore safely assume that
although the labour of very young children had started to disappear
from the mills in the late 1870s and 1880s, children continued to be
employed within the home throughout the entire period. Of course
the textile mills were employing large numbers of boys and girls
between the ages of 12 and 18: in 1887 in some of the larger woollen
mills 16% of the work force was made up of boys and another 3% of
girls in that age category.[41] In 1901 compulsory education was
instituted for children under the age of twelve, but in 1913 an inquiry
by the Child Welfare Office indicated that large numbers of children
were still engaged in domestic industrial activities before and after
school hours.[42] It is most likely that this was common practice also in
Tilburg where the textile industry at that time still provided ample
opportunities for domestic work.

The textile industry has traditionally been one of the major employers of female labour, and this was no different in Tilburg. In the
1950s and 1960s, 30 to 40% of the town's working population in
textiles consisted of women;[43] for 1887 and 1899 the share of female

[38] Only one violation of the law was established; in the local stone factory children
under the age of 12 were said to be employed in the carrying of pieces of stone.
[39] van Doremalen, 'Tilburg', p. 81.
[40] Wagemakers, 'Over buitenwevers', p. 119.
[41] These figures may only be used tentatively; they are based on the information
provided by the labour inquiry of 1887 on sixteen of some of the major mills. See de
Jong, 'Enige sociale aspecten', p. 186.
[42] de Regt, *Arbeidersgezinnen*, p. 111.
[43] van Doremalen, *Arbeid*, p. 59.

to leave the mill. In the latter case, however, the young man would be banned from all other mills.[56] Whatever the effect of these and other measures may have been, it is evident that in the nineteenth century illegitimacy in Tilburg was rather low when compared with other major towns in the same province.[57] Moreover, Tilburg children born outside of marriage were more likely to be made legitimate eventually by their parents' marriage.

2.4 Housing conditions

Deplorable housing conditions are one of the other inevitable associations which nineteenth-century towns usually evoke. No doubt the housing situation of the Tilburg working classes, particularly considering their low standard of living, must have been poor and unhygienic. As late as 1902 the health authorities reported: 'It is not rare to see 8 to 10 persons in one single filthy room, where they live, sleep and work.'[58] Some of the people questioned by the inquiry committee in 1887 maintained that housing conditions were generally better for domestic weavers than for those working in the mill. Most of the weavers, it was reported, would own their own houses which in addition provided more room, air and light.[59] Some of them added that this applied in particular to those workers living on the outskirts of the town.[60] Domestic workers, in contrast to factory labourers, were also described as having small plots of land next to their houses.[61] Yet, the evidence offered by the 1887 inquiry is scanty and probably to some extent biased.[62] Some more concrete evidence is found in the State Inquiry into conditions in the domestic industry of 1910. This report indicated that the majority of the 344 domestic weavers who were still there in Tilburg were living in two or three-roomed houses and that 39% of them owned their own homes.[63] It was stated also that nearly all cottages had a small strip of land used for the cultivation of potatoes or the raising of some cattle.

---

[56] Sterkens, 'De zorg', p. 220.
[57] Vermunt, 'Buitenechtelijke geboorten'. Quite intriguing in this connection is that J. Humphries ('. . . The Most Free') demonstrated that a close statistical relationship exists between the rate of illegitimacy and the degree of sex segregation at work in nineteenth-century England.
[58] Cited by van de Put, *Volksleven*, p. 3.
[59] *Enquete*, Tilburg, question 10671.
[60] *Enquete*, Tilburg, question 10205.
[61] *Enquete*, Tilburg, question 10706.
[62] The questions were framed rather tendentiously. See also: Wagemakers, 'Over buitenwevers', p. 122.
[63] *Onderzoekingen*, III, p. 35.

The crowding of large numbers of families in run-down districts enclosed within the narrow confines of city walls was definitely not characteristic of the nineteenth-century development of Tilburg. The town's spacious layout provided ample space for building. This may have been the main reason why, despite its growth during the second half of the nineteenth century, the housing situation at the end of the century was still relatively favourable in quantitative terms.[64] Rents and the price of land were still low in 1890. Nine years later 23% of the Tilburg population was reported to be living in single-room houses. This proportion was somewhat higher in some of the towns in the north and west of the country: 58% for both Groningen and Rotterdam, and 38% for the Amsterdam population.[65] Other towns in the province of Noord-Brabant also appear to have had a larger proportion of the population packed away in single rooms. In 1909 the single and two-room housing in Tilburg had declined even further.[66] Of course these figures do not necessarily indicate that prior to these dates, especially during the heavy in-migration of the sixties and seventies, housing shortages did not occur. However, this is not likely to have been the case given the fact that the annual municipal reports of that period, while referring to the tremendous growth of the community's population, stated that the sharing of houses by more than one family did not occur.[67]

Nevertheless, in the 1910s a serious shortage in the housing market did occur due to the continued increase in the number of families and the collapse in private building.[68] In addition World War I brought a large number of military and Belgian refugees into the town, but they were only of minor influence on the total shortage.[69] A municipal inquiry into the situation held in 1917 indicated that a 10% shortage in houses existed and that in 11% of all cases at that time two or more families were sharing a house.[70] The shortage occurred in all rent categories but was greatest at the bottom of the scale. Towards the end of the decade the authorities began to develop a municipal building programme which was to eliminate the deficit in the housing market. Until that time building had been entirely private.

---

[64] Rossen, *Het gemeentelijk volkshuisvestingsbeleid*, pp. 122, 272.
[65] van den Dam, *Arnold Leon Armand Diepen*, p. 73.
[66] Rossen, *Het gemeentelijk volkshuisvestingsbeleid*, p. 272.
[67] Cited in van den Dam, *Arnold Leon Armand Diepen*, p. 78.
[68] Rossen, *Het gemeentelijk volkshuisvestingsbeleid*, p. 279.
[69] van de Put, *Volksleven*, p. 18.
[70] Only co-residing couples (with or without children) or a co-residing one-parent family with children were included in this count. Such cases as a co-residing widowed grandmother were not regarded as an expression of a housing shortage. See: Rossen, 'Het Tilburgse volkshuisvestingsbeleid', note 14.

2.5 Labour relations

A Dutch sociologist once described relations between the Tilburg industrialists and their workers in the nineteenth century as being characterized much more by an awareness of solidarity rather than by an awareness of opposition.[71] The rather secluded Brabantine society of the nineteenth century continued to be based on the traditional principles of class into which a capitalist type of class struggle simply did not fit. Most industrialists were not merely distant providers of capital, they were visibly involved in the mill's productive activities on a daily basis. The small scale of the average enterprise, which made possible a much more personal relationship between the mill owner and his labourers, and the strong influence of Catholicism, stressing the moral responsibilities in the divinely ordained social order, further worked towards the continuation of traditional paternalistic relationships. This description may be said still to apply to the Tilburg situation in the second half of the century despite all the industrial developments that had taken place.[72] It is best illustrated by the comment one of the overseers of the railroad construction yard provided in 1887: 'In Tilburg it has the character of one big family. Workers remain with one patron and by inheritance continue in the same family's service. The patrons I know are like fathers to their workers.'[73]

Whatever the truthfulness of these and other similar statements may have been, it is clear that they do not reflect an atmosphere in which labour unions and socialist ideologies would easily take root. Social protest and collective action remained a largely unknown phenomenon within Tilburg society until well into the twentieth century. Only a few cases in local history are found that may possibly be described as instances of workers resisting a deterioration in working conditions or standard of living in any organized way.[74] It was not until 1917 that strikes and collective action were first introduced to the Tilburg textile industry.

A very early attempt to initiate the Tilburg workers to socialist ideology took place in 1871. Three workers of the railroad construc-

---

[71] van de Weijer, *De religieuse practijk*, p. 153.
[72] van den Eerenbeemt, *Ontwikkelingslijnen*, pp. 95–6.
[73] *Enquete*, Tilburg, question 11235.
[74] Some social unrest is reported to have accompanied the introduction of the first steam-engine in 1827, but machine-breaking did not occur. In 1855, 1864 and 1872 some minor wage disputes arose leading to one-day strikes. Only the first of these conflicts applied to the textile industry, the other two concerned bricklayers and carpenters. See: van Doremalen, 'Sociale onrust'.

tion yard, all three recent migrants from Utrecht and members of the International Workers Association, were caught while canvassing for support among their fellow workers. They were immediately dismissed. The incident relates to one other important element responsible for the continuation of traditional relations: the 'foreign' element in the town's population was weak or nearly missing. Whereas other nineteenth-century industrial towns experienced heavy inflows of migrants from all parts of the country, in Tilburg the native-born made up the greater part of the population. At the turn of the century 75% of all Tilburg inhabitants were born and bred there.[75] The introduction of new ideas and attitudes thus could proceed only slowly.

From 1895 onwards trade unions were being established in Tilburg which aimed at the improvement of working conditions. At first they met with strong opposition from employers and clergy alike. It is significant again that the Catholic weavers' union could only come into existence due to the activities of an outsider, a German immigrant who, being a worker at the national railroads yard, was not subject to the measures of disqualification of the textile employers. However, part of the clergy realized in time that they needed to take the lead and work towards the creation of a solidly Catholic social movement throughout the principally Catholic provinces of the south of the Netherlands.[76] They knew quite well that this was the only way to prevent the Church from eventually losing its hold over the mass of the working population. Given the combination of elements described above, a transformation of social economic relations in Tilburg along more capitalist lines was effectively prevented.

2.6   Concluding remarks

In summarizing I will try to assess the nature and extent of the changes transforming nineteenth-century Tilburg. To what extent are both change and continuity present within this process of transformation and to what extent did this development conform to the pattern found in other industrial centres? This is particularly important since the industrial town that had come into existence by the beginning of

[75] Rossen, *Het gemeentelijk volkshuisvestingsbeleid*, p. 150. This could also explain the diverging experience of Eindhoven, also situated in Noord-Brabant, where the large-scale immigration of workers to the Philips factories favoured the early foundation of socialist parties, see: van den Dam, *Arnold Leon Armand Diepen*, p. 132.
[76] Nineteenth-century Tilburg was a solidly Roman Catholic community: throughout the century 96% to 97% of the population described themselves as such.

the twentieth century was the tenth largest city in the Netherlands, but did not conform to the classical concept of a nineteenth-century industrial city.

First of all, it lacked any degree of compactness and density. Towards the end of the century the pattern of the many little hamlets from which Tilburg had developed was still conspicuous. Due to its special urban genesis the town preserved a kind of rural atmosphere until the beginning of the next century despite the industrial developments and the considerable growth rate of its population in the second part of the century. City airs and style were fundamentally absent. There was no recognizable city centre in which political, economic and social functions were concentrated, rather the town consisted of a series of smaller centres which continued to be the primary focal points of its inhabitants. In this context related urban turmoil such as overcrowding, and appalling sanitary and health conditions were either non-existent or much less extreme.

Secondly, the town had largely developed from 'within': at the end of the nineteenth century three-quarters of its population was of native origin. Transiency and high rates of population instability were fundamental characteristics of most other industrial centres at the time. For instance, in Enschede, a cotton mill town in the east of the country, only 44% of its population in 1899 was of native origin. In mid-nineteenth-century Preston in England, just to mention an industrial town for which family patterns have been extensively investigated, as many as 70% of the resident population consisted of migrants. The modest share of migrants in the total Tilburg population must have greatly contributed to the sense of continuity and cohesion of its inhabitants. Most likely it was also responsible for the slow transformation of social and economic relationships in a direction which effectively excluded the introduction of socialist ideologies.

Thirdly, although the town's productive structures had undergone a slow, but nevertheless fundamental change over the century, these changes at the same time incorporated important elements of continuity. The industrialization that had taken place was of a small-scale character: massive concentrations of workers in huge industrial plants did not exist. The Tilburg mills were indeed a far cry from, for instance, the Amoskeag mill in Manchester USA employing thousands of workers at the same time, or indeed even from the textile mills in the east of the Netherlands. Moreover, the transformation of economic structures was only partial; during the entire century traditional domestic production continued to occupy an important position within the textile industry. It is likely that throughout the period under study considerable sections of the Tilburg working population retained the outlook of small property holders as a result of home-ownership and the possession of small plots of land. Thus, industrialization in Tilburg was not accompanied by a thorough and rapid process of proletarianization transforming its working-class population into a mass of propertyless, unskilled factory labourers with few roots in the local community. The large numbers of men, women and children involved in the domestic weaving economy retained important ties with a preindustrial culture in which work and family had overlapped, a culture in which the family had combined subsistence farming with domestic industrial production.

The minor importance of female factory work may conveniently be listed as a fourth element distinguishing Tilburg from other industrial nineteenth-century towns, and in particular from other textile towns in the period. As was pointed out before, this is strongly related to the continued importance of the domestic industry which provided young girls and, in particular, married women with abundant opportunities to contribute financially to the family budget. This dual local labour market may easily have led to a large number of families combining industrial wage work, for instance by its chief male breadwinner and some adult children, with domestic industrial activities employing the wife and the family's younger children. Employment patterns of this type are undoubtedly of considerable consequence for family life and family composition.

It would seem then that both change and continuity were integral parts of the process of transformation taking place in nineteenth-century Tilburg. It is likely that a strong sense of continuity enabled the working classes of Tilburg to cope with those discontinuities that did occur. How did all this affect family life? Was family life equally dominated by continuity? We might speculate that this particular industrializing context may have been highly favourable to the continuation of normative kinship relations. Strong family and community values originating from a small peasant culture may have continued to shape people's lives in spite of the large number of factory chimneys arising throughout the town and affecting the lives of many. However, change was evident, and it did offer new opportunities to individuals. Young men and women may have seized upon these opportunities with both hands, greeting every chance at increasing individual freedom. Or did family values continue to prevail among young adults? If industrial turmoil was largely absent and households continued to be embedded in a strong local family and community network, what effect did this have on family patterns? If indeed 'critical life situations' were comparatively absent from working-class family life in Tilburg, this may have had a decreasing effect on the incidence of household extensions. Perhaps normative family values were shaped into new family patterns better suited to fit the demands and opportunities offered by the changing context. How indeed did nineteenth-century Tilburg families experience the small and big changes of their times?

3

Sources and methods

In this third chapter I shall discuss the source on which this study is based, the Dutch nineteenth-century population registers, and the quality of the data used for this study. The construction of the different samples used for analysis is outlined and in addition a number of methodological and analytical problems involved in the analysis of longitudinal family histories are dealt with.

3.1 Static versus dynamic

Within family history it has become widely accepted that the family should be considered as a dynamic concept. In the last volume of articles produced by the Cambridge Group, Sieder and Mitterauer concluded that the importance of a dynamic approach in the historical study of family and household was no longer in dispute.[1] When studying aspects of family and household the developmental stage of the household has to be taken into account. Unfortunately, the methodological realization of this goal is not always straightforward. Family historians are considerably hampered by the static character of their source material. Historians are mostly forced to rely on census listings which only render a frozen image of the household. As Laslett and Wall put it in their introduction to *Household and Family in Past Time*: 'We find ourselves for the most part forced to discuss a process as if it were in fact a state.'[2] The cross-sectional approach misses the essential processes that produce the particular manifestations of household composition as presented by the census.

However, while the theoretical advantages of a dynamic approach are universally acknowledged, the advocates of this view have not yet

[1] Sieder and Mitterauer, 'The reconstruction'.
[2] Laslett and Wall, *Household*, p. 34.

50

been able to devise a satisfactory general methodology for its implementation. In an attempt to break away from the static approach most scholars have employed the synthetic cohort method which relates the structure of the household to the age of its head. This method, which was first introduced by Lutz Berkner,[3] appears to present people's co-residential experiences in a life-cycle format but it remains unclear to what extent it covers the actual experiences of any individual or cohort over its life time.[4] Clearly, the synthetic cohort method is based on the ahistorical assumption that co-residential processes remain unchanged over generations. Studies of the life cycle based on single cross-sectional listings are, therefore, totally unsuitable for the purpose of relating family change to macro-level historical forces such as the process of industrialization.

In trying to escape from the severe limits of cross-sectional data some historians have embarked upon the laborious road of linking households and individuals from one census to the next. Katz's study of Hamilton is a good example of this approach as he linked households from the census of 1851 to the next in 1861.[5] The more recent volume produced by the Cambridge Group also contains three studies using this technique by Andorka and Faragó, Danhieux, and Sieder and Mitterauer.[6] This approach represents an improvement over studies based on a single enumeration, in particular if the inter-censal periods are relatively short, as is the case in the study by Sieder and Mitterauer who worked with yearly censuses. Nevertheless, problems remain. Not only is this type of record linkage extremely time-consuming, there is also the problem that data are lacking for the period in between the censuses. In addition, there is the problem of deciding what unit in the second census is to be regarded as the continuation of the household found in the first. This issue will be returned to later in more detail.

Unlike census material, the Dutch nineteenth-century population registers enable the historian to develop a genuinely dynamic approach. On the basis of these continuous registers, which mostly run up to 1910 or 1920, it is possible to follow the development of a large number of households from day to day at the level of a single community. They enable one to unravel the intricate dynamics of family life and the underlying processes producing different types of

---

[3] Berkner, 'The stem family'.
[4] See for an elaborate discussion of these problems: Kertzer and Schiaffino, 'Industrialization', pp. 364–9.
[5] Katz, *The people*.
[6] Andorka and Faragó, 'Pre-industrial household'; Danhieux, 'The evolving household'; Sieder and Mitterauer, 'The reconstruction'.

household structure and composition. The richness of this type of longitudinal record has already been demonstrated for Belgium by Van de Walle in his study of marital fertility in La Hulpe in the mid-nineteenth century and, more recently, by George Alter in his study of the female life course in Verviers.[7] The Dutch population registers, however, have hardly been touched. Moreover, those researchers who have used them, have not fully exploited their unique potential.[8] In part this reflects a lack of interest on the part of Dutch historians in individual and family histories, but may also be due to the complex, longitudinal organization of the registers themselves and the overwhelming amounts of data they contain.[9]

In this study of family life in nineteenth-century Tilburg I will be making use of the town's population registers while trying to adopt a dynamic perspective on family and household. This involves both a new way of thinking about households and families, and a search for new analytical techniques in order to grapple with the ever-changing complex process of the family. Some of the issues involved are discussed below. To begin with, a completely new and dynamic definition of the household has to be outlined. In the following sections I will first discuss the most pressing conceptual and analytical problems involved in longitudinal research on the family. After that I will briefly outline the nature of the population registers, the problems they posed and the samples of households that were used for analysis.

3.2   A dynamic definition of the household

What does the concept of the 'household' entail, and, even more important, when can a household be said to start and end? Most researchers in the field of family and household history do not have to concern themselves with the second of these questions. More or less forced by their sources, they use a cross-sectional approach. At most they have to ask themselves what constitutes a household at a

---

[7] Van de Walle, 'Household dynamics'; Alter, *Family*.

[8] We consider the real potential of the registers to be that they permit the reconstruction of entire life courses of large groups of people who usually did not leave behind any other concrete evidence of their existence. Also see Gutmann and Van de Walle, 'New sources'.

[9] Apart from this, the association with problems due to inadequate and or insufficient registration will play an important role. There are periods of bad or minimal registration in population registers, some elements even suffer permanently from underregistration, so that it becomes necessary to consult other sources such as the civil registration and the income tax registers for the benefit of correction. See for this the Gutman/Van de Walle article, mentioned in the previous note.

specific moment. In contrast, the longitudinal study of the family requires a dynamic definition of the concept of the household.

Clearly, several factors must be taken into account. Historical validity is one. It is evident that a definition of the household that bears no relationship to the historical reality of the households in question, turns this concept into an empty and useless instrument.[10] Similarly, the source material itself also stipulates a number of constraints. A definition of the household as a unit of consumption, for instance, is not feasible on the basis of population registers alone.

Taking these considerations into account I arrived at a definition of the household which is based on two elements. First, the household is defined as a co-resident domestic group, living at one particular address. This should not run us into too much trouble in the case of the Netherlands, as the primary structuring principle of the population registers is based on address.[11] Of course, we still need to remain sensitive to the possibly distorting influence of the opinions of the civil servants who went through the town deciding who was living with whom at a given address. The second element in the definition is constituted by the concept of the conjugal family, the family unit of parents and their unmarried offspring. There are societies where such an approach would be problematic, but Tilburg is not one of them. The conjugal family unit, more or less complete, formed the core of most of the town's households during the nineteenth century. Households consisting of unrelated co-residing individuals scarcely existed. Of course households headed by single persons did exist, but they are best considered as households of individuals who were the last surviving members of the conjugal family they belonged to. In most cases these were households of widows or widowers.

Following this definition a household begins with the independent establishment of a married couple indicated to be heading the household at a certain address. During the period over which the household exists, co-resident kin, servants, lodgers and others may be part of it, if they are registered at the same address. The conjugal unit of this couple and their unmarried offspring heading the household may be called the primary conjugal unit. The household is considered as remaining in existence as long as the function of head of the household is performed by those persons belonging to this conjugal

---

[10] We must realize however that such a cultural embedding of the concept household will impede possibilities for comparative historical research.

[11] Simple as this criterion appears, it may nevertheless not be easy to apply in certain areas of Europe. See for instance Wall in his introduction to *Family forms in historic Europe*, pp. 6–13.

unit. At first this will be the husband, after his death it will be passed onto the wife, and after the death of both parents onto the remaining unmarried children.

Other, and therefore secondary, conjugal units, may temporarily reside in the household. It is possible, for instance, for a son or daughter to marry while remaining a resident within the parental household, together with his or her partner. The parental household obviously remains in existence, provided that one of the parents is still registered as household head. If, for whatever reason, the son or daughter who married into the parental household takes over control of the household to become the new head, the parental household is considered to have ended, while that of the child has just started. The parents in their turn now constitute a secondary unit in the new household of their child. Another example may further clarify the working of the definition. After the death of both parents, the remaining unmarried children continue living together under the charge of the eldest brother or sister. After a short while, however, the eldest child decides to marry and to bring his or her partner into the household, while the younger brothers and sisters remain resident. At that moment the history of the independent conjugal unit of the child that marries begins while that of the parents' ends. Thus, our definition of the household is based on the history of the independent household of one conjugal unit of parents and their unmarried offspring living at one and the same address.

But this does not end our problems. What are we to do when one of the parents decides to get married after his or her partner has died? The following rules, admittedly somewhat arbitrary, were decided upon to deal with this type of situation. If the remaining parent decides to move, possibly with children, in order to form a new household together with his or her new partner at another address, then the original household is taken to have ended. But should the new spouse simply move in with the remaining parent, then this is considered to constitute a continuation of the original household.

The difficulties involved in deciding what constitutes one and the same household over a period of time have led a number of scholars to renounce the household as the appropriate unit of analysis in family history, mostly in favour of the individual life course.[12] They

---

[12] See for instance Kertzer, Schiaffino, 'Industrialization'. Sieder and Mitterauer ('The reconstruction') opt for the use of the individual farm or property as the longitudinal unit of analysis, which however would lose its efficacy in the urban context where most of the property is more or less continuously sold to strangers, or divided and dissipated.

argue that when linking census listings over time it is impossible to decide which household in the second census should be regarded as the continuation of the household in the first listing. Consider the following example. In one census we find two married brothers co-residing together with their respective families. In the intercensal period the brothers decide to split households for some reason so that in the next census they will appear as two separate households. Which of the two households should be regarded as the continuation of the original household of the two brothers?

Continuous population registers enable the researcher to avoid these pitfalls, in that they actually tell you who moved out from whom. But they cannot automatically resolve all difficulties. The historian is still required to exercise judgement as to when some households end or begin. This inevitably leaves room for disagreement in some circumstances. Households of two co-residing married brothers and their families simply did not exist in Tilburg, but a similar case arises where an ageing couple co-resides with married children. After some time the two units split up and each moves to a new address. Following my definition of the household, I would consider the unit headed by the parents, which was the primary conjugal unit we started off with, to be the continuation of the original household. Of course, the same principle might be applied to the case of the frérèche as described above. It is only dependent on the possibility for the historian to decide in all cases who is the head of household.

Another, arguably more serious, problem facing the household as the unit of analysis is the claim that it obscures the individual and the extent to which they pass through certain life course transitions such as marriage, headship of a family, parenthood or widowhood.[13] If one wanted to examine the extent to which individuals experienced these stages in their lives, it is clearly essential to incorporate individual level analysis. At one level, this is merely a matter of adjusting the research strategy to the questions that are being asked. However, more generally, it is surely incorrect to assume that individual lives are the result solely of individual decisions. Even under conditions of increasing individualism this is not a tenable view. Rather, individual life courses are embedded within a familial context without which they are impossible to understand.[14] As Tamara Hareven rightly points out, the life-course approach should

---

[13] Kertzer and Schiaffino, 'Industrialization', p. 365; Elder, Jr, 'Families'.
[14] See for instance: Segalen, 'Life course patterns'.

not lead historians to focus on the individual to the exclusion of the family.[15]

If the aim of the historian should be, therefore, to study both the family and the individual, then the approach suggested here is highly suitable. A household-based approach using population registers still enables the researcher to examine individual-level phenomena such as the departure of children from the home or the extent to which parents were forced to give up headship of their household in old age. In fact I would contend that the combination of individual and household analysis provides deeper insights than either taken in isolation. For example, when studying the extent to which parents and children maintained relations with their extended kin and with each other, the strength of nineteenth-century family life can be seen in a meaningful and coherent context. In short, the form of analysis suggested here seems to be well suited to answering the questions of most interest to family historians.

While there are many valuable aspects to the definition of the household suggested here, inevitably there are also drawbacks. The first relates to the size of the study. If it is not possible to include the entire population of a community, and analysis is based on a sample, then some valuable information will be lost. For example, when co-residing married children take over the headship of the parental household it comes to an end, and we consequently lose sight of the parents. What happens to them? Do their children lovingly look after them or do they get rid of them by sending them to another household or an old people's home? When studying the functioning of a kinship system, questions like these can not be easily disregarded. In fact the same problem exists for those children who leave the household. We may know where they go, but what happens to them after that remains unknown. Nevertheless, it is important to stress that these problems do not arise from the defects inherent in the definition itself. They only arise if we have to confine ourselves to samples of households. If the entire population residing within the town could be included, departing parents moving to their children's households, or parents handing over the headship of the household to their married children, would from that moment onwards have been included into the latter's household history. This 'downstream' household could then seamlessly be joined to the household history of the parents. With comprehensive data on the entire population, no

---

[15] Hareven, 'Family history', pp. xiii–xv.

forms of household, or to put it another way, not a single period of time in the life of an individual, would have to fall outside the scope of our dynamic definition of the household.[16] It would then become possible to trace individuals on their march over time through subsequent household histories.

However, even when a sample of households is used, it is possible to keep track of departing individuals to a limited extent. Moreover, other research requirements of the present study necessitated at least a partial recording of the whereabouts of departing sons. The analysis of social mobility patterns of the fathers and sons required tracking down their occupations and income in municipal income tax listings. These listings are accessed by address, thereby requiring information on all addresses within Tilburg to which sons moved after leaving their parental home. In addition to these addresses various other types of information were recorded while the same was done for daughters residing outside the parental home.

3.3 The analysis of longitudinal household data

Having defined the nature of a household history, how does one analyse its intricate dynamics when we are concerned with a large number of cases? In their examination of longitudinal data on nineteenth-century Austrian peasant families Sieder and Mitterauer charted and discussed the individual development of thirteen households over time.[17] The way they presented their material is very similar to the representation of the history of one of the Tilburg families in figure 3.1. It would be patently impossible, however, to present any large number of household histories in this way, discussing the peculiarities of each household's development. We would in no time lose ourselves in the 'morass of detail and small numbers' envisaged by Richard Wall as being all too easily the result of dynamic household studies.[18]

What concepts and techniques should we then employ in the study of a large amount of longitudinal household data? Few examples exist today of studies in which households are analysed dynamically with reference to comparable research questions. Clearly, the methodology of analysing longitudinal household data is still poorly

[16] That is with the exception of the time people resided in institutions such as convents and prisons which could not in any way qualify as households.
[17] Sieder and Mitterauer, 'The reconstruction'.
[18] Wall, 'Introduction', p. 3.

HHNR 267

ppnr:	name	date of birth
3125	driessen, martinus bern	14-02-1845
3126	oostendorp, maria	24-11-1848
3127	driessen, gerardus bern	19-05-1873
3128	driessen, theodorus herm	14-06-1876
3129	driessen, wilhelmus mart	11-11-1878
3130	driessen, johannes mart	27-09-1881
3131	driessen, johanna ma	28-10-1883
3132	driessen, hermanus mart	10-04-1885

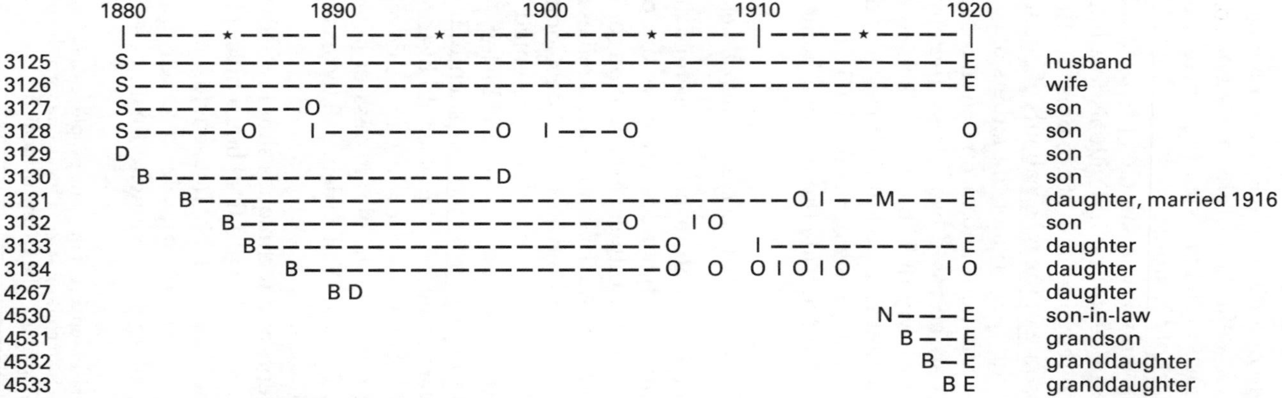

ppnr:	name	date of birth	relation
3133	driessen, antonia ma	28-09-1886	husband
3134	driessen, gerarda joh	20-06-1888	wife
4267	driessen, dina sus	08-04-1890	son
4530	v lieshout, henricus jos lamb	17-09-1887	son
4531	v lieshout, maximinus mart ma	20-07-1917	son
4532	v lieshout, maria cath ant	09-08-1918	son
4533	v lieshout, catharina jos ma	04-10-1919	daughter, married 1916
			son
			daughter
			daughter
			daughter
			son-in-law
			grandson
			granddaughter
			granddaughter

```
        1880      1890      1900      1910      1920
          |---------|----*----|----*----|----*----|----
3125    S----*-------------------------------*-------E
3126    S-----------------------------------E
3127    S--------O
3128    S----O---------------O----------------O
3129    D
3130      B----------------D
3131        B-------------------O----O I----M----E
3132        B-----------O I O-------------O I O--I
3133                              O O--O I O I----E
3134                              O----------O----E
4267                          O----O I O I--O----I
4530                                      N------E
4531                                        B----E
4532                                        B----E
4533                                          B E
```

Explanation of symbols:

S = present at start of register
E = present at closing of register
B = entry by birth

D = exit by death
O = exit through migration
I = entry through migration

M = marriage
N = entry through marriage

Note: when successive entries and exits occur within a single year only the final move is displayed

Figure 3.1. The history of a household

developed.[19] Hence, a great deal of time and energy had to be devoted to thinking out appropriate analytical strategies, and subsequently to developing the corresponding computer programs. Only with these tools could an effective understanding of the development of nineteenth-century households emerge. In spite of the time taken in their development, the concepts and methodology outlined in this study should be looked upon as a first effort towards a more comprehensive and penetrating methodology for the longitudinal study of historical households.

The analytical concept which seems best suited to form the basis for further elaboration is that of the family cycle. The sociological concept of the family cycle was introduced in the 1960s and 1970s in order to incorporate a dynamic element in the historical study of the family. Traditionally, the family cycle provided a sequential perspective on the development of the family whereby the family moved through a number of fixed stages of parenthood, beginning with the marriage of the couple, the birth of the first child and so on, until reaching the stage of the post-parental, ageing family.[20] However, historical families frequently fail to correspond to the orderly twentieth-century patterning of the classical family cycle model.[21] It is entirely possible, however, to apply family cycle approaches without making use of a sequential model with rigidly predetermined stages. The family cycle in this more flexible usage serves to depict the trajectory through time followed by the conjugal unit of parents and their offspring after their establishment as an independent household. The family cycle then indicates the passing of time for a cohort of married couples and their unmarried offspring during the period they are heading their own households. The use of the concept in this way makes possible a stylized representation of the co-residential experiences of a cohort of married couples.

Events relating to the changing composition of the households, such as the entry of extended kin members or the departure from home of sons and daughters, can then be charted along this trajectory to determine their timing. Moreover, by counting the number of times a certain event occurs over the entire cycle or parts of it, its frequency may be established. Or, in an alternative framework, we

---

[19] Contemporary demographers are more familiar with such data and its analysis, but their substantive interests rarely coincide with those of historians, see Keilman, Keyfitz, 'Recurrent issues'.

[20] See e.g. Hill, Rodgers, 'The developmental approach'; Anderson, *Family structure*, applied the life-cycle model in this way to Preston families; p. 49.

[21] Segalen, 'The family cycle'.

may measure durations, e.g. the length of time extended kin members spent co-residing in the household. This time-based perspective can be supplemented by a cross-sectional type of analysis in an attempt to illuminate the reasons why specific household structures arise. Thus, we can examine the structure of the household at the time when married children entered the household of their parents at any point along the household's cycle or during any specific period of that cycle. By looking at the longitudinal perspective in this way, it is possible to reveal some of the mechanisms that underlay nineteenth-century household formation.

Central to an effective and lucid application of the method discussed here however is the use of age-cohorts of married couples. The households in the two main samples in this study are all headed by married couples within the 30–35 age group at the start of the period of observation of their households. All households are therefore in comparable developmental stages from the moment their history comes under observation. This has the advantage that all households are more or less simultaneously moving through biological time, family time as well as historical time. All couples are exposed to similar historical influences and similar family events during more or less the same periods. This makes it possible to reduce the histories of the households of this age-cohort of married couples to the common denominator of the more abstract time scale of the family cycle. If we were to include all households headed by couples or widowed individuals of whatever age present in the community at a certain date and follow them forwards through time from that moment on, additional structuring principles would have to be brought to bear. Some of the difficulties arising from this will be seen in chapter 8 where I proceed to analyse households headed by factory workers and domestic weavers. Although these two smaller samples also contain histories of households headed by married couples at the beginning of those histories, they do not all begin at the same historical moment, nor the same moment in the individual life course of the couples.

3.4 *The population register and the quality of the data*

Continuous population registers in the sense of bound documents with non-removable pages were prescribed in the Netherlands by the Royal Decree of 22 December 1849. The registers were to record the population legally residing within the community. This was changed in 1861 so that from then on the registers recorded the *de facto* population.[22] In most communities population registers in the traditional sense remained in use until 1910 or 1920, after which date a new form of continuous registration system was introduced consisting of loose sheets, the so-called *gezinskaarten* (family-cards), based on the registration unit of the family as opposed to the household.[23] In Tilburg the registers continued to be used up to and including 1920.

The census taken on 19 November 1849 served as a starting point for the first population register. The communal authorities copied the census returns onto the population register, and from then on all changes occurring in the resident population in the next decade were recorded. With each subsequent census the procedure was repeated so that every single register covers a time span of ten years in between the different censuses. Each household was entered on a double folio page, with the head of the household first, then his wife, children, relatives and other members of the household, such as servants or lodgers. For each individual the register recorded a number of items of information: date and place of birth, relation to the head of the household, sex, marital status, occupation and religion. Additional columns were provided to record information on in-migrants (former residence and date of arrival), out-migrants (future residence and date of departure) as well as on date of death. New household members arriving after the start of the register, through in-migration or birth, were added to the list of individuals already recorded on the page, in the order of arrival, while those moving out or those that had died were simply crossed out with reference to place and date of migration or date of death. When someone returned to the household after having lived elsewhere for a period, he or she was always entered again together with all personal information at the bottom of the list. Finally, the register also recorded the address of the household.

The population register thus combines census listings with vital registration in a particularly convenient way. It presents information on demographic events in an already linked format on the entire population, even the very mobile, and it facilitates the computation of a wide range of demographic rates. The population register further enables the historian to follow the evolution of the family and the household on a day-to-day basis throughout the entire period 1849–1920. This is made possible by linking the entire series of registers by using alphabetical indexes which exist for each separate register. The indexes list all individuals, giving their full name, their year of birth

[22] *Geschiedenis*, p. 82.
[23] For this period see: van den Brink,'The Netherlands'.

and all volumes and pages on which information concerning this individual is found in that particular register. Another interesting aspect of the registers is that they can be used in combination with other sources which may greatly expand the amount of information available. In this study I have used the registers in conjunction with municipal income tax listings and militia registers in order to appreciate more precisely the social and economic position of the household and the individuals within it.

How accurate and complete were the Tilburg population registers? In the following pages I will discuss the registers' strengths and weaknesses which have become apparent in the course of this study. First, there is the problem of the lack of accuracy in the registration of occupations which is generally acknowledged to be the case for all Dutch population registers. Usually occupations were recorded upon entry into the register but were not updated afterwards. In quite a number of cases the only occupation entered concerned the head of household. The wife's occupation was recorded only occasionally, while registration of children's occupations was very erratic. In addition to the possibility that some of the occupations were out of date at the time of entry into the register, there is also the problem of vague categories: the entry 'merchant' may at the same time refer to a very rich and successful businessman and a marginal trader barely able to keep the family out of Poor Relief. Additional information about occupation and above all income is therefore extremely valuable.

Information on the relationship of individuals to the head is always stated clearly and correctly, with the exception of the first register covering the period 1849–59 which did not include a separate column on relationship. However, inferences about the most likely relationship to the head of household were in almost all cases relatively easy to make on the basis of such factors as order of registration, sex, and name and age. The fact that married women were always registered by their maiden name greatly facilitated identification procedures, though in some cases recourse had to be made to the vital registration. The good quality of the registration of relations in the later registers, however, does not rule out the possibility that some more distant kin relations may have been passed off falsely as servants. The relationships between individuals is often implicitly but sometimes also explicitly recorded, such as in cases where a married couple not heading the household is present: the two individuals concerned are always explicitly indicated to be man and wife.

Internal migration is heavily underrecorded in the registers prior to 1880 but only as far as movements of households between addresses is concerned.[24] Individuals moving between households were normally accurately recorded although some unrecorded cases did exist in the final years of some registers when young people moved to other households in order to become servants. However, internal migration of individuals not accompanied by demographic events, such as marriage, was registered without reference to a date, so that the timing of the move had to be inferred from other entries on the page.[25] Internal migration of individuals resulting from a marriage and the establishment of a new household, however, was always accurately recorded, including the date. This is in marked contrast with the Belgian registers, or at least those of La Hulpe.[26]

A further serious problem is general underregistration of new arrivals as well as of people moving out either by death or migration. The problem is most urgent in the case of the most transient segment of the population, domestic servants and lodgers. In all probability a large number of in-migrating servants were not recorded at all, while subsequent moves within the town of those servants who were entered may have remained unrecorded. This was probably due to either a lack of interest on the side of the registrars or a failure to report the move on the part of the population. This aspect is of some importance to the present study in that it relates to the time at which children left the parental household. Underregistration of children leaving the parental household to become servants in other households within the town would cause an upward bias in the mean age for leaving home. The only way positively to identify underregistration of this type occurs when children disappear at the start of a new register or turn up in other people's households without being crossed out in the parental household. Fortunately, few such cases were encountered. By making use of the information available on the household concerned inferences were generally easy to make as to the timing of departure. Sometimes acceptable estimates of the timing of exit were also made possible by checking the annual tax listings which recorded the number of children present under the age of 16. Nevertheless, the possibility remains that the early exits of some children went unnoticed. We have to assume that their weight in the large number of observations in this study was only small.

Underregistration of co-residing extended kin members was also

---

[24] Until 1910 the address stated did not refer to a specific street or house number. All households were simply numbered sequentially within their neighbourhood, which 'address' was also used in other sources such as the tax listings.

[25] In these cases imputed dates were given, see also note 28.

[26] Gutmann and Van de Walle, 'New sources', p. 136.

apparent in a few sudden appearances and disappearances between registers. However, the small number of cases seems to assure that underregistration of extended kin was a considerably less pressing problem. Some of the unrecorded exits of extended kin, which mostly occurred during the final year of the existing register, could be resolved by checking the death registers. For instance, in the case of disappearing grandparents this usually provided correct dates and types of exit. Nevertheless, estimates of the frequency of extended family households based on these data are probably biased downwards. In addition to the vital registers, the annual tax listings could be used to cross check the population registers on the presence of adult co-residing extended kin. The municipal income listings usually recorded the head of the household as well as those adult members not belonging to the head's immediate family. These extended kin were considered to be responsible for their own upkeep. This category included the head's parents or parents-in-law and siblings of the head and his wife, regardless of their age, sex and the amount of income they actually earned. In a few cases the tax listings were successfully consulted as a means to date entries and exits of kin more accurately, although these listings did not record all cases of kin co-residence.

In general it is reasonable to assume that the registers were fairly accurate in reporting demographic events such as births, deaths and marriages, but were a little less accurate in reporting migration. This becomes understandable when we consider the fact that the reporting of births, deaths and marriages necessitated registration in the vital registers, which were far more conscientiously kept up to date. On such occasions it required less of an effort to realize registration in the population register as well. Little notes arriving at the registrar's office reporting the out-migration of individuals were easy to let slide, resulting in delays in registration, and leading sometimes to the failure to record at all. The practice of entering births, deaths and marriages simultaneously into the vital registers and the population registers is evident from the fact that the events in the population register mostly are assigned the date of the certificate which in the case of births and deaths usually differs from the event itself by one day.

The high quality of the population registers in recording demographic events such as births is indicated by checking the registration of births in the population register against the birth registers for the two smallest samples of households used in this study. Results are presented in appendix 1. In 'normal' times at the most 0.2% of all births occurring within the decade were not entered in the population register. All such cases concerned children dying soon after birth.[27] However, appendix 2 also indicates the period in which a serious crisis affected the system resulting in a total neglect of the population register. The seven births that went unrecorded in the decade 1860–70 all fell in the few years between 1865 and 1868, marking the beginning and end of the authorities' failure to keep the register updated. A final judgement as to the reason for this failure is impossible; however, it is most conspicuous that the crisis coincided with the heavy influx of migrants during the second half of the decade. The in-migration of the sixties, on a scale unparalleled in Tilburg before or since, may have given the registrar difficulties in carrying out all his administrative duties. The absence of high-quality accurate registration was self-evident, even without compiling the appropriate statistics, in the otherwise complex and minute recording of the registers. In order to compensate for this underregistration a systematic check of all households under study was run for the entire period 1860–69 by way of the annual income tax listing, to detect underregistration of kin and missed exits of children under the age of 16. The difficulties in this period led to a relatively high percentage of events of which the date could not be established with complete certainty.[28] The figures concerning the number of events for which dates were uncertain in all samples are given in appendix 1.

The final register, covering the period 1910–20, presented a different problem to the study of households which had until then remained quite unnoticed. It seems as if in this period the registrar was already experimenting with a family-based registration system, which after 1920 was to replace the household-based system of the registers. The 1910–20 register initially recorded all those co-residing in one household together on the same page as was usual.[29] However, some of the changes occurring after 1910 were recorded on the basis of the nuclear family as the primary administrative unit.

---

[27] This is considerably better than the La Hulpe registers in which 9.2% of the births in average remained unrecorded, see: Gutmann and Van de Walle, 'New sources', p. 140.

[28] In those cases in which dates were uncertain or unclear from the register, estimated dates were used. The following guideline was followed. If there was no certainty as to month and day, the fictitious date of 31 June is recorded; should the date be completely unknown, then the estimated year is recorded, with the entry 00 for both day and month. When analysing the information contained in the database these uncertainties may be taken into account, when appropriate.

[29] With the exception of servants and lodgers for which a separate register was started in 1910, no doubt in relation with the forthcoming introduction of the family-based registration system.

While processing the households of the 1880–1920 cohort and their children it became clear that some of the married children, although recorded on different pages in the register, were actually living at the same address as their parents. Consultation of the income tax listings confirmed the co-residence in all cases.[30] This discovery necessitated a check of all addresses of parents against those of their children revealing a large number of temporary extended family arrangements. The new set-up of the 1910 register inevitably means that I may have missed some incidences of co-residence in those cases where the ageing parents of the 1880–1920 cohort co-resided with relatives other than their own married children and grandchildren. However, whilst it was rather exceptional for families to have more distant kin in the household in all stages of its history, this was particularly so in the final stages. I therefore assumed that only a tiny fraction of the co-residing kin in that period fails to appear in the database.

To conclude, I would like to stress that the overall quality of the register and the elaborate attempts at correction wherever necessary provide sufficient confidence in the data to embark upon their analysis.

3.5   The samples

The core of the study is formed by two samples of households headed by couples who at the start of each period of observation, 1849 and 1880 respectively, were in the age range of 30–35 years old. It was further specified that both husband and wife were either both born within the town or both outside it. These two samples are the age-cohorts of married couples referred to earlier in this chapter. Households headed by married couples formed the overwhelming majority of all households in and below this age range, see appendix 33. Couples of mixed geographical descent were excluded. The first cohort group of households covers the forty-year period between 1849 and 1890, and consists of 361 households of which only 51 had co-residing kin present at the end of 1849. The entire cohort of parents, being relatively small, was used for analysis.

The following cohort was to consist of households in which the couples were aged 30–35 in 1880, and whose histories were to be traced until, at the latest, the end of 1920. Considering the size of the

---

[30] The tax listings were then also used to determine which of the two couples, the parents or the married children, were heading the household. We assumed the first name entered to be the head of household.

town's population in 1880 the use of a sample for this second cohort group was required. Considering the few absolute cases in which extended kin were present in 1880, it was decided in favour of a disproportionately stratified sample with an overrepresentation of extended households. Thus, all eighty-six households extended in the beginning of 1880 and belonging to this cohort group of parents were accepted into the research group while the nuclear households were sampled. The sampling was carried out in two steps. A first round of sampling, drawing one in every three migrant households and one in every five of the native households,[31] was executed for the purpose of a preliminary study of family and household in Tilburg.[32] In order to increase the absolute number of observations for the present study a second round of sampling was implemented: of the remaining nuclear households of migrants every second household was added to the existing sample and every fourth of the native nuclear households. This made a total of 389 households in which the weight of households having kin in the beginning of 1880 was almost doubled. For some parts of the analysis therefore this group was corrected by randomly excluding the required number of households of the latter type, resulting in a total group of 343 households of which 40 households had co-resident relatives present.[33]

The final part of the present study makes use of two smaller samples which were headed by domestic weavers and factory workers. The way these two latter groups of households were constructed is explained in detail in chapter 7.

[31] For sampling all households were listed in the order of their appearance within the register which recorded households by neighbourhood. This ensured a sample representative of all the different neighbourhoods of the time.

[32] See: Janssens, 'Industrialization', p. 39. In the first round of sampling households that could not be observed continuously for at least ten years were excluded. For the present study this rule was dropped while the few households that had been excluded in that way in the first round were readmitted to the sample in exchange for their former replacements.

[33] Survey of the 1880 research cohort of households headed by 30–35 year-old parents of either native or migrant origin:

Total cohort	total households	747
	nuclear	661
	extended	86 (11.5%)
Uncorrected sample	total households	389
	nuclear	303
	extended	86 (22.1%)
Corrected sample	total households	343
	nuclear	303
	extended	40 (11.6%)

The data for all household histories were processed and analysed by computer. A methodology was devised which made it possible to feed the data directly into a micro-computer, without any intermediate processing by hand. A description of this so-called 'direct-entry' methodology is given in appendix 4.

4

Family structure through time

In this chapter the results of the comparative analysis of the developmental family cycle of two age-cohorts of married couples in nineteenth-century Tilburg will be presented. This constitutes the first of the four strategies, discussed in chapter 1, that I have chosen in order to deal with the problem of the relationship between developments within the family and the process of social change. Here I will concentrate on the following question. To what extent did the second half of the nineteenth century and the beginning of the twentieth witness a decline in family cohesion, as expressed in the relative occurrence of extended kin in the household and the strength of generational links between parents and children? Methodologically, the dominant perspective is a dynamic one: co-residential family arrangements will be analysed over the course of the family cycle.

4.1   Family structure along the cycle

In chapter 1 the assumption made in traditional family theory, that the process of industrialization has a disruptive effect on kinship relations beyond the immediate family, was discussed at some length. According to one sociological theory, the internal dynamics of the industrial system required an occupationally and geographically mobile reservoir of workers. Hence, family solidarity in industrial society necessarily had to be restricted to the members of the nuclear family only. This was done by segregating the family from the economic system. Thus, the process of industrialization necessarily implied a process of nuclearization of the family group. Competing theories suggest either a continuation of existing family patterns, or even a rise in traditional complex family households. According to

69

this second view families do not just passively adapt to the social and economic changes surrounding them, they actively make use of traditional family patterns to cope with the 'critical life situations' created by the process of change. Thus, people act on traditional values in their confrontation with modern problems.

I shall begin by measuring in various ways changes in the extent to which families received extra-nuclear kin members into their homes. Attention will also be given to the question of what caused families to live with kin, and what functions the extended family structures may have had. Next, I will examine changes in the generational relationship between parents and children. A strong, normative link between generations may be regarded as the linchpin of the extended family system. If the relationship of children towards the family of origin permits a greater autonomy of the child, one major force making for extended family co-residence will be removed.

I look first at the frequency with which families in Tilburg co-resided with kin. The innumerable studies of household structure in north-west Europe have produced frequencies of extended households, ranging from about 10% to about 20%. Tilburg seems to fit into this regional pattern perfectly well, with an overall percentage of extended households of 10% in 1849 and 9.7% in 1880.[1] Dutch household structure in the nineteenth century however seems to resemble much more the situation in preindustrial England, for which Laslett established a frequency of 10%,[2] than the English urban-industrial household pattern. For Rotterdam and Groningen in the second half of the century, for instance, figures of household extension have been put forward ranging from 6% to 13% for the former and 11% to 14% for the latter town.[3] These are both much lower than the 23% for Preston and 21% found for York in the mid-nineteenth century.[4] Finally, extended households in nineteenth-century Tilburg appear to be as frequent as in the rural Brabantine areas a century earlier. Klep found 10% of the households in late eighteenth-century West-Brabant to be co-residing with kin.[5]

---

[1] These percentages should be handled with care since they relate exclusively to households headed by marital couples. Solitaries and households headed by unmarried individuals or those widowed were excluded. Households headed by widows or widowers may have contained quite a number of cases of kin co-residence, so that the total number of extensions is biased slightly downwards. For survey of household structure in 1849 and 1880 see appendix 5.

[2] Laslett, 'Mean household size', p. 149.

[3] van Dijk, *Rotterdam*, p. 284; Kooij, *Groningen*, p. 26.

[4] Anderson, *Family structure*, p. 44; Armstrong, 'The interpretation', p. 72.

[5] Klep, 'Het huishouden', p. 73.

However, it is possible to go beyond such purely static approaches to the issue of household structure by looking at kin co-residence from the perspective of the history of the household. For this purpose I will be using the two cohort samples of households covering complete 40-year histories for each cohort. The first cohort spans the period from 1849 to 1890 and contains 361 households, while the second cohort of 389 households runs from 1880 to 1920. For reasons connected with the sampling procedure, described in chapter 3, the latter group will on certain occasions be restricted to 343 households.[6] Where this is the case it will be indicated in the text. The couples heading these households were all aged 30–35 at the beginning of the two periods of observation, that is in 1849 and 1880 respectively, which makes these two groups two successive age-cohorts of married couples. The heads and their wives of 1880 could well have been the children of those heading the households of 1849. Indeed some actually were.

As would be expected the developmental stage the household had reached was of some importance to its structure. This is reflected in the slightly higher frequency, compared with other age groups, with which the two cohort groups we will be studying here were living with kin in 1849 and 1880: 14.1% for the former cohort and 11.5% for the latter.[7] What happened to family structure after these two initial points in time? In my efforts to outline the relative importance of kin co-residence in a longitudinal perspective I will be using a number of different approaches, which may roughly be divided into those relating to frequency and those relating to duration. To begin with let us have a look at the problem of frequency. Having measured the percentage of extensions in the initial years, 1849 and 1880, we could go on to chart the percentages in all of the following years throughout the entire family cycle; this yields the number of extensions by family cycle year. This procedure could indicate sudden falls or rises in the number of those living with kin and can, for instance, be used to detect relations with historical events intersecting with the history of the household. Important as this technique may be, it does not properly inform us on the crucial question of how many of the families were actually sharing specific co-residential experiences. I therefore add observations on the number of families that had ever received extended kin into their homes. Finally, the same principle may be applied to different stages in the development of the household, for

---

[6] For further details on data collection, sampling procedure, and other methodological and conceptual issues the reader should turn to chapter 3.
[7] See appendix 5 for survey of household structure in 1849 and 1880.

instance when the number of households containing co-resident kin during the first ten or twenty years of the cycle is computed. This then indicates the number of families sharing a particular co-residential experience at particular stages of the family cycle. Before proceeding to the issue of duration, I will first examine the various measures of frequency.

To begin with, I will investigate the relative incidence of extended households by year of the family cycle. To this end the number of extended family households was plotted as a percentage of all households present for each year of the family cycle for both groups. The count in this procedure was 'optimistic' in the sense that the household was considered to be extended for a particular year when at some time during that year a relative had been present, even if it were only for a fraction of the year. The result is presented in figure 4.1. Throughout the first thirty cycle years the 1849–90 cohort, starting off from the level of 14%, displays a remarkably stable number of extensions by year: just above 10%. Towards the end of the family cycle, however, we witness a gradual rise in the number of extensions to 16% at the most in some of the final years. It is clear that the proportion of extensions by year is very modest indeed for this cohort group. What is perhaps more interesting is its stability, particularly in respect to the period between the fifteenth and twenty-fifth year of the cycle which coincided with the period of heavy in-migration of the late sixties and early seventies. The absence of increases in the number of extensions seems to suggest that there were no housing shortages at the time. But we must also realize that in this period the elder sons and daughters of these households were reaching the marriageable age. If housing shortages did occur, due to the influx of young migrant families, the results of figure 4.1 may be taken to indicate that the sons and daughters in the earlier cohort were postponing marriage rather than marrying into the parental household. Finally, the fact that the number of extensions for this cohort hardly rose at all during the final years of the cycle would appear to suggest that kin co-residence did not become any more frequent as parents reached old age.

The later cohort deviates only slightly from the level of their predecessors during the first thirty years during which the number of extensions tends to fall slowly to 5% or 6%. There are, however, two conspicuous, if small, peaks in this period, one in the tenth and the other in the twentieth year which are both coincidental with the start of new registers. As each new population register started off on the basis of the census returns these peaks clearly indicate incidences of

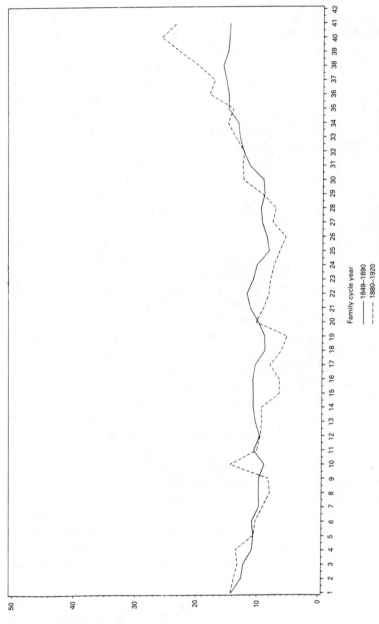

Figure 4.1. Proportion of extended family households by family cycle year for two age-cohorts of married couples (corrected sample for 1880–1920 cohort)

Family cycle year

1849–1890

1880–1920

underregistration occurring towards the final years of the previous register. The two peaks suggest that perhaps the number of extensions for this group in reality remained as high as 14% to 15% during the first ten years after which it slowly fell to the level of 10% during the second decade. This apparently small deterioration in coverage is surprising and not easy to explain, given the assumption that the earlier registers were probably of lesser quality than the later ones, and that these peaks do not appear in the 1849–90 cohort. Towards the end of their cycle the families in the later cohort experience a steady rise in the number of extensions up to a level of 25%. In this period, between the thirtieth and fortieth year of the cycle, parents were reaching old age, they were beyond sixty, and it is likely that almost all of their children had left the parental home. In addition, this cycle stage coincides with the severe shortages in the housing market arising after 1912. Obviously, these considerations would suggest that many elderly parents started to co-reside with their married children who in this way were resolving their housing problem. Before going on, it is important to stress that the different historical experiences these families were undergoing during their history did not result in widely diverging levels of extensions by year or entirely different courses over their cycle. The level of extensions as represented in figure 4.1 is determined by both the number of households with kin and by the duration of the time these households remained extended. As a consequence the two relatively similar curves could theoretically be the result of very dissimilar numbers of households going through the experience of household extension. One curve may be the result of a marginal group of households who are more or less continuously co-residing with relatives, while the other could relate to large numbers of households in which kin co-reside only once and for only short periods of time. In other words, the graph does not inform us as to the relative distribution of the tendency to live with kin throughout both cohorts. The percentage of households ever extended by decade may help to provide an indication for the relative distribution of the phenomenon of kin co-residence during different periods of the cycle. It is computed as a percentage of all households present at the beginning of that particular decade.

Table 4.1 presents the figures resulting from this operation.[8] It

---

[8] Some examples may clarify the construction of this table. All households attaining an extended structure during the first ten years of observation contribute to the percentage of extensions in this period. If, however, one of these households became extended for a second time within the same period it still contributed only once to the number of extensions occurring in the first decade. Finally, to take one

confirms the moderate importance of extended family co-residence for the cohort of families from 1849 to 1890. Per decade, the percentage of extensions in this group ranged from 17% to 21% for all households present. In the second cohort, kin co-residence during the first ten years of the cycle appears to be a little more frequent: almost a quarter of all households were extended. On the whole, however, their cycle only begins to diverge significantly from the former cohort's experience towards the end. During the final decade 42% of all households still present at the beginning of that decade experienced a phase of extended family living. As they grew older, parents of the 1880–1920 cohort took in relatives much more often than did parents belonging to the earlier cohort. Compared with their parents' generation they doubled the percentage of extended family households during the later years of their household history. As was indicated above, this may have been connected to the shortages in the housing market arising after 1912. Other family history studies have suggested that households are most likely to be extended in both their early and later years.[9] While the latter cohort does indeed show this pattern, such peaking at the beginning and end of the family cycle did not occur for the earlier cohort. Kin co-residence was spread more or less evenly over the entire cycle.

What the values in figure 4.1 come down to is that, when all extensions are taken into account, a majority of the households in the 1880–1920 cohort passed through an extended phase at some point along the household history.[10] Of all 343 households in this group 56.9% co-resided with kin at some point.[11] The generation of their

example, in the case of kin members entering the household during the ninth year in order to leave again in the twelfth year of observation this specific household would contribute to the number of extensions in both the first and the second decade of observation.

[9] Van de Walle, 'Household dynamics'.

[10] This echoes Berkner's conclusion in his study of the eighteenth-century peasant household in Austria (Berkner, 'The stem family', p. 406).

[11] In an article on previous work on the 1880–1920 cohort the number of households ever extended in this cohort was estimated to have been 64% (see Janssens, 'Industrialization'). This percentage is higher than the one computed here because of the different cycles used. That article makes use of the 'parental cycle' instead of a 'family cycle' because at the time I could not for all families distinguish between households still headed by the parents I had started off with in 1880 and those households in which married children had become the new head of household. Further archival research made possible the distinction between the different types of households. See chapter 3 note 30. On the basis of new calculations our previous estimation concerning extensions during the parental cycle proved to be correct. In the 1880–1920 cohort 67.3% of all parents experienced kin co-residence at least once at some time during their life in their own or their children's household. For parents in the earlier cohort this percentage amounted to 42.9%.

Table 4.1 *Extension by kin during the family cycle by decade for two age-cohorts of married couples*

	Decade			
	1st	2nd	3rd	4th
1849–1890				
% Extended	17.5	18.0	19.9	21.5
N	361	339	317	275
1880–1920				
% Extended	24.8	18.6	21.6	42.0
N	343	330	320	257

parents did so to a lesser degree: 39.1% of all households in that cohort received kin into their homes at least once. These diverging percentages are mainly the result of the much larger number of households in the later cohort extending themselves to include kin in the final decade of their cycle. To some degree the number of extensions in the earlier cohort may be biased downwards somewhat as a result of incomplete registration prior to 1890. As was indicated in chapter 3, it seems that registration was imperfect during the 1860s and early 1870s. But it seems doubtful that underregistration of co-residing kin could account entirely for the difference in total number of extensions ever found between the two groups.

The conclusion that 40% to 60% of all households did at some time experience extension is of some importance. It indicates that kin co-residence was by no means an experience to be lightly passed off as marginal to nineteenth-century family life. Clearly, these results should warn us against rash conclusions on the basis of static measurements of household structure showing percentages of only 10% of extended households.

As we have only few studies available that are based on longitudinal material, there are commensurately few possibilities for comparison. We do have some longitudinal figures on Italian and Spanish family structure, however. In the eighteenth-century southern Italian town of Agnone, William Douglass found that 74% of 382 households attained an extended structure at some time during the course of a 34-year period. Douglass also traced twenty Basque households over the lengthy period of 118 years at 10–15 year intervals between 1842 and 1960.[12] He found only one household failing to extend beyond the nuclear family at some point in time. Probably in both cases, but definitely in the latter, the concept of household was defined in ways that differed from the one used here. Undoubtedly, the histories of the twenty Basque families could easily span the cycles of at least three successive marital units. We must therefore handle these results with care. Moreover, the examples cited above were concerned with households in an agrarian setting. The presence of landed property and the labour requirements of agrarian households are generally believed to have stimulated the formation of traditional family structures. Family property, and to a lesser extent labour requirements, may also have exercised a decisive influence on household structure in an industrializing context. In this study these relationships will be examined in chapter 5 and 7.

As might be expected given the results we have been looking at so far, in the 1880–1920 cohort a greater number of households go through extended phases more than once. Some of them are not only extended in the beginning of the cycle but also at some point in the final years. Table 4.2 presents figures concerning the number of times households were extended. If a household in the 1849–90 cohort came to be extended, this usually happened only once.[13] No more than 6.6% of all households did so for a second or third time. This provides a clear contrast with the later cohort in which 21.8% lived with kin for a second or a third time, or even more frequently than that.

As was explained earlier in this section the longitudinal perspective on household structure allows measurements of duration in addition to measurements of frequency. Duration of kin co-residence is important, not only because it provides further evidence of the relative importance of the phenomenon itself, but also because it may suggest its place and meaning in the lives of those concerned. Again, different possibilities are at hand, we may want to consider both the amount of time individual kin members resided in the household and the total time the household spent in extended structures over its history. The latter result may then be related to the 'period at risk', i.e. the period during which the household could be observed, which yields a relative measure of the 'proportion of time spent extended' by the households concerned.

[12] Douglass, 'Cross-sectional'; and: 'The Basque stem family'.
[13] Separate phases of uninterrupted extension are counted, which do not coincide with the number of individual co-residing relatives. If two kin members are present in the household during partially overlapping periods of time, only one phase of separate extension is the result.

Family and social change

Table 4.2 *Frequency of phases of extension by kin for two age-cohorts of married couples*

number of phases	1849–1890	1880–1920
0	60.9	43.1
1	32.4	35.0
2	5.5	12.2
3	1.1	6.7
4 ⎤		
5 ⎬	—	2.9
6 ⎦		
N	361	343

In general, not only frequency but also duration of kin co-residence will have been determined by a great number of variables. I shall consider briefly two of these. The first to consider are the functional characteristics of the extended structures. Kin may, for instance, be brought into the household in order to pass over family property from one generation to the next. On the other hand, extension may also occur as the result of the addition to the household of young migrating individual kin members looking for jobs. The length of kin co-residence is likely to vary considerably between these two examples. Second, demographic characteristics of the population concerned may exert a decisive influence. If household extensions occur at all, high levels of mortality and a fairly advanced age at first marriage will create short phases of extension in the first example. With these considerations in mind we turn to the question of the total duration of extension for which data are presented in table 4.3.

It is evident that the extended households from the 1849–90 cohort were more 'solidly' extended in the sense that this group contained a relatively large number of households which were extended for a long time. More than 40% of them were extended in all for ten years or more, some even for more than twenty years. This rarely happened in the second cohort of married couples. In this latter group most extensions occurred for only a short period: for almost a quarter of all extended households even less than twelve months. All this is clearly reflected in the mean duration of total extension for all households. The time spent extended for the earlier cohort is almost double that of the later cohort. The same pattern results when only separate phases of extension are considered: a mean of 7 years for the 1849–90

Table 4.3 *Mean length of time of total extension by kin
for two age-cohorts of married couples*

length of time	1849–1890	1880–1920
< 12 months	8.5	24.1
1–4 year	30.5	38.5
5–9 year	19.1	22.6
10–19 year	33.3	10.3
20–> year	8.5	4.6
mean in years	8.2	4.9
N	141	195

cohort and 3.2 years for its successor. The lower mean for the later cohort is heavily influenced by the much larger proportion of households that experienced extension by kin in the final years of their cycle. A note of warning is appropriate here however. The under-registration which was a more frequent problem in the earlier registers may have exaggerated the duration of extension in the first decades. It is likely that differences in duration were a little less extreme.

In interpreting these results, however, it is important to remember that the two cohorts experienced differing demographic circumstances, which would affect the duration that households remained in observation. It is very likely that the life expectancy of parents in these two cohorts was rather different, increasing over time, with the effect of shortening the relative period of observation for households in the first cohort. In other words there might be a difference in 'period at risk'. This indeed proved to be the case, although the difference is only small.[14] In order to take into account differences in 'period at risk' between the two groups a 'rate of extension' was constructed which indicates the relative duration of the time the household spent in extended structures.[15] Despite the fact that the 1849–90 cohort counted fewer households-ever-extended as well as a slightly shorter period at risk, this group had a slightly higher rate of extension compared with the second cohort: 9.6 against 8.8. This result could be read as follows: the earlier cohort spent almost 10% of its total period at risk living with kin, while the later cohort did so for

[14] The households in the earlier cohort were under observation for a mean number of 24.5 years, against 25.4 years for the later cohort.
[15] Rate of extension: (number of days of extension/number of days at risk)*100.

a little less than 9% of its total period at risk. The rate of extension conveniently indicates the shift between the cohorts from a restricted group of households characterized by rather long periods of extension, towards a larger number of households in the later cohort increasingly characterized by short periods of extension, confined for the most part to the end of the household history. In the following section on co-resident kin I will discuss some of the factors which may have been responsible for this effect. As a final observation on the rate of extension, we could note that the time during which these Tilburg households displayed extended structures appears to have been somewhat shorter than was found in eighteenth-century Alphen, a rural community in Brabant near Tilburg, where households were extended for 16.2% of the time.[16]

These first explorations into the development of nineteenth-century Tilburg households seem to justify the tentative conclusion that extended family living in this nineteenth-century textile community was certainly not a marginal phenomenon. Two-thirds of the households in the first cohort and almost half of the households in the second cohort lived with kin at some point. The later cohort comprised an increasing number of households which were extended only briefly during the final stage of the household history. As a result a larger proportion of households in this group was found to have been extended at some time. Furthermore, it is important to consider the evidence in the light of the rather different social and economic contexts these families were operating in, which was outlined in chapter 3. The families of the first age-cohort of married couples were still largely caught up in a traditional and economically unstable rural type of community which was only just beginning to move away from home-based production and showed slow rates of demographic growth. Part of the experience of this cohort was the heavy in-migration of the late 1860s and early 1870s which did not give rise to higher levels of extension. Did problems simply not arise because of sufficient housing opportunities, or were some of the youngsters in the community at that time postponing marriage because of the pressures resulting from the influx of migrants? The families in the second cohort, in contrast, were operating during a period in which the community finally embarked upon full-scale industrial production and the completion of the process of proletarianization. Moreover, this was also a period in which the town experienced vigorous demographic growth rates and was slowly and

[16] Lindner, 'De dynamische analyse', p. 81, note 17.

cautiously shaking off its geographic isolation. In the next section it will become clear that some of the developments resulting from this process of change were responsible for the considerable increase in the number of extensions occurring in the households of the second cohort of married couples.

4.2   Co-resident kin

Understanding extended family arrangements must necessarily include a closer look at the relatives involved and the mechanisms by which kin co-residence was brought about. It is one of the advantages of the longitudinal character of the population registers that they facilitate this. In this section I will describe some of the elementary characteristics of the kin found to be co-residing in the Tilburg households. Their relation to the household head, their age and marital status, the way they entered and left the household and so on, should throw light on the reasons people had for co-residing with relatives. This type of information is crucial when we eventually get to the question of the function of kin co-residence in the nineteenth century and the relationship between family structure and social change.

The ties between members of the nineteenth-century primary family were certainly very strong. The relatives found to be co-residing in the households of both cohorts almost all belonged either to the family of origin of husband and wife, or to their own family of procreation. A survey of kin members entering the households of both cohorts at various stages of the household history is provided by figure 4.2. This indicates not only the type of relationship of the co-residing kin member to the head of the household, but also the timing of their entrance into the household, and, most important, the percentage of households experiencing entries of a particular kind of kin during different periods of the cycle.[17] For instance, of all households of the later cohort who were present during the first four cycle years 8% experienced at least once the entry of co-residing parents of the head or his wife, while in another 7% a co-residing brother(in-law) or sister(in-law) entered the household. This may have occurred partly within one and the same household and partly in different households. For instance the co-residence of married children and grandchildren will mostly have concerned the same households.

In both cohorts parents and siblings are the two main categories of

[17] Separate entries instead of individuals were counted, so that when one and the same individual kin member entered the household twice but during different periods in the household history, this contributed to the count of entries in both these periods.

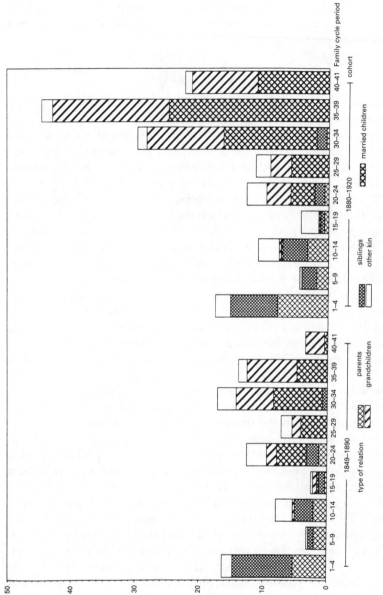

Figure 4.2. Proportion of households with entries by kin by family cycle period for two age-cohorts of married couples (corrected sample for 1880–1920 cohort)

kin during the first twenty years or so, after that married children and grandchildren rapidly take over. In the earlier cohort relatives are spread more or less evenly over the different stages of the household history, and over the different categories of kin. On the whole there is no sharp dichotomy in the occurrence of kin co-residence between the first and the last half of the household history such as we find for the households belonging to the 1880–1920 cohort. In the second cohort the great bulk of co-residing kin consisted of married children and grandchildren entering the household during the second half of the family cycle. These figures strongly reflect the substantial rise of extended households in the 1880–1920 cohort during the last ten years of the family cycle rather than a shift in the preference for a certain type of kin to live with. For both cohorts it is evident that if families lived with kin, they lived with immediate family members: parents and siblings, and married children and grandchildren. (See also appendix 7.)

Almost all the parents that we see entering during the first two decades of the family cycle in both cohorts were widowed and well into their sixties or even seventies. Mothers of husband or wife were more common than fathers in the households of the 1880–1920 cohort in contrast to the experience in the earlier cohort (see appendix 8). Co-residing parents were in general present for a considerable number of years and they stayed until they died. In this respect there were no major distinctions between the two cohorts.

Brothers and sisters constituted the second main category of kin with which people lived in the first half of the household history.[18] Co-residing siblings in both cohorts were single and were mostly in their 20s or 30s. Co-residing siblings could be of either sex, though there was a clear preference for brothers and brothers-in-law (see appendix 8). In the households of the 1849–90 cohort some of the brothers and sisters were present for quite a long time: 54% for ten years or more. In contrast, in the later cohort 70% of the siblings had left before their fifth year of co-residence. About the same proportion of all siblings in this cohort left because of migration to other households within or beyond the town. This seldom happened in the earlier group where brothers and sisters disappeared from the household either because they got married or because they died.

What caused families in both cohorts to live with a widowed parent or unmarried sibling? Did families try to attract kin members in order to share poverty or pool resources? Were they in need of baby-sitters?

---

[18] See also appendix 7.

Or were co-residing kin present because they needed the care and support of their families? In the case of the co-residing grandparents it is difficult to think of any reason other than the need for care in old age which provided the stimulus for their living in the households of their married children. As we have seen, the grandparents concerned were well above 60 years old, in both groups the majority was over 70 at the time they entered the household. It is not likely that many exercised an occupation at such an age.[19] Even if we assume that all grandparents did work, their economic contribution to the family, considering their advanced age, can only have been marginal.

Co-residing grandparents, however, also may have enabled both husband and wife to go out to work for wages in that they provided child-care facilities. Both Hareven and Anderson opt for this line of reasoning and it seems this was indeed also the case in a number of Dutch factory towns.[20] In Enschede and Maastricht married women working in factories took in their mothers or mothers-in-law to help them with household duties and child care. Day-care centres did not exist at all in these industrial centres so that support from relatives and neighbours was essential for married women to enter into factory work.[21] In Tilburg, however, we do not always find a clear preference of grandmothers over grandfathers. This was certainly not the case in the 1849–90 households: the mother of either husband or wife made up only 57% of all co-resident grandparents. In the next cohort, however, we do find a clear majority of grandmothers over grandfathers: two-thirds of all co-residing grandparents were grandmothers.

Still, it is a dubious assumption that these grandmothers were taken in by their children to provide child care so as to enable the mother to go out to work. In Tilburg married women hardly ever worked for wages outside their household. In chapter 2 I described the strong opposition within the Tilburg community against factory employment of married women. Factory work was commonly considered to be a threat to the moral well-being of married and unmarried women alike. The population registers record occupations for only 63 of the 406 wives in the first cohort, and 53 of the 366 wives of the second cohort. This is not to say they did not do any productive

---

[19] The defective registration of occupations in the population registers makes it problematic to use these entries in even the most tentative way: for 86% and 96% of the co-residing grandmothers and 63% and 61% of the grandfathers in the two respective cohorts no occupational entry was given.

[20] Anderson, *Family structure*; Hareven, *Family time*.

[21] de Regt, *Arbeidersgezinnen*, p. 58; van Rijswijk-Clerkx, *Moeders*, pp. 46–89.

work. The population registers were particularly prone to underregister women's occupations. In general, we may assume that most wives in the lower social classes contributed to the family budget by doing outwork such as darning for the textile factories or running a small shop. Productive work in the household made it possible for these wives to contribute to their family's standard of living, while at the same time providing for the household and children. A co-residing grandmother could be very useful in these circumstances, but was not as crucial to the working mother of Tilburg as she probably was to her counterparts in Preston. Finally, we may point out that the effects of a higher life expectancy for elderly women compared with men, as well as a lesser tendency for elderly widows to remarry, created a larger number of grandmothers available to cohabit. This may explain the preponderance of co-residing mothers over fathers in the households of the second cohort. This issue will be discussed in chapter 6 on households and migration.

Co-residence with siblings of the husband or wife could effectively improve the balance between consumers and producers during the first, formative years of the family cycle. At this stage almost all households had many unproductive mouths to feed, while the mother had less time to spend on paid work. We have seen that co-resident siblings were mostly aged between 20 and 40, economically an individual's most productive phase of life.[22] However, there are additional considerations weighing against the assumption that co-resident siblings were recruited solely for the purpose of an economic contribution to the household. Especially in the case of the earlier cohort we must bear in mind that brothers and sisters co-resided in the household for quite a long time until they eventually departed either to get married or because of death. When seen along with the very low marriage frequencies for men and women in the province of Brabant in the beginning of the nineteenth century, this suggests that these siblings were taken in because they were on their own and not yet married.[23] The economic crisis of the 1840s which had seriously slowed down demographic growth, in Tilburg as elsewhere in The Netherlands, must have created a much larger reservoir of celibate men and women in the 1850s. If they had lost their parents before marriage finally became feasible again, they were on their own. Cultural values and economic constraints made it

---

[22] Still, of all co-resident brothers (in-law) 19% to 34%, for respectively the younger and the earlier cohort, had no occupations recorded. As could be expected, for co-residing sisters these percentage are very much higher: 75% and 58% respectively.

[23] Hofstee, *De demografische ontwikkeling*, p. 203.

almost impossible, especially for women, to live independently outside a familial context. Unmarried men and women, if they could no longer live with their parents, thus lived with their married siblings whenever possible. The same pattern has been shown to have existed in Verviers, Belgium, by George Alter when describing the experience of unmarried women.[24] In the 1880–1920 cohort co-residing siblings were apparently a more mobile group. They did not stay for very long in the households of their kin, and a large majority moved out again to other households, some in Tilburg, others outside. Young unmarried individuals seemed to have used the households of their married siblings as stepping stones to facilitate migration. An increase in siblings using the households of their kin for migratory reasons probably offset the decline in siblings needing to stay in the households of their kin because of the postponement of marriage. I will consider this particular class of co-residing kin again in chapter 6.

Another way to approach the question of why people co-reside with kin is to try to assess the consumer-producer balance within the household, which is mostly done by computing the ratio of the number of family members with and without occupation. This approach is based on the idea that families facing the necessity of raising large numbers of children will try to attract adult kin members able to make economic contributions to the household. The defective registration of occupations in the population register, however, would make such an exercise extremely unreliable in the present case. I have already pointed out that it was not common to list occupations for women, and married women in particular, or for co-residing elderly people, nor was this often done for people under the age of about 20. We will have to satisfy ourselves, therefore, with a rather crude measure based on a comparison of the number of children in households in which kin co-resided during the first twenty years of the cycle to the number of children in all other households. For working-class parents this was definitely the worst period: families grew to their final size and included a large number of small children. Only by the time they reached the tenth year of observation could one or two of the elder children begin to contribute modestly to the well-being of the family. If many mouths needed to be fed, a co-residing parent or sibling could either bring in additional income or enable the mother, by relieving her of some of her household duties, to acquire additional income in domestic production.

However, if we consider the total number of children ever born to a

---

[24] Alter, _Family_.

family there are no observable differences between households with co-residing parents and siblings and those without. Nuclear and extended families in both cohorts had the same median number of children, six in the first cohort, seven in the second. Still, some families may have been more successful than others in the boarding out of children at a relatively young age, thereby crucially influencing their consumer-producer balance; or some families may have had higher levels of infant or child mortality than others. A comparison of the mean number of children who were actually present in the household by cycle year for all first-phase extended and nuclear households could be the way to investigate this issue. Figure 4.3 and figure 4.4, however, only confirm my earlier conclusion; in both cohorts families with co-resident parents or siblings during the first twenty years were not necessarily those with a large number of unproductive mouths to feed. Other researchers have come to similar conclusions. Among them are M. Katz and colleagues, who found the greatest number of relatives and boarders in households in Hamilton among families with no children at all or with working children.[25]

Regrettably, on the basis of these data, this is as far as we can get towards answering the question why families should co-reside with their ageing parents and unmarried siblings. It would seem that although the material contributions these kin members would be making to the receiving household were no doubt very welcome in most cases, they were probably not decisive. There is no evidence that they were the reason why kin were invited into the household in the first place, although clear material advantages may have arisen out of the situation for both parties concerned.

We will now focus our attention on those kin members co-residing in the later stages of the household history. Figure 4.2 indicated that, for both cohorts of families, married children and grandchildren were the main categories of kin present at this late stage. The graph shows this type of kin co-residence to be far more frequent for families in the later cohort as a result of the larger number of extended families during the final years of the family cycle.[26] There is, moreover, an additional factor contributing to the sharp dichotomy in the 1880–1920 cohort. The procedure used to generate information for figure 4.2 involved a count of all entries of kin irrespective of whether it concerned the same individual or not. Co-residing relatives who were

---

[25] Katz, Doucet and Stern, *The social organization*, pp. 293–6.
[26] We should be aware of the fact that, of course, the households in which married children enter do almost all overlap with those in which grandchildren enter. But then, this is so for both cohorts.

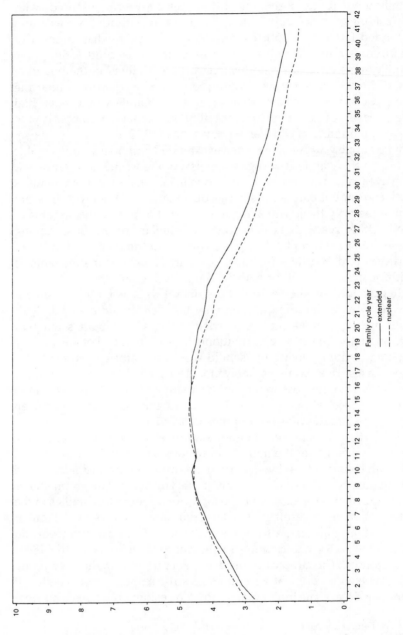

Figure 4.3. Mean number of children present in the household by family cycle year first-phase nuclear and extended families, 1849–1890 age-cohort of married couples

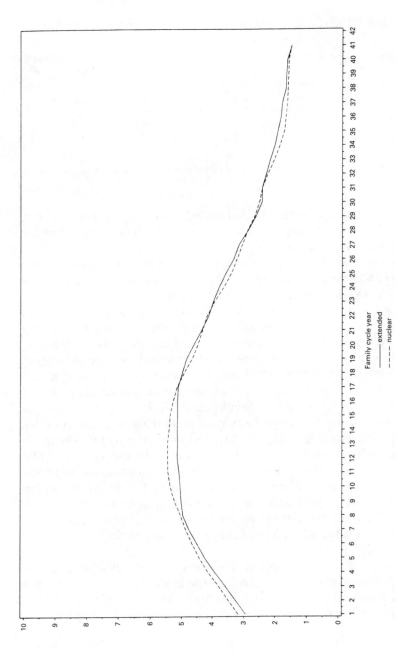

Figure 4.4. Mean number of children present in the household by family cycle year first-phase nuclear and extended families, 1880–1920 age-cohort of married couples (corrected sample)

Table 4.4 *Reason for entry of co-resident married offspring for two*
age-cohorts of married couples

entry	1849–1890		1880–1920	
	sons	daughters	sons	daughters
migration	16.7	7.7	46.3	46.8
marriage	83.3	92.3	53.7	53.2
N	12	26	67	79

coming and going frequently contributed to the count every time they
entered the household, provided these entries occurred in different
periods of the cycle.

Coming and going, staying only for a short time, was exactly what
some of these married children in the 1880–1920 cohort were doing in
the last two decades of their parents' households. As we shall see
later on, most children of the later cohort left their parents' household
either for migratory reasons or at marriage. For some reason many of
them returned to their parental household after their marriage,
mostly with spouse and children, and some did so more than once.
Of all co-residing ever-married sons and daughters in this cohort 13%
entered their parents' household on more than one occasion. About
half of all married sons and daughters did so for migratory reasons.
As table 4.4 shows, a large proportion of all married children in this
cohort entered by way of migration. While their mobility was much
greater when compared with the sons and daughters of the first
cohort, the time they spent living with their parents was relatively
short. Almost two-fifths of co-residing married children left within
the same year, whilst only one in twenty stayed on for five years or
more. They left in order to migrate afresh to other places (23.8%), or
in order to establish independent households of their own within
Tilburg (38%).

If married children took up residence in the households of the
1849–90 cohort they did so only once and in almost all cases this was a
consequence of their marriage into their parents' household.[27] Most
married children stayed in their parental households for periods of

[27] If all co-residing married children (including in-laws) are taken together, we find
that in the 1880–1920 cohort two-thirds of these children had entered the household
by way of migration while the remaining one-third did so by way of marriage. For
the 1849–90 cohort this ratio was exactly the reverse.

Table 4.5 *Structure of the household at time of entry of married offspring for two age-cohorts of married couples*

	1849–1890		1880–1920	
	Sons	Daughters	Sons	Daughters
1 parent only	8.3	3.9	1.5	7.7
1 parent + sibling(s)	66.7	65.4	55.2	42.3
2 parents only	—	—	13.4	6.4
2 parents + sibling(s)	25.0	30.8	29.9	43.6
N	12	26	67	79

between one and five years, while one-third stayed for more than five years. After that time they either became the new heads of household or left to form households of their own. Accordingly, the great majority of the 1849–90 cohort's grandchildren were born into the household, whereas most grandchildren in the following cohort in-migrated in the company of their parents.[28]

It was indicated in figure 4.2 that married children started to enter their parents' household during the later periods of the family cycle. This might suggest that co-residence came about in order to assist elderly parents who were increasingly being confronted with problems resulting from old age. For the first cohort this may indeed have been the case. When married children entered the household this was mostly at a time when only one parent survived, as can be seen from table 4.5. The experience in the 1880–1920 cohort, however, was rather different. Half of all married children in this cohort entered the parental household when one of the parents had already died, therefore the other half had both parents still alive at the time. This implies that in the second cohort there were additional mechanisms at work, creating co-residential arrangements with married children in the final stages of the parental life course. I will return to this issue below. There can be little doubt as to the precarious situation of elderly widows and widowers living by themselves in the nineteenth century. Research into nineteenth-century Poor Relief in Alkmaar, in the province of Noord-Holland, has indicated just how critical the presence of wage-earning children in the household could be for this

---

[28] For the 1849–90 cohort 75% of all grandchildren were born into the household. This was true for only 29% in the 1880–1920 cohort.

group.[29] If we are correct in assuming that elderly widowed parents did indeed require the support of their married children, this does not mean that they will not also have valued their independence. The fact that the widowed parents in the 1849–90 cohort could make their married children come and live with them, rather than the other way around, could be seen as a sign of this wish for continued independence even in old age. Moreover, it should also be seen as evidence of the strong position of these elderly parents in the process of inter-generational bargaining.

The figures presented in table 4.5 must be understood in relation to two different developments. For one thing, the life expectancy of parents in the earlier cohort was lower than for their successors. The median age at death for heads and their wives was 61 and 58 in the 1849–90 cohort, as against 63 and 61 for the later group. Similarly, survival rates were also much higher for the 1880–1920 cohort of parents.[30] The 1849–90 households, therefore, stood a greater chance of having lost one of the parents by the time that married children, for whatever reason, took up residence in the parental household. Further on in this section we will see that most parents in this first cohort did indeed die before the end of their household history. A second, and probably more important factor to consider is the role of migration. Married children in the 1880–1920 cohort were present in their parental households to some extent for their own migratory reasons. We have already seen that about half of them entered the household by way of migration, while a considerable proportion of them either moved on for the same migratory reasons (23%) or for the purpose of establishing their own households within Tilburg (38%). To put it more strongly, married children in the later cohort often used their parental homes more or less like boarding houses or relay points in their quest for better opportunities. In these cases the structure, and thus the needs, of the parental household will have played a minor role, if at all, in the decision to co-reside with parents on the part of these children.

The mobility of the sons and daughters of the second cohort, especially between 1910 and 1920, is one of the consequences of the gradual lifting of the isolated geographical position of the town which had continued throughout the nineteenth century.[31] Only around the turn of the century did Tilburg begin to link up with larger networks

[29] van Loo, *Armelui*.
[30] At age 70 for heads in the elder and later cohort: 38.6% and 55.5% respectively. Of the wives at age 70 36.3% and 47.5% were still alive.
[31] van de Weijer, *De religieuze practijk*, p. 130.

of labour mobility. During the 1910s both in-migration and out-migration surpassed earlier levels.[32] Some of these sons and daughters even took part in the boom in overseas migration occurring in the later 1910s,[33] migrating to Canada or the United States. At that time the local economy was rapidly expanding because of the large orders for military cloth issued before and during World War I. Thus, these migrating sons and daughters and their families were clearly not pushed out by a downward economic trend. What is more likely, however, is that the tightness of the housing market in this period prompted many young families to search for independent family housing elsewhere. The booming local economy of the later 1910s may have enticed a number of them to return to Tilburg. For this return-migration they conveniently made use of the services of the households of kin. Whether they were on the move to acquire jobs or housing, it is clear that some of these co-residing married children used the parental household as a baseline from which to prepare for migration or to fall back on for support if things went wrong.

From table 4.5 it seems clear that the 1849–90 cohort of married couples displayed a clear preference for co-residence with a married daughter and her family (68.4%) as opposed to co-residence with a married son. In the later cohort, however, the difference had become minimal: 54.1% of entries into the parental households were of married daughters. In addition to married children, there were also a number of widowed sons and daughters entering the households of both cohorts, though widowed sons made up the large majority (see appendix 9). The entry of these young widows and widowers needs no elaborate explanation. Faced as they were by the difficult task of raising a number of small children on their own, the widowed sons in particular were in need of domestic support. They simply had nowhere else to go. Gender differences in kin co-residence did thus exist, sometimes as a result of domestic and practical impossibilities as in the case of widowed sons, and at other times as a result perhaps of an emotional preference as in the case of married daughters. It has been suggested that in urban industrial society kinship links were primarily maintained along the female line due to the continuity in activities between mothers and daughters.[34] Occupational mobility and differentiation, and we might add proletarianization, had on the contrary led to an increasing number of fathers and sons who no longer shared occupational or property interests.

[32] Ibid., p. 114.
[33] Hofstee, 'Demografische', p. 91, see graph 9.
[34] Young and Willmott, *Family*, p. 43.

Table 4.6 *Reason for final exit from household for parents aged 60 and over for two age-cohorts of married couples*

	1849–1890		1880–1920	
Reason for exit	Fathers	Mothers	Fathers	Mothers
death	85.7	82.2	61.8	56.7
move to hh of child	2.9	5.9	17.4	19.1
give up headship	0.7	1.7	7.9	8.3
move to kin	—	—	0.6	—
move to others	—	—	4.5	2.6
migration	3.6	2.5	5.1	8.3
move to institution	2.9	2.5	2.8	3.8
marriage	2.1	0.9	—	1.3
unknown	2.1	4.2	—	—
N	140	118	178	157

Table 4.6 can be read as showing that parents in the 1880–1920 cohort co-resided with married children a great deal more often than did those of the earlier cohort. If we include co-residence of parents with married children in either their own household or the household of their children we find that in 48.1% of all the 1880–1920 households parents lived with married children at some point in time. For the earlier cohort this happened for only 16.7% of all households. This increase over time arose not only from a larger number of parents taking married children into their own households, for which the percentage had risen from 11.9 for the first cohort to 31.7 for the second cohort, but even more strongly from a larger number of parents moving into the household of one of their married children.[35] This development marks an important break in the life-course experience of parents during the nineteenth century. In only 5.4% of all households of the 1849–90 cohort did parents eventually face the necessity of shifting to the household of a child. In the following cohort this proportion had risen to as much as 27.9%, a direct consequence of the fact that more parents in the earlier cohort survived

[35] This also comes out in the increasing number of children of the second cohort living with kin in the first stages of their household history: 12.7% for the earlier cohort's children, and 30.2% for the younger. The share of (grand)parents in these cases of co-residence increased from 29% to 33%. Differences cannot have resulted from a shorter period at risk for the children of the earlier cohort: the figures were 13.5 as opposed to 12.3 years.

after the breakup of their own households. The increasing number of parents in the second cohort who survived until the end of the history of their own household is also borne out by table 4.6. Consequently, a larger number of ageing parents were confronted with the departure from home of the last of their children.

What did elderly parents do when they saw that the end of the history of their household was imminent? In the 1849–90 cohort we see a slight preference on the part of parents, mainly the mothers, towards joining one of their married children, or, inviting a married child into their own household after which the son, or son-in-law, became the new household head. The rest mainly migrated. 'Unknown' exits must in this case also be considered as undocumented migratory exits since there is no plausible alternative explanation. In the later cohort we find that the growing number of cases in which parents 'survive their own households' do not distribute themselves evenly over the options available. There is virtually no increase in parents who were placed in institutions for the old and the infirm, religious or otherwise, though there was a modest increase in the number of parents who were forced to move into households of unrelated persons. The greater part of these surviving parents moved in with children or handed over their households to children moving in with them. Interestingly, this suggests that in the course of the nineteenth century, children became more important to ageing parents, presumably as a result of increases in life expectancy.[36]

I may summarize this section by stating that kin co-residence in nineteenth-century Tilburg was mainly restricted to the members of the immediate family. Widowed parents and unmarried siblings were usually present during the first twenty years, while married children and grandchildren started to enter the parental household during the last ten or twenty years of the household history. This pattern existed for both cohorts. Poverty of the receiving household does not appear to have been the primary reason for inviting parents and siblings into the household. We can assume, therefore, that unmarried siblings were primarily taken in because of the economic and practical difficulties of living independently. In addition, and this was much more pronounced for women, cultural values required familial supervision for young unmarried individuals.[37] Young adults residing outside a

---

[36] Between 1865 and 1915 the average age at death in Tilburg rose from 38 to 50, from which figures infant mortality is excluded. See van de Put, *Volksleven*, p. 267.

[37] In 1906 Amsterdam housing authorities still voiced the opinion that women belonged with their families and therefore did not require independent housing. See: Rossen, 'Huize Lydia', p. 101.

familial context were extremely rare in nineteenth-century Tilburg. In 1849 only 1.2% of all households was headed by an unmarried or widowed individual under the age of 30. In 1880 this proportion was even lower at 0.5%.[38] For the earlier cohort of married couples it is probable that the number of unmarried siblings available for co-residence was much greater than later in the century due to the economic crisis of the 1840s. Co-residing siblings in the second cohort were also more often present as a result of migration. For the co-residing elderly in the households of both cohorts it is most likely that they had found it impossible, because of failing health or poverty, to maintain solitary households any longer. Towards the end of the family cycle the balance was tipped: kin co-residence, mainly with married children, served to strengthen the economic basis of the receiving households. This comes out most clearly in the households of the 1849–90 cohort into which married children mostly entered after the death of one of the parents. In the later cohort many of the co-residing married children were present for what could be seen as their own reasons; they were in need of a secure basis from which to venture out into the world or to return to in case of failed migration. Co-residence of parents and their married children further increased as an effect of rising life expectancy. In the first cohort very few parents had been faced with the necessity of moving out of their households in old age. Most of them died before that juncture was reached. For the second cohort housing supply must also have been influential in their residence decisions, prompting co-residence with married children during the final years of the family cycle. In this section we have begun to observe some of the effects of changing social, economic and demographic circumstances on kin co-residence. It is as if the more dynamic society which came into being towards the end of the century created a more dynamic system of mobile individuals relying more heavily, but only temporarily, on the assistance of kin in the matter of residence.

---

[38] See appendix 33. In this type of household other household members might be present and often were. The mean size of households headed by unmarried or widowed individuals under the age of 30 was 2.2 in 1849 and 3.1 in 1880. These solitaries were likely to be either widows or widowers with kin or others, or households consisting of co-residing unmarried brothers and sisters. In the northern and western parts of the Netherlands solitary householders appear to have been more common than in the south (see: van der Woude, 'De omvang', p. 227; Kooij, *Groningen*, p. 19). Klep has established this Brabantine tendency towards 'family households' for late eighteenth and early nineteenth-century rural areas (Klep, 'Het huishouden', p. 64).

4.3 *Intergenerational relations*

Industrialization is often thought to have loosened generational links between parents and children, as growing economic opportunities in the labour market created possibilities for children to acquire a living independently. For some families industrialization destroyed the connection with the land or the family enterprise. Their family economy was, if sometimes gradually, sometimes abruptly transformed into a family wage economy. Therefore, the argument continues, industrialization undermined the complex of interrelated familistic, economic and property interests which had tied all members of the family group together. According to structural-functionalist theory this enabled young men and women to leave the parental home to set up their own family to which all future solidarity would henceforth be confined. A growing autonomy of children in relation to their parents would thus inhibit the formation of extended families. Children would no longer feel any responsibility towards parents and siblings to help them cope with poverty, old age or the other hardships of life.

For historians like Edward Shorter the growing opportunities for wage work outside the household carried with it more than just a growing independence of young people in respect of their parents. This development also led to the sexual 'liberation' of young women, who were escaping traditional family control, with a consequential rise in the level of illegitimate births.[39] Similarly, Michael Anderson has argued that industrial city life created changing relationships between parents and children in Preston. It introduced a calculating element into intergenerational attitudes, making youngsters either bargain or leave, when, for instance, they felt parents were charging too much for board and room.[40]

Other opinions have been voiced. Although he believes industrialization to have seriously undercut relations between parents and children, Braun qualifies this view in several interesting ways.[41] The preindustrial labour market, he writes, often forced family members to find work many miles away from home, even at a tender age. By creating job opportunities in the home town and village, proto-industrialization and then industrialization proper perhaps prolonged the period unmarried children spent in their parental homes. Katz and Davey found that this is precisely what had happened

[39] Shorter, *The making*, pp. 79–119; Shorter, 'Illegitimacy', pp. 250–1.
[40] Anderson, *Family structure*, p. 135.
[41] Braun, 'The impact', p. 64.

happened during the early industrialization of Hamilton, Canada.[42] Between 1851 and 1871 the age at which half of all young men had left home rose from 17 to 22, while correspondingly the age for women increased from 17 to 20.

In her book on Dutch working-class families in the period between 1870 and 1940, Ali de Regt concluded that the moment children started contributing to the family budget through independent wage work the balance of power between parents and children inevitably tilted in favour of the child. Parents lost part of the power they had over their children, whose contributions had often been essential to the family's survival. De Regt suggests that the idea that once children earned a fair wage they would leave parents to their fate may also have caused parents not to opt for extended schooling for their children.[43] However, patterns of continued solidarity of sons and daughters with their families were found by many scholars. Among them is John Bodnar who stressed that children were forced to sacrifice individual ambitions to the well-being of their families.[44] When tensions arose from this, the children frequently got the worst of it, he assures us.

Even if children did leave home earlier than in industrial times, it did not necessarily involve increased autonomy for the child. As Tilly and Scott, and many others have confirmed, children, particularly daughters, continued to feel a strong sense of responsibility and attachment to their families of origin. They actively tried to keep up family ties and handed over a considerable part of their hard-earned wages to their mothers. Family values that had taken shape long before industrialization thus continued to define individual behaviour. By raising this point Scott and Tilly have rightly indicated that failure to co-reside should not be simply equated with failed family responsibility.

This section is concerned with the extent to which industrial developments in Tilburg altered the relationship between parents and children. Late nineteenth-century parents often voiced their fear of wage earning children walking out on them.[45] How justified were their fears? Perhaps children in late-nineteenth-century Tilburg were abandoning their parents earlier and more frequently than had been the case before because of the expanding labour market. There can be

[42] Katz and Davey, 'Youth', p. 91.
[43] de Regt, *Arbeidersgezinnen*, pp. 118, 130–5.
[44] Bodnar, *Workers' world*; see also Hareven, *Family time*; Scott, Tilly, 'Women's work'; Alter, *Family*; Cross and Shergold, 'The family economy'.
[45] de Regt, *Arbeidersgezinnen*, p. 118.

little doubt that the children of the second cohort were surrounded by many more opportunities for industrial wage work than their predecessors. One of the crucial changes which came about during the life course of the later cohort's children is the almost total disappearance of the domestic weaving economy. During their life time textile production was finally removed from the home into the factory. Darning and burling continued for a long time to be done within the domestic economy to some extent, but this provided employment mainly for married women. Factory employment increasingly offered attractive opportunities to the male adolescents and young adults of the second cohort. Factory work provided rather high wages relative to artisanal work, especially at young ages. What effect did the changing labour market of the community have on the behaviour of these youngsters?

We can begin to assess changes in intergenerational relations by looking at the ages at which children left home, and the extent to which they continued to co-reside with elderly parents. Age at marriage may also be regarded as an important indicator of the strength of intergenerational links. As long as children remained unmarried, whether they were still living at home or were in service far away from home, parents could exercise their power to extract all or most of the children's wages. The marriage of a child, however, often meant a severe financial loss to parents. Marriage removed the child from the parental home and transferred his or her financial contributions to a new family, all this occurring at a time when the child had reached his or her full earning potential. Parents will consequently have dreaded the marriage of the last of their remaining children. A well-known observer of late-nineteenth-century family life in Brabant, P.A. Barentsen, also mentioned the fact that parents feared the loss of income through early marriage of their children.[46] This was one of the motives for parents in subjecting their children, particularly their daughters, to a strict discipline. Parents in Tilburg may have tried to keep their children from marrying early. For working-class children, however, early marriage must generally have been an attractive alternative; marriage brought with it the possibility of applying hard earned wages to his or her own use.

I will first examine the age at which children left home for the first time. In the following calculations I have excluded those departures by children caused by death as well as those coinciding with the end of the household history. This leaves all cases in which a son or daughter departed to leave parents and siblings behind, thus con-

---

[46] Barentsen, 'Het gezinsleven', p. 29.

stituting a break away from the family of origin. In nineteenth-century Tilburg children left their parental home at quite advanced ages in comparison with present day patterns. The following tables and graphs show the extremely strong ties which bound sons and daughters to their families of origin. The experience portrayed is quite similar to that described by George Alter for the women of Verviers, Belgium. Alter cites Janet Salaff when he concludes that 'Each woman reconciled her obligations to her family with the pull of nonfamilial opportunities in a different manner, yet each did so in favor of the family.'[47] He could well be describing the past experience of young men and women in nineteenth-century Tilburg.

During the years under examination here, however, sons and daughters did begin to leave the parental home earlier. The median age of first departure from home for sons fell from 25 to 22 between the two cohorts. Between the two cohorts the timing of first exit for daughters also fell by three years: from 24 to 21 years. Figures 4.5 and 4.6 illustrate the distribution of first exits of children over the different age categories and the types of exit concerned. In the first cohort there were two major groups of years in which both sons and daughters started to leave their parental homes. A little over 40% of the sons left home between the ages of 25 and 29; together with those leaving in the age group 20–24 years, this made up 70% of all first exits for sons. In the second cohort first exits by sons in the age groups 10–14 and 15–19 more than doubled, while those leaving between 25–29 years only constituted 27% of all exits. For the daughters we find comparable patterns. The number of daughters leaving between the ages of 10–14 and 15–19 doubled, while the percentage leaving aged 25 or over fell from 45 to 29.[48] On the whole daughters in both cohorts left a little earlier than sons. First cohort sons and daughters for the greater part stayed home until they married. Table 4.7 shows that 60% of sons and 63% of daughters left home for the first time at marriage.

In the 1880–1920 cohort most children left to join other households, either within Tilburg or elsewhere. Even if we consider all 'unknown' exits for all groups to be exits because of out-migration, which they probably were, there still is a significant difference.[49] The difference is

[47] Alter, *Family*, p. 162. Salaff, *Working daughters*, p. 120.
[48] For table see appendix 10.
[49] 'Unknown' exits may either be exits to other households in Tilburg or the result of out-migration. They cannot be exits as a result of marriage and subsequent settlement of the young couple within the town. These would have been detected in the Tilburg population register in all cases. However, some of these unknown exits may have been the result of cases where the child married and settled elsewhere.

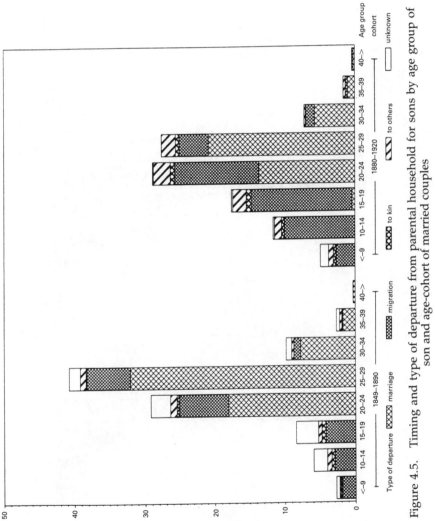

Figure 4.5. Timing and type of departure from parental household for sons by age group of son and age-cohort of married couples

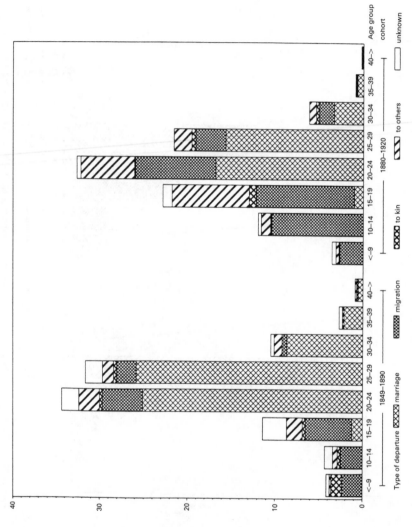

Figure 4.6. Timing and type of departure from parental household for daughters by age group of daughter and age-cohort of married couples

Table 4.7 *Reason for first departure from parental household for offspring of two age-cohorts of married couples*

Reason for departure	1849–1890		1880–1920	
	Sons	Daughters	Sons	Daughters
move to kin	1.8	2.9	3.1	2.1
move to others	3.7	7.2	8.5	19.2
migration	23.2	17.4	44.8	38.8
marriage	60.4	63.8	42.9	37.7
unknown	11.0	8.6	1.7	2.3
N	626	556	946	872

especially remarkable for the girls: in the first cohort 63.8% of them left because they got married, while thirty to forty years later this had fallen to only 37.7%. The rest either out-migrated or went into service in other Tilburg households.

The larger proportion of exits from the parental household involving out-migration for the later cohort's children may be related to the gradual disappearance of the family economy which must have made it more difficult to employ children at home. Moreover, economic prospects facing the children of the two cohorts were entirely different. Children of the first cohort, in particular the older ones born between 1840 and 1850, were reaching the ages of 15 to 20 at a time when local employment opportunities were rapidly expanding. By contrast, the tight economic circumstances of the late 1880s and early 1890s may have required children born between 1870 and 1880, of the second cohort of parents, to find employment elsewhere. An alternative explanation could be that the second cohort of parents found it impossible to accommodate them any longer in the crowded family home and were forced to send some of their children out to other households. The latter motive is suggested by the fact that the second cohort of families were on average blessed with many more children.[50] Although the greater frequency of infant and child death in the later cohort helped to keep down totals, the mean number of children present by family cycle year (see appendix 12) indicates that families of the second cohort still had a larger maximum number of

[50] In the earlier cohort 6 children were born to the average family, in the later cohort this had risen to 7.2.

children.[51] Parents may have welcomed rather than feared the early departure of their older children. Of course, both economic circumstances and the increase in the number of children born may have worked to create the pattern of earlier exits established for the second cohort's offspring.

The earlier departure from home of the children in the second cohort probably did not offer them earlier independence from parents. The first departure from home did not always entail a final co-residential break with parents and siblings. Sons and daughters in the second cohort showed themselves to be a lot more mobile than those in the first. They left home at an earlier age to migrate, but they also frequently came back, in order to leave again after a short stay. First cohort daughters seldom returned: for 90% of them their first departure was also their last. This proportion fell to 70% in the second cohort, while almost 10% of the later cohort's daughters made three exits or more. The same picture emerges for sons. Of the sons in the earlier cohort 83% left home only once, never to return again; this happened to only 65% of their later counterparts.[52]

Although children started to leave their parental homes at an earlier age than before, this would in general not have involved an immediate loss to the parents of the financial and practical support of the child concerned. In between jobs and migratory moves children kept coming back, and it is likely that they continued contributing financially to the parental household. Hard evidence concerning the Tilburg situation, however, is not available except for a few stray remarks of contemporaries. In 1887, for instance, a local physician commented upon the quality of the relationships between parents and children: 'In Tilburg there is a good spirit; the children hand over their wages to the parents. . .'[53] There can be no doubt that parents expected children to contribute to the family income until they married, even if the child worked away from home.[54] The extent to which

[51] Cumulative percentages of deaths of children by age group:

age	1849–1890	1880–1920
< 1	4.2	9.6
< 5	10.0	15.9
< 10	13.0	17.7
< 15	15.0	18.8

[52] For table see appendix 11.
[53] *Enquete*, Tilburg, question 10717.
[54] de Regt, *Arbeidersgezinnen*, p. 130.

they did so is unclear. However, when children in the later cohort left for the last time, they did so at an age which was comparable to that in the first cohort. The median age for final departure from home decreased between the two cohorts by only one year for both sons and daughters. First cohort sons and daughters finally departed from their parental home at the ages of 26 and 25 respectively, their successors at 25 and 24. Departure from the parental home in Tilburg proved to have been a very gradual process in the nineteenth century.[55] There was no set age for this life course transition, which could occur at age 15 but equally well at age 30. Additionally, those who left early might return to the parental home, as happened in the case of the second cohort's sons and daughters, in order to leave permanently at some later date.

The age at leaving home may, however, not tell the whole story. If children died before they could leave home, or if children did not leave at all but stayed home until the end of the period of observation, they were left out of the above calculations. These latter cases especially may have contained many instances of one or two sons or daughters postponing their independence in order to take care of their, by then, elderly parents. In an attempt to trace patterns of this type, the proportion of sons and daughters who were still at home at different ages was computed, both before their first and final departure from home. Results are presented in detail in appendix 13. The main conclusions follow below.

Compared with our twentieth-century families children did not leave home at an early age. Even if only first exits are considered we find that 17% of the sons and 20% of the daughters in the older cohort were still living with their parents at the age of 30. They had not lived away from home even once before. The final break from home came at an even later age; at age 30 nearly one-quarter of both sons and daughters had not yet broken away permanently from their family of origin. In the second cohort this had changed to a certain extent, since children were leaving home for the first time in much larger proportions. Only 10% to 11% of children reached the age of 30 before making the first break from home in the later cohort. Almost half of all 20-year-old sons and daughters had already been away from home, a considerable change from the previous cohort's experience. However, as far as final departures are concerned the differences are less pronounced. While almost one-quarter of all children in the 1849–90 cohort had not yet left permanently by the age of 30, this had fallen

---

[55] See also Wall, 'The age'; Modell, Furstenberg and Hershberg, 'Social change'.

to 19% and 21% for sons and daughters respectively in the following cohort. For all 25-year-olds we found a decrease of only 6–7% in the proportion of sons and daughters still living at home. Although the process of breaking away from the parental home did undeniably start at much earlier ages towards the end of the nineteenth century and must have enhanced the risk for parents of a lonely old age, the damage appears to have been restricted.

The earlier age at which boys and girls in the second cohort started to leave home may have generated the wish for more autonomy in these children. Most out-migrating boys would probably have lived with other families as boarders or as co-resident kin. These two forms of residence were in practice the only possibilities. In nineteenth-century Tilburg there were no large boarding houses in which young people resided in great numbers without any form of familial supervision. With some exceptions, this will have applied to most of the smaller and middle-sized towns in the Netherlands. When the girls left home however, they went into domestic service. In almost all of the exits by daughters to 'others' within Tilburg and the larger part of the exits by migration this will have been the case. Despite the familial context in which both boys and girls continued to reside after they left home, this may have involved a relaxation of parental supervision. If we add to this the much improved economic prospects around the turn of the century and the increased opportunities for industrial wage work we might expect marriage frequencies to rise and the age at first marriage to fall in the later cohort of sons and daughters.

However, this did not happen. In both cohorts sons and daughters married at comparable ages and, as we shall see later, in comparable frequencies. The median age at first marriage was 25 for women, and 26 for men in both cohorts. Mean ages are 27.0 for sons in both cohorts, 26.1 for daughters in the 1880–1920 cohort and 26.2 for those in the earlier cohort (see appendix 14). Clearly, there does not seem to have been any trend towards a lowering of the age at first marriage either for women or for men. Compared with the countryside of the province of Noord-Brabant, marriage in Tilburg was quite an early phenomenon in the life course of men and women. In a number of villages in the eastern part of the province marriage came at the age of 31 for men and 27 for women in the later parts of the century. In Nuenen, a village not far from Tilburg, farmers married at the age of 32.6, while their wives were 29.5 years old.[56] In the still-rural com-

---

[56] van der Heijden, 'Gezin', p. 139.

munity of Eindhoven the median age of marriage in the nineteenth century was 29 for men and 27 for women in the same period.[57] Town life in general in this southern province, independently of the particular economic character of the town concerned, appears to have stimulated a lower age at first marriage. Men and women in Breda for instance, a town not marked by any industrial development, married at exactly the same age as found in Tilburg.[58] For the country as a whole, the mean age at first marriage declined in this period by about one year for men and two for women. Men born between 1810 and 1814 married at the mean age of 28.8, women born in the same period did so at the mean age of 27.4. For the cohort group 1895–99 these figures had fallen to 27.4 and 25.7 respectively.[59] Consequently, in a comparative perspective it would appear that age at marriage in Tilburg had already fallen considerably in the first half of the century. During the following decades it did not decline further, so that towards the end of the century national and town averages converged.

I have already mentioned that there were no major shifts in the frequency of marriage between the sons and daughters of the two cohorts; the proportion married rose only very slightly for sons and daughters of the later cohort. In particular, differences in frequencies for sons were minimal (see appendix 15). The largest difference was found for the age of 34 when 21% of sons and 23% of daughters in the later cohort group had not yet married, as opposed to 25% and 28% for the earlier cohort. At the age of 49 almost 10% of the earlier cohort's daughters were still single, whereas daughters in the later cohort had all married by then. For sons at the age of 49 the figures were: 6.7% and 8.3%. Marriage frequency in Tilburg was considerably higher compared with other towns in the south of the country.[60] It must also have risen substantially when compared with the beginning of the century. However, apart from some minor differences we must conclude that in a general sense marriage patterns between the two cohorts were remarkably stable. Neither the greater mobility of young adults and adolescent children, the rising level of incomes, nor the expanding industrial labour market of the town had discernable effects on marital behaviour. It is remarkable that the different economic prospects facing the respective birth cohorts of 1850–59 and 1880–89 had so little influence on age at marriage and hardly any at all

[57] Boonstra, 'De dynamiek', pp. 95–6.
[58] Engelen and Hillebrand, 'Vruchtbaarheid' p. 258.
[59] Frinking, 'Demografische analyse'.
[60] van Poppel, *Stad*.

on marriage frequency. Men and women born between 1850 and 1859 were confronted by the slump of the late 1870s followed by the crisis of the 1880s at the time they reached their twenty-fifth birthday. The cohort born between 1880 and 1889 by contrast was able to profit by improved economic conditions and expanding employment opport-unities in the textile mills.

If we are right in assuming that sons and daughters of the second cohort could have married earlier, it remains difficult to say why they did not do so. Were they consciously postponing marriage so that they could continue to co-reside with and support their parents? Although this may not have been a genuine option, they could in principle have solved the problem by combining marriage and con-tinued co-residence in the parental household. However, if continued support of elderly parents was their motive, they should have post-poned marriage even longer than they did. After all, parents in the second cohort increasingly survived to older ages than before and with increasing departure rates of children many more of these parents came to reside on their own. Of course, the cohort born between 1890 and 1899 may have found it difficult to find a family home considering the shortages in the housing market, but this obstacle can hardly have applied to the two previous cohorts. Perhaps, considering the fact that age at marriage in Tilburg had already dropped considerably in earlier decades of the century, it may be that the sons and daughters of the second cohort were, unconsciously, adhering to generally accepted cultural, or Catholic, values concerning the appropriate minimum age at marriage.

The conclusion that marital patterns had not changed is of some importance here. It indicates the continuing strength of ties between parents and children in the early stages of industrialization. It also means that the rise of extended households towards the end of the family cycle cannot have resulted from a change in marital patterns of sons and daughters. After all, given the fact that extended house-holds partly arise out of the need to take care of elderly parents who are living alone, a fall in the age at marriage and/or a rise in the frequency of marriage of children would have influenced the number of extended households occurring in the final stages of the history of the household.

Children were indeed of the utmost importance to parents. For both cohorts of married couples we may say that children were generally present in the parental household until the very end. In general, parents succeeded in keeping their children living with them until they died or until the very end of their household history. This was even the case for parents in the later cohort, where the combined effects of a larger total number of children born, a higher child mortality rate, higher departure rates for children, and in addition a longer life expectancy of parents created an only slightly higher percentage of households in which parents came to reside on their own in old age. Most of the parents were still living with one or more children in the last phase of the household history. For all heads and wives in the 1849–90 cohort who had ever had children born to them, only 27.2% ended up living on their own, for the later cohort this was 33.7%. If parents were not living with their children, they either had a spouse, or some other kin or unrelated person present in their household. In only 17.9% and 22.4% of all cases in the older and the later cohort respectively did we find a parent living on his or her own at the end of his or her household history.[61] Now it might be suggested that the higher percentages found for the second cohort reflected a development towards neglect of elderly parents on the part of their children. The larger number of parents living without children, however, is merely the result of the larger number of parents surviving to see their children leave home. And, we already know from the previous section of this chapter, most of the parents who survived their own household moved over to the households of their married children, or migrated to other related households.

Thus, elderly people were largely being cared for by immediate relatives, if they had any. It would appear as if the words of one of the local physicians carried at least some truth when he claimed that 'when the father or mother stays behind on their own, if all other children have left, the remaining child many times assumes responsibility and stays with his parents when they need him'.[62] All this is not to say there was no friction between parents and children as a result of which parents may have been neglected or had to fend for themselves in their old age. For instance, among the later cohort we do find some parents repeatedly being passed from the household of one married child to that of another. The fact that married children were giving residential support to widowed parents does not tell us anything about whether they actually liked doing so. Cases are recorded in Tilburg of children trying to have an ageing parent put away in a mental institution at public expense.[63] Children taking care of elderly

---

[61] The percentages offered here apply to parents who ever bore children and whose households were observed for at least fifteen years. These figures relate to the household headed by the parent only.

[62] *Enquete*, Tilburg, question 10717.

[63] van de Put, *Volksleven*, p. 73.

parents also seems to have been general in the Devonshire parish of
Colyton, England. Here too, elderly people in their sixties and seventies are found co-residing with, above all, unmarried children. If the
latter were not available they lived with a spouse or with married
children. In late-nineteenth-century Bertalia, one of the parishes of
Bologna, virtually no widows or widowers of 65 years and over were
living without at least one of their children.[64] Other material on
elderly people in The Netherlands in the first half of the twentieth
century strengthens the idea of the representativeness of the Tilburg
pattern. Although elderly people of 60 years and over in Groningen
and Limburg sometimes are seen to have been living alone for a
while, they eventually came to co-reside with their (married)
children.[65]

4.4   Conclusion

Family life in Tilburg showed no clear sign of weakening under the
pressures of the town's changing social and economic structure. The
breakdown of traditional productive structures which had accelerated
in the final decade of the nineteenth century appears to have had no
major impact upon family behaviour in general. The expansion of
wage work in industry and improved economic conditions around
the turn of the century might be supposed to have led to individuals
loosening the bonds between family members. This did not happen
in any observable way. Families continued to receive extended kin
into their homes and the majority of children were not seen to
abandon parents in old age.

   In the middle part of the century a considerable proportion of all
families were taking in kin members at some point in their developmental cycle. In this period families found to have co-residing kin
generally embarked upon a commitment lasting for quite some time,
especially when parents and siblings were taken in. Throughout the
period under study, if households were augmented with co-residing
relatives, this was by their immediate kin only. Parents and siblings
were found to be present in the first twenty years, while ever-married
children and grandchildren entered the household during the last
two decades. In the later part of the nineteenth century, and at the
beginning of the twentieth, kin co-residence came to be a more
frequent phenomenon in the lives of the families of Tilburg. A
majority of the households that started off on their developmental

---

[64] Robin, 'Family Care'; Kertzer, *Family life*, p. 97.
[65] Bulder, *Household structures*.

cycle somewhere in the 1870s appeared to have been extended at some point in time between 1880 and 1920. Of course, we must bear in mind that some families may also have been extended before and after the period of observation, so that the percentages of households ever extended cited in this chapter must be considered a minimum. The increase in the frequency of kin co-residence came about because of a larger number of parents co-residing with their married children towards the end of the developmental cycle.

Household extension in the period under study could serve different purposes. During the first part of the developmental cycle kin co-residence primarily served the function of providing for the young and the old who had lost the support of their own families. Co-residence of unmarried brothers and sisters of the head or his wife resulted from restrictions on independent residence of young adults, in particular for women. Economically unfavourable periods characterized by low marriage frequencies and relatively high mortality rates could thus result in larger numbers of young men and women seeking accommodation with their married siblings. This was more often the case in the households of the first cohort. Offering accommodation to those without the support of their family likewise applied to widowed parents. The inability to form economically viable independent households will have necessitated their co-residence with married children.[66] Families did not appear to have taken in their parents and siblings in order to redress the balance between relative numbers of producers and consumers, although hard evidence is admittedly not available on this issue. Nor is it likely, considering the particular local circumstances, that parents or siblings were present so as to enable the wife to go out to work for wages.

Towards the final stages in the history of the household the balance of dependency started to change. At the point when almost all of the children had left the household, and when in addition one of the marriage partners had already died, it was the members of the receiving household, rather than the incoming relative, who were most in need of support. In the 1849–90 cohort almost all parents died before the last of their children had left the household. This was the combined result of high levels of mortality, high ages at marriage, low marriage frequencies, and a protracted span of childbearing. If, however, parents did find themselves living on their own for a time, they eventually arranged to co-reside with one of their married children. It is important to stress that these extensions usually came

[66] See Haines, 'Industrial work'.

about in the parental household. Ageing parents clearly preferred to ask their married children to come and live with them rather than to move over to the household of the child. Parents presumably valued the independence this afforded them and tried to retain headship of their own households for as long as possible.[67] This probably still held for the second cohort of parents except that they more frequently ran into the problem of solitary living. More parents in this later cohort survived their own household, and, despite their larger number of offspring, more of them saw the last of their children leave as a result of higher mortality and higher rates of departure. This development apparently compelled an increasing number of parents to give up their own households and move into the households of their married children.

While the process of industrialization gained momentum, kin co-residence seemed to have served a second and quite different purpose. Among the households of the second cohort, extended family structures also came about as one step in the migratory process of individual kin members. This is likely to have been so for some of the co-residing siblings present in the first decades who frequently moved out again after a short time in order to migrate to other places. In chapter 6 I will discuss these kin members in more detail. However, increased levels of migration were clearly responsible for a large number of the extensions occurring in the final decade of the second cohort's family cycle. We found that quite a number of married children in this stage of the cycle were migrating in and out of their parental homes. After 1910, these migratory moves not infrequently took the form of international migration for entire families particularly to Canada and the USA, sometimes giving rise to quite complicated patterns of exchange of individuals between kin-related households. Finally, there can be little doubt that the shortage in the housing market occurring after 1912 reinforced the necessity for these mobile individuals and families to seek co-residential help from parents. Apart from the married children who were using their parental households as stepping stones for migration, some of the remaining children may of course have stayed in the household to assist their parents in old age.

Within the period covered by the present study we have witnessed an increase in the relative frequency of extended households in

[67] De Regt mentions the fact that co-residing elderly parents valued highly the introduction of a state pension, for those over the age of 70, in 1913. This addition to the family budget increased their sense of independence. See de Regt, *Arbeidersgezinnen*, p. 133.

Tilburg. Two separate processes are believed to have been at work. With marriage patterns remaining largely constant during the period of observation, with departure rates of children rising and the life expectancy of parents increasing, many more parents ultimately came to face the economic insecurity of the 'empty nest'. As a result parents increasingly had to resort to co-residence with married children, either in their own or in their children's household. The longer time span of the parental life course also increased chances of parents co-residing with married children if necessary, for other less structural reasons. The Tilburg households thus confirm findings and assumptions of Ruggles and Hubbard who both stress the influence of demographic factors when accounting for the rise in nineteenth-century extended households.[68]

Yet, other influences were at work. The emergence of industrial structures may also account for the growing number of extended households, since these necessarily gave rise to an increase in opportunities for communication and mobility. Accordingly, not only did the mobility of married children increase, but young unmarried sons and daughters in their teens are seen to migrate more than did their predecessors. While the mobility of individuals rose, it is unwise to assume a corresponding increase in the number of resources mobile individuals could turn to in order to facilitate migration, acquire jobs and secure appropriate housing. In the nineteenth century kin relations still provided the main network for aid and assistance, not only for the aged and the lonely, but also for the young and the mobile.

Dissolution of kin ties as a result of industrialization could not be confirmed when focusing on relations between parents and children. In the majority of households children were present until the end of the family cycle. In the course of the century young people started to leave the parental home at an earlier age, and also migrated to a larger extent. They may have been expelled from the household by their parents to earn a living elsewhere or to make room in the family home. For the moment it is difficult to be decisive on this question. They may even have gone out of their own free will. Whatever their motives may have been, the important thing to stress here is that their greater mobility did not result in large numbers of solitary, uncared for parents. The proportion of sons and daughters who had not yet left permanently at the age of 25 or 30 remained high, although it did show a limited tendency to fall.

Breakdown of the family did not become apparent from the

---

[68] Ruggles, *Prolonged connections*; Hubbard, 'Forschungen'.

examination of age at marriage and marriage frequency. The changing economic tide towards the end of the nineteenth century, the gradual expansion of the industrial labour market and increased levels of mobility in the final decades did surprisingly little to change overall marital patterns. Children married at very much the same ages as they had done before and almost in the same numbers. It appears to be difficult to suggest a plausible reason for this remarkable stability. Before speculating further on the issue of marriage, however, I shall proceed in the next chapter to the question of social class. Nevertheless, at this stage it seems fair to suggest that economic developments did not produce change in marital and family patterns as quickly as might be expected. Moreover, we also have to consider the relatively large number of parents who moved into the households of their married children. That these married children were taking in their parents strongly suggests the survival of a kin support system until at least the 1920s. These sons and daughters certainly challenge Peter Laslett's doubts about family care for the elderly before our present day.[69]

Summarizing the results from the first analytical strategy I must conclude that industrialization in its early stages did not appear to have weakened kinship ties in Tilburg. Structural-functionalist theory expects the mobility of individuals, which is so vital to the establishment of industrial society, to be inimical to the maintainance of extended kinship ties and thus the formation of extended families. Therefore it is all the more remarkable that at this stage the increasingly dynamic behaviour of young people in Tilburg appears to have stimulated rather than inhibited the formation of extended households. However, these conclusions must be taken as tentative, pending the analysis of later chapters. In the following chapter I will introduce the important element of social class which may greatly have affected family patterns. An examination of the influence of social class on families and individuals may perhaps help to resolve some of the issues which remained unresolved.

[69] Laslett, *Family life*, see chapter 5.

5

Family life and the social structure

This chapter is concerned with the second of our four research strategies: the study of the relationship between the family and the social structure of an industrializing society. Through the examination of class position in relation to the structural evolution of the household a better understanding may be gained of the relationships between the macro-processes of social change and the micro-processes affecting the family. Again the perspective employed is a dynamic one. This is not only because different aspects of the family along its cycle are involved, but also because the relationships between the family and the social structure are analysed through time. To begin with I will look into the issue of social class and family structure. Next, the relationship between parents and children is further discussed, this time taking into account the social background, while the final section of this chapter deals with family structure and social mobility.

5.1 *Family and social class*

In the previous chapter we dealt with family and household disregarding social and economic variables. However, the historic evolution of the family cannot be fully understood in isolation from the social and economic structure of the society of which it is part. This by now widely accepted point of view in fact constituted one of the major points of criticism on the early work of the Cambridge Group which tended to abstract households from their social and economic context.[1] The need to distinguish between different socio-economic groups becomes especially urgent when examining the interrelationships between the family and the processes of change. Class position

[1] Anderson, 'The study', p. 50; Berkner, 'The use and misuse', pp. 734–6; Medick 'The proto-industrial family economy', p. 295.

115

may be looked upon as an intermediary variable determining not only the direction and strength of the influence of changes but also the way people interpret them and act upon them.

As was explained in the introductory chapter, the relation between the family and the social structure lies at the heart of structural-functionalist family theory. From this viewpoint, the modern family is given its specific shape and structure through the effects and demands made upon it by the social structure of industrial society. The theory maintains that high rates of social, occupational and geographic mobility necessitated the emergence of the nuclear family form which allows the individual freedom to move. Nuclear families in industrial society have realized most completely the supposed 'structural fit' between family and society; they have adapted themselves best to new demands made upon the family and will therefore also be most successful in terms of social and economic position and occupational or social mobility. Following structural-functionalism, thus, with the onset of industrialization we may expect the middle and upper classes, who are by definition the most successful social groups, to be the first to adopt new family patterns. As the process of social change continues and more groups are effectively integrated into the industrial system the ideal of the nuclear family will be spread with it.

Paradoxically, however, empirical evidence suggests that in fact higher social classes in most societies conform less to this ideal type of the nuclear family than do other social groups. The functionalist sociologist William Goode regards this as one of the disharmonies between the nuclear family system and industrial society.[2] Higher-class families in all societies, Goode observes, not only have the resources with which to resist the undermining pressures of industrialization on their kinship ties, they also have most to lose by relinquishing them. For example, middle and upper-class parents may successfully lay heavy claims to their children's loyalty when providing the means for extensive professional training. These youngsters would in their turn have a considerable interest in keeping intact such an active and useful family system. For the lower classes the situation is reversed: they have something to gain from letting go of kinship ties. Consequently, William Goode assumes that in an industrializing process both the peasant and the proletarian 'are forced to adjust their family patterns more swiftly to the industrial system, and find at least more immediate opportunities in it'.[3]

---

[2] Goode, *World revolution*, pp. 12–15.
[3] Goode, 'Industrialization', pp. 244–5.

This contrasts sharply with the views of those historians who believe the nineteenth-century urban extended family household to have been related to the economic pressures of the industrialization process on the lower economic strata of society. Extended family households in the industrial city were no longer an expression of wealth of resources and an instrument to preserve family property, as they had been in agrarian societies. They now came to fulfil the need to cope with the hardships of proletarian family life. The dangers and uncertainties of industrial wage labour, high levels of migration, mortality and fertility, and the lack of formal institutions providing aid and services meant an increased dependence upon kin among working-class people. Modern urban economic development may thus have been accompanied by family patterns considered to be traditional by the prophets of modernization theory.[4]

This discussion also raises the important issue of diverging meanings of apparently uniform household structures. The same type of family pattern may have one meaning or purpose for the proletarian family, but quite a different one for the peasant family or the middle and upper-class bourgeois family. This consideration is one more reason to be very sensitive to the specific social setting of the households involved.[5]

We will continue our study of the cohesion of kin relations under the pressures of early industrialization with a careful examination of family patterns among different social groups in nineteenth-century Tilburg. The question which I will look into in this chapter is the way in which the dynamic process of the family in various social strata interacted with the transformation of the town's social structure. Using the comparative perspective yielded by the two age-cohorts of married couples we will study the, perhaps changing, relationship between household processes and the social structure of an emerging industrial society.

For this purpose we will have to stratify both groups of households. The construction of a nineteenth-century model for social stratification was a much debated subject in Dutch historiography during the 1970s, involving both theoretical and practical problems.[6]

---

[4] Wrigley, 'Reflections', p. 81; Anderson, *Family structure*, pp. 162–9; Hareven, *Family time and industrial time*, pp. 85–119.

[5] Segalen, 'The family cycle', p. 227; Anderson, 'The study', pp. 47–81; Medick, 'The proto-industrial family economy', p. 295.

[6] The debate in chronological order: Giele and van Oenen, 'De sociale structuur'; van Tijn, 'Voorlopige notities'; Diederiks, 'Klassen'; Giele and van Oenen, 'Wel discussie'; Lucassen and van Tijn, 'Nogmaals'; Giele and van Oenen, 'Theorie en praktijk'; Lucassen and van Tijn, 'Naschrift'; de Belder, 'Beroep of bezit'.

The key question of this debate concerned the issue of whether we should distinguish categories of status or social rank, or make use of the (neo-)Marxist concept of class, or construct a combination of both. For those researchers who prefer to stratify on the basis of social status there was the additional issue of the number of status categories. Should mid-nineteenth-century Dutch society be divided into two social ranks, of the rich and the poor, or would three, four, five or even more yield a better model of stratification? Moreover, on the basis of what criteria do we decide to include people in one of the status categories decided upon: professional prestige, income, consumption, political power and so on? The debate on these topics came to no clear conclusion. Some scholars threw up their hands and called it complete confusion, while others discerned at least a little progress. In practice Dutch social historians regularly make use of models implying a combination of categories of class and social rank, distinguishing between an upper bourgeois class of bankers, merchants and industrialists, a middle class of self-employed artisans, shopkeepers and schoolmasters and a lower class of labourers.[7] They may insert one or more other categories between these groups, such as a lower-upper class of academics, higher civil servants and smaller merchants, and a separate class of skilled workers in between the lower and the middle classes. Placement in one of the categories usually proceeds on criteria such as profession, income or property, or sometimes the number of servants.

In this research I will likewise make use of a model of social stratification combining elements of social status, in this case professional prestige, with level of income derived from taxation data. The latter criterion is used in order to categorize more accurately such vague occupational titles as *koopman* (trader). Additional corrections were necessary to provide for other occupations which were affected by changes in social status or financial rewards towards the closing of our period of observation.[8] For an elaboration of the criteria for social stratification as they have been used in this research the reader should turn to appendix 16. The model that emerged involves the following social and economic groups:

---

[7] See e.g. van Dijk, *Rotterdam*, chapter 3; for a good summary of debate and research practice see also Kooij, *Groningen*, pp. 27–33.

[8] This was the result of the combined effects of structural shifts in the Dutch economy and a general rise in the level of incomes, both observed to have been national trends (see van Tijn, 'Het sociale leven', pp. 306–14) and the emergence of new and lucrative possibilities in some professional sectors of the Tilburg economy.

Class I and II: Upper classes
Consisting for the most part of factory owners, merchants, and the professions.
Class III: Middle class
Mostly consisting of self-employed artisans and shopkeepers, but also includes school masters, foremen and overseers, and administrative personnel with lower qualifications.
Class IV and V: Skilled and unskilled labour
Contains the working classes, where class V consists mainly of day labourers and unskilled factory workers while class IV includes artisanal workers and skilled factory labourers.

Families were placed in one of the above categories on the dual basis of the occupational status of the head of household and the family's income, both of which were usually derived from municipal taxation records. Placement in category III was conditional upon being above the tax threshold, except in the case of schoolteachers, so that marginal shopkeepers and tradesmen were excluded and relegated to class IV. Further income criteria were used for categories I and II. A detailed explanation of procedures used and of the nature of the sources is contained in appendix 16. This stratification will be used for all following allocations of social class and social mobility.

In all, five separate allocations of social class have been carried out. Two of them relate to the heads of household, of which the first indicates the heads' social and economic position at the start of their household history in 1849 and 1880 respectively, when they were about the age of 35. The second allocation was made when the heads turned 50. These two allocations of social class will hereafter be referred to as the heads' initial and final class position. The remaining three concern the social position of the sons; they are used to assess the degree of intergenerational mobility which I shall be dealing with in the final section of this chapter.

In the following section a number of aspects of the developmental cycle of the household will be related to social class. In order to permit statistical analysis I have to bring some order to the apparent chaos of household dynamics. The principal categories I propose to use relating to household structure are 'first-phase household structure' and 'second-phase household structure', which refer to respectively the first and second twenty years of the history of the household. From the previous chapter we know that this division corresponds to the two main kin co-residential periods in the history of the household. Thus, when examining the relationship between social class and

household structure we may relate the household's first-phase structure to the head's initial social class. Likewise, when looking at social
mobility patterns of the heads of nuclear or extended household
structures, all households will be divided according to structure during the first twenty years of the history of the household.[9] This
coincides with the period during which the social mobility of the
heads is measured. In addition, when discussing social mobility patterns a further check on the relation between upward mobility and
family structure is introduced by distinguishing between all first-
phase extended families and those that were extended for at least five
years. Almost all the tabulations presented in this chapter concerning
household and social class use the initial class position of the household rather than its final one. Whenever using the final social class
position, as opposed to the initial class position, yields completely
different results this is indicated and discussed in the text.

Around the middle of the nineteenth century extended household
arrangements in Tilburg were certainly not a specifically working-
class phenomenon. As table 5.1 indicates, if families co-resided with
kin they were most likely to be found among those belonging to the
middle strata of society.[10] Extended family households were a typical
component of middle-class family life in Tilburg throughout the
nineteenth century. Middle-class households in the 1849–90 cohort
were twice as likely to be living with extended kin as were skilled or
unskilled labourers. There is, however, no simple linear relationship
between social class and kin co-residence in the sense that extended
households become more numerous as the social standing of the
household rises. Upper-class households contained co-resident kin
only slightly more often than households of unskilled labourers,
almost a third had kin living with them during the first twenty years
of their domestic cycle. In the first cohort skilled workers were the
least likely to be living with kin at all at that stage.

Considering the fact that in the first cohort the middle classes were
almost entirely made up of self-employed artisans, shopkeepers or
small entrepreneurs, it would be tempting to suggest that extended
family living arose out of the need for additional cheap family labour.

[9] The sample of households covering the period 1880–1920 contains an overrepresentation of households that were extended in 1880. For some analyses in the present
chapter the entire sample is used in order to increase absolute numbers for the group
of extended households, while other parts of the analyses cover only the corrected
sample for this group. If the latter is the case a reference of this is made in the text.
For further details on this problem see chapter 3, pp. 66–68.

[10] For the 1880–1920 cohort in table 5.1 the corrected sample was used.

Table 5.1 *Proportion of extended households during first phase of the family cycle by initial class of head for two age-cohorts of married couples*

Class	1849–1890		1880–1920	
	%	N	%	N
upper class	29.2	24	31.6	19
middle class	51.0	49	53.7	54
skilled labour	18.0	194	30.8	159
unskilled labour	24.5	94	23.4	111

At a later stage in this chapter, however, it will become apparent that this is probably too simplistic an interpretation.

In the second cohort roughly the same pattern relating to family and social class reappears, although with some modifications. Again the middle classes display most clearly a tendency towards extended family living during the first twenty years of the developmental cycle. Largely because of a remarkable rise in the proportion of extended housholds among skilled labourers, a slightly less polarized picture emerges with as many extensions among skilled workers as among upper-class households at this time. Nevertheless, we must conclude that kin co-residence was not primarily a working-class affair for either age-cohort of married couples.

Within the agrarian setting a clear and definite relationship between family and social class appears to have existed. The larger the farm and the greater the wealth, the larger and more complex the household would be. This relationship was established by Berkner when writing about eighteenth-century Austrian households, as well as by a number of other scholars for nineteenth-century American and English agrarian households.[11] We also know that household size and complexity were positively correlated with social class in seventeenth- and eighteenth-century agrarian households in the provinces of Holland and Brabant.[12] But, while large farmers and other upper-class households in the English countryside around Nottingham in 1851 took in extended kin more often than did the lower classes, the same relationship could not be established for the textile town of Nottingham itself.[13] In the case of urban communities we may be

[11] Berkner, 'The stem family'; Laslett, 'Social change'; Smith, 'Early Victorian'.
[12] van der Woude, 'Variations', p. 316; Klep, 'Het huishouden', p. 84; van den Brink, 'De structuur', p. 40.
[13] Smith, 'Early Victorian'.

dealing with a more complex relationship between the two variables. Hubbard could find only a weak positive relationship between a higher social status and complex household structure for the town of Graz in 1857.[14] However, Steven Ruggles insists that nineteenth-century extended families were unambiguously associated with the higher social strata, not only among Erie County farmers in the United States but for town and city dwellers in the latter area and in the Lancashire textile towns as well. He finds a clear linear relationship between the two, with the percentage of persons residing in extended families steadily decreasing with the social status of the head. In addition, Michael Katz observed the same relationship to have existed in nineteenth-century Hamilton, Canada.[15] The Tilburg case seems to provide only a partial confirmation of the findings of both Ruggles and Katz when looking at extended households during the first half of the family cycle. Extended family arrangements in Tilburg should in the first place be associated with middle-class family life.

The pattern changes, however, when we take into consideration household structure during the second half of the cycle and relate it to the head's initial social position. Results on this are presented in table 5.2.[16] Middle-class parents belonging to the 1849–90 cohort do still co-reside with extended kin significantly more often than other social groups; as we have seen in the previous chapter, co-residence at this stage of the family cycle was mostly with kin from the categories of married children and grandchildren. Results for labouring and upper-class households do not differ greatly in this group. Class distinctions, however, seem to disappear almost entirely for the second cohort of married couples. In all social groups almost half of the households take in extended kin at some point during this period. This surprising result suggests that in the final half of the period under study the extent to which married children were taken into the household when parents grew older was not as clearly determined by social class as it had been before.

However, we need to exercise a certain caution in this regard. In the first place, when the head's final social position is used, in table 5.2, rather than the initial status, the difference between social classes in the first cohort largely disappears. The upper classes on this basis had about 34% of extended households while results for lower and middle classes remain largely unchanged. For the later cohort there is

---

[14] Hubbard, 'Städtische Haushaltsstruktur'.

[15] Ruggles, *Prolonged connections*, pp. 31–42; Katz, *The people*, pp. 232–6.

[16] This table again includes only the corrected sample for the 1880–1920 cohort.

Table 5.2 *Proportion of extended households during second phase of the family cycle by initial social class for two age-cohorts of married couples*

Class	1849–1890		1880–1920	
	%	N	%	N
upper class	15.0	20	42.9	14
middle class	42.5	40	45.1	51
skilled labour	29.2	171	42.7	150
unskilled labour	26.7	86	46.7	105

no such effect; results do not differ substantially when the final class variable is introduced. There is a further reservation to make concerning the high percentage of extensions for upper-class households in the later cohort during the last twenty years. This was not the result of an increase in upper-class parents taking in married children, perhaps to help with problems of old age, for these parents were in fact co-residing with kin beyond their immediate family. I will return to this when discussing further results.

We begin by considering the percentage of extended households ever, in other words households in which extended kin were present, if only once and/or for a short time in whatever stage of the family cycle. The strong tendency for households to be extended at any stage among the middle classes is clearly born out by table 5.3.[17] In both cohorts the middle classes provide the highest percentage of extensions, to such an extent that in the second cohort almost three-quarters of such households were extended for some time. This figure is very high and conveniently summarizes the enormous importance of kin co-residence for this particular social group. Clearly, household extension by kin in nineteenth-century Tilburg was a structural phenomenon for the middle class. But, we must not overlook the fact that the incidence of extended households among the working classes also rose considerably. In the 1849–90 cohort only about one-third of working-class households came to be extended, while in the later cohort this increased up to the level where one in every two households co-resided with kin at some point. Finally, I should stress that households in the upper strata of society were the least inclined to be extended taking their whole family cycle into account. This pattern persisted throughout the period.

[17] Corrected sample was used for the 1880–1920 cohort.

Table 5.3 *Proportion of ever-extended households by initial class of head for two age-cohorts of married couples*

Class	1849–1890 %	1880–1920 %
upper class	33.3	36.8
middle class	59.2	72.2
skilled labour	35.6	54.7
unskilled labour	37.2	55.9

Tables 5.1 and 5.2 were designed to convey the degree of diffusion of the tendency towards household extension within each social rank. Table 5.1, for example, answers the question of how many households within a certain social rank ever realized extension during the first twenty years of their existence. Figures 5.1 and 5.2 on the other hand examine the number of extensions occurring within each social group for every single year of the family cycle. These two graphs indicate the distribution of household extension over the cycle for different social groups. These figures also indicate what the chances were of finding households in different social groups containing co-resident kin if a purely static approach were adopted, as would be done by taking snap-shots at several points along the cycle.

The two graphs generally confirm the findings above, but figure 5.2 also indicates why table 5.2 might in some respects be somewhat misleading. However, let us look at the two graphs for a moment. Figure 5.1 substantiates once more the importance of extended kin co-residence for middle-class households for every single year of the family cycle in the first cohort.[18] Compared with both lower and upper-class households the percentage of extensions is quite high in each year, varying mostly between 20% and 30% during the first twenty years and stabilizing at a little under 20% during the last period of twenty years. Upper-class households in this cohort were slightly more likely to be extended than were those of the working class in the first half of the cycle. After that point the number of extensions becomes negligible and falls below the level for working-class households. As we shall see later on this is a result of the small number of ageing upper-class parents taking married children into their households. The group of working-class households in this

[18] Household structure for both figure 5.1 and 5.2 is measured by the head's initial social class.

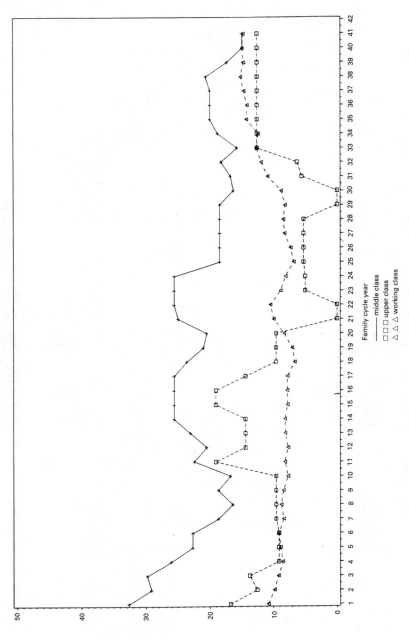

Figure 5.1. Proportion of extended family households by initial social class and family cycle year, 1849–1890 age-cohort of married couples

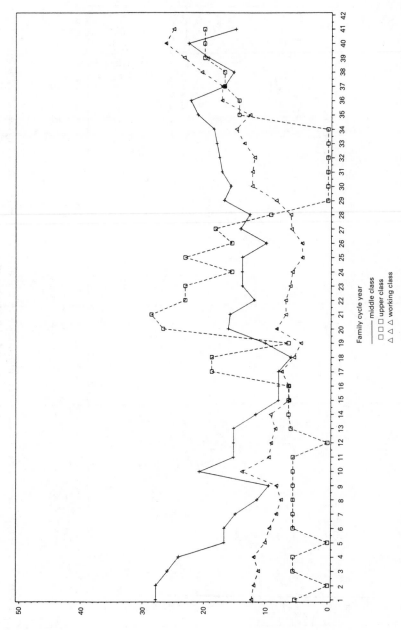

Figure 5.2. Proportion of extended family households by initial social class and family cycle year, 1880–1920 age-cohort of married couples (corrected sample)

Family cycle year

——— middle class
☐ ☐ ☐ upper class
△ △ △ working class

cohort displays a remarkable stability in the number of extensions by year. It varies only modestly around the 10% level, slowly rising towards 15% during the last decade. The greater stability of the pattern for working-class households as compared with the other social groups is, of course, partly a function of the larger absolute numbers. However, the conclusion is inescapable that for both working and middle-class households extension in this cohort is not at all cycle-specific. We have to maintain a fair amount of caution about upper-class households because their numbers are small. It would probably be best to restrict ourselves to suggesting that household extension in this group occurred mostly in the first half of the cycle, and was nearly absent in the second half. (For a survey of absolute numbers of households for different years along the family cycle of both cohorts see appendix 32.)

Table 5.1 shows that in the 1880–1920 cohort the tendency towards extension among upper-class households was about the same as it was among the working classes. When measured by year, as in figure 5.2, upper-class households were less likely to be extended when compared with working-class households. This implies that although working and upper-class households may have had similar chances of forming extended households, once working-class households became extended, they remained that way for a much longer time. Kin co-residence among the upper classes was apparently more temporary, resulting in lower percentages of extended households at any one point in time. Middle-class households showed themselves to be very prone towards co-residence with extended kin in both periods. The overall level, however, is slightly lower in the second period than in the first. This is explained by the fact that more households experienced shorter phases of extension (see tables 5.1 and 5.2).

Returning to the second cohort's upper-class households in figure 5.2, we notice a high peak in extension between the seventeenth and twenty-seventh year of the cycle. This peak did not arise because of co-residence with married children, but was mainly brought about by co-residence with more distant kin: cousins, uncles and aunts. This peak, occurring at a perhaps unexpected moment during the family cycle, was for the greater part responsible for the large number of upper-class extensions during the second half of the cycle, as shown by table 5.2. It is illogical to assume it to have been caused by problems of old age because when time advanced, between the twenty-eighth and thirty-fourth year, almost no extension occurred in this group. The short, steep rise during the last six years does not remove the difficulty. To explain upper-class patterns for this cohort I can only advance the hypothesis that extension in these households was not determined by life course crises such as old age. Rather, it was the need of the individual kin member, the loss of his or her own family-household, or a temporary inability to reside in that household, as opposed to the need of the receiving household, which caused families to take in relatives. This has to be a tentative judgement, of course, given the small absolute numbers of households in this particular social group.

Finally, there is the pattern of the 1880–1920 cohort's working class to discuss. In the first half of the cycle the number of working-class extensions is a little higher than it was in the earlier cohort, which is in accordance with results from table 5.1. The percentage is nevertheless considerably below that of the middle classes and clearly above that for upper-class households. During the first half of the cycle the working classes of the second cohort clearly occupy a middle position, but then, from a very low level in the third decade, they slowly start to rise towards the high point of 27% in the fortieth year. This upward curve during the last decade may help explain the high level of extended households in the second half of the family cycle reached by lower-class families in this cohort, as indicated in table 5.2. The last four years in particular enabled the households of workers, as it were, to catch up with the others. There can be little doubt as to the reasons for this pattern. The increasing shortage in the housing market after 1912, worsened for lower-class people to some extent by the temporary upheavals of World War I,[19] were in all probability mainly responsible. These effects may have been made more pronounced by the coincidence with physical and financial problems of elderly parents who were living longer than in preceding times.

To what extent these factors were working on middle and upper-class households as well is difficult to say. It seems reasonable to suggest that more affluent households were less affected by housing shortages or by the effects of national mobilization during World War I. Greater financial resources may not only prevent the occurrence of problems of old age, but may also diminish dependency on extended kin. Indeed, the relatively high level of extensions from the midpoint of the family cycle onwards, suggests that middle-class households were less influenced by the historical developments occurring between 1910 and 1920. Similar statements concerning the experience of the second cohort's upper-class households between 1910 and 1920 are a hazardous undertaking because of their small absolute num-

---

[19] van de Put, *Volksleven*, p. 18.

bers. Nevertheless, results of the 1917 housing count revealed co-residence (of two or more families) to be only a little less frequent among higher rentable value categories than among lower ones.[20] The upheavals of the final decade therefore do not seem to have left middle and upper-class households entirely unaffected. Part of the gradual rise in the curve for the middle classes and the sudden, short rise in the curve for upper-class households during the final years of the cycle may thus be explained.

By way of conclusion, it is important to stress that the data do not indicate that living in extended families was typical for the working classes in the nineteenth century. When measured by family cycle year, skilled and unskilled workers in both cohorts had fewer co-resident relatives than the middle and upper classes taken together. Although the number of extensions among the lower strata of society rose considerably between the two cohorts, kin co-residence remained a more common feature of middle-class family life throughout the period. Upper-class households, however, were, like working-class ones, not very likely to have co-resident kin. This tendency was as persistent throughout the entire period of observation as the high level found for the middle classes. It is important to stress that upper-class families did not in any way contribute to the trend towards a higher frequency of kin co-residence in our period of investigation. In fact, the upper classes appear to have been the least affected by the processes of change transforming late nineteenth- and early twentieth-century society. Furthermore, while the tendency towards extension does not appear to have been family cycle specific in the first cohort for any of the social groups, this was increasingly the case for lower-class households in the second cohort. For these households, problems of old age in combination with unique historical circumstances may have caused the number of extensions in this cohort to rise at the very end of the household's history.

Before going on to an examination of the type of kin members co-residing in the households, I still have to deal with the possibility raised above, that extended family co-residence among middle-class households may be connected to the need for cheap family labour. The assumption has it that extension would be typical of households engaged in small-scale, household-based production or commercial activity. This suggestion is furthermore connected to the hypothesis that families functioning as work groups or productive units may be

[20] Rossen, *Het gemeentelijk volkshuisvestingsbeleid*, pp. 296–7; van de Put, *Volksleven*, p. 19.

distinguished in structure from those that were not.[21] It is also closely related to the functionalist point of view on the importance of the separation between the occupational and the familial sphere, without which the modern nuclear family would not have emerged. It may be remembered that Parsons considered American farming families to be a major exception to his model of the isolated nuclear family precisely because of the pronounced and persisting overlap between the two spheres in these households. The need to hand down the family enterprise undivided to successive generations may also have led to the formation of extended households, very much as it had always done in agrarian society. This relationship between family and property for agrarian households was originally advanced by Le Play, and after him by many others.[22]

The lack of appropriate sources makes it extremely difficult to examine these issues in detail. All we can do is to distinguish between heads of household running a family enterprise and those who were wage-dependent among the middle and upper classes.[23] Unfortunately, however, this would yield a comparison containing so few cases that it would be impossible to say anything meaningful. Figures are nevertheless given in the footnote.[24] On the basis of the present data, therefore, it is impossible to address the question of family property and the family work group among the higher social strata. The issue of the family work group and its consequences for the structural evolution of the lower-class household will be given extensive attention in chapter 7.

If we turn our attention to the type of kin people accepted into their households, we find that co-residence patterns differed significantly

---

[21] Tilly and Scott, *Women*; Laslett, 'Family and household'; Braun, *Industrialisierung*.
[22] Le Play, *L'Organisation*; Braun, *Industrialisierung*; Berkner, 'Inheritance'; Nimkoff and Middleton, 'Types of family'.
[23] In order to do this I have to rely on the occupational details contained in the taxation listings. For instance, someone described as being a manufacturer is assumed to be (co-)running a family enterprise and to be self-employed. Teachers, overseers and a technical engineer were among those considered to be wage-dependent.
[24] Proportion of extended households during the first phase of the family cycle by initial occupational status of the head for middle and upper classes, for two age-cohorts of married couples:

status	1849–1890		1880–1920	
	N	%	N	%
self-employed	28	45.2	43	54.4
wage dependent	4	36.4	6	75.0
total	32	43.8	49	56.3

Table 5.4 *Proportion of households with co-residing parents by initial social class of head for two age-cohorts of married couples*

Class	1849–1890 %	1880–1920 %
upper class	12.5	26.7
middle class	37.0	43.3
skilled labour	37.0	43.1
unskilled labour	29.6	41.7
N	108	165

between upper-class households and other social groups. Upper-class families during the first twenty to twenty-five years of the family cycle had in almost all cases brothers and sisters co-residing with them rather than parents, which was the other major category of co-resident kin during that stage. Table 5.4 shows that the proportion of extensions involving parents increased between the two cohorts for all social groups.[25] This fact is undoubtedly related to the general rise in the age at death, which lengthened the period that parents could co-reside with their children, and possibly also to a fall in the proportions unmarried, thereby reducing the numbers of unmarried men and women who after their parents' death had to be taken in by their married siblings.[26] The most important information contained in this particular table, however, is the small role in the extension of upper-class households played by co-residing (grand)parents. Of all upper-class extended households, only 12% in the first and 26% in the second cohort were actually taking in ageing parents at any time. Commercial and industrial entrepreneurs in nineteenth-century Tilburg were above all extending their households to include unmarried brothers and sisters.

This pattern is repeated at a later stage of the family cycle, although only for the households of the second cohort, when the couple heading the household might co-reside with their married children. Again, from table 5.5,[27] we notice an overall increase between the two

[25] This table indicates the number of households co-residing with parents as a proportion of all households ever co-residing along the family cycle with all types of kin, except (ever) married children and grandchildren.

[26] This was discussed in chapter 4; see p. 85.

[27] Computed as a proportion of all households in which at least one child was ever born.

Table 5.5 *Proportion of households with co-resident*
married children by initial social class of head for two
age-cohorts of married couples

Class	1849–1890 %	1880–1920 %
upper class	8.7	8.3
middle class	9.1	32.2
skilled labour	13.7	35.5
unskilled labour	12.4	28.8
N	339	374

cohorts in the number of households ever extended through the addition of married children to the household. Such extensions were least evident in upper-class households. How should these socially diverging co-residence patterns be explained? While upper-class parents may have been more successful in avoiding co-residence with their married children, on the other hand both parents and married children in the upper strata of society may simply not have been faced with the necessity to co-reside.

We will return to this question at a later stage. For the moment I will confine myself to the statement that upper-class parents in all probability seldom needed to co-reside with their married children because they had other, unmarried children still at home. According to this line of reasoning, married children entered the household after all or most of the other, unmarried children had already departed, leaving ageing parents more and more in need of kin assistance of some kind. Or perhaps, when parents wanted to avoid the precarious situation of a lonely old age, the last child to marry would be invited to come and live, with spouse, in his or her parental household. In addition, table 5.5 brings out the much stronger pressures exerted by the housing shortage after 1912 on young lower and middle-class married couples, causing more of them to live with parents.

5.2 Parents, children and social class

Did industrialization weaken intergenerational ties? In the previous chapter we concluded that as far as actual behaviour goes this is hardly likely to have been the case. The age at marriage of sons and daughters remained virtually unchanged. Final exits from the parental household did take place at a somewhat earlier age in the second half of the nineteenth century, but not to such an extent as to suggest a breakdown of intergenerational ties. Parents, so it seemed, continued to rely on their children for care and support in old age. To some degree, though, this general picture obscures differences between social classes which will be explored in this section.

Goode suggested that working-class intergenerational relations would be weak, when compared with those of the upper classes, because working-class children had no substantial support to expect from parents, let alone from other kin, which would help advance them socially. Consequently, their children were expected to leave the parental home at much earlier ages and to be less inclined to accept responsibility for elderly parents. Tentative historical support for this hypothesis is advanced by Anderson's work on Preston. Working-class children of poorly paid parents tended to leave home earlier than children whose fathers earned higher wages because, as Anderson put it, 'they had most to gain and least to lose by such a step'.[28] In this, he effectively paraphrased William Goode's position. In conformity with the Preston results, Katz and Davey found in Hamilton that the higher the occupational status of the father, the longer the time children resided in the parental home. In addition, the timing of marriage in Hamilton appeared to have been influenced by occupational status, those in clerical and professional occupations marrying relatively late and labourers relatively early. Katz and Davey concluded that 'if saving and the postponement of pleasure made sense to the clerk or the professional, it had no foundation in reality for the early industrial laborer'.[29]

Although postponement of marriage made no sense to young labouring men and women, we must realize that to working-class parents it could make all the difference. Working-class parents were in general dependent in their old age upon the earnings of adolescent and adult children. In some cases this was the only way to fight off destitution. Quite clearly, however, proletarian families had no ways of exacting subordination of the child's individual interests to those of the family.[30] This hypothesis underlies most of the literature concerning the effects of (proto-)industrialization on marital patterns and family structure.[31] In addition we have to consider that for working-

---

[28] Anderson, *Family structure*, p. 129. Admittedly, Anderson's approach is more sophisticated than this; he also takes into account the wage level of the child concerned. He then suggests that well-paid children of poorly paid fathers will leave first.

[29] Katz and Davey, 'Youth', pp. 102, 113–14.

[30] Anderson, *Family structure*, pp. 91, 123.

[31] Medick, 'The proto-industrial family', p. 303; Braun, *Industrialisierung*, pp. 59–89.

Table 5.6 *Mean age at first exit from home of sons and daughters by initial social class of head for two age-cohorts of married couples*

Class	1849–1890		1880–1920	
	N	Age	N	Age
Sons				
upper upper class	24	16.6	20	14.4
lower upper class	24	19.4	28	14.8
middle class	72	24.9	146	20.3
skilled labour	340	24.6	443	22.2
unskilled labour	160	24.3	308	22.5
Daughters				
upper upper class	29	18.0	20	18.7
lower upper class	29	22.4	29	18.2
middle class	63	24.2	123	18.7
skilled labour	291	24.2	386	21.6
unskilled labour	141	23.2	311	21.5

class children, and to a lesser extent also for those in the middle classes, the possibility of continued co-residence in the parental home was largely determined by the local labour market and employment opportunities in other households.[32] There is, therefore, every reason to expect class differences to have been present in intergenerational relationships in nineteenth-century Tilburg. Various social groups may also have followed diverging patterns over time.

Considerable socio-economic differences did exist in the age at which sons and daughters began to break away from home. From table 5.6 it is evident, for both cohorts and for both sexes, that children from upper-class families left home at substantially earlier ages than working-class children.[33] The age variation between social groups is especially great for sons. Most young men in working-class families of the first cohort left home at about the age of 24, while upper-class sons departed when they were still in their teens. In the 1880–1920 cohort sons from all social groups left at younger ages. The variation between the classes, however, did not change; in the second

[32] Employment opportunities in other households gradually declined in rural Brabant between 1750 and 1850, leading to a fall in the number of domestic servants and a rise in the number of children co-residing with parents, see Klep, 'Het huishouden', pp. 66–9.

[33] Table 5.7 excludes all exits through death as well as all of those coinciding with the end of the history of the household as these were mostly quasi-exits.

cohort upper-class boys left home for the first time aged only 14, while most working-class sons did not leave until they were 22.

In his well-known work on Preston, Anderson suggested that working-class boys would leave home and gain independence at earlier ages than their sisters.[34] The fact that in general boys were better paid than girls, which was the case in Tilburg just as it was in Preston, would not only encourage their drive for independence but would also increase opportunities to do so. The data on Tilburg do not support this assertion. Table 5.6 indicates that in both cohorts daughters with working-class fathers actually tended to leave home at slightly younger ages than their brothers. In general it may be said that while the sons were expected to find jobs in the local textile factories or workshops, most parents preferred their girls to find positions as domestic servants.[35] This would often involve a move away from the parental household by the girl. These patterns, then, result from different employment opportunities as well as cultural ideals concerning suitable types of paid work for boys and girls.[36] While working-class girls on average left one year earlier than working-class boys, most likely in order to become a life-cycle servant in another household, girls with more affluent parents stayed home longer than their brothers. On the whole, however, the life-course transition of a first departure from home for girls in both cohorts did not vary to such a large extent between social classes as it did for boys. Furthermore, it is interesting to note that while in the first cohort middle-class sons and daughters followed the working-class pattern, they clearly distinguished themselves, especially the girls, from the lower classes towards the end of the period.

Such a pattern is initially surprising, contradicting expectations based on theory and historical evidence. Instead of leaving home at much younger ages, working-class boys and girls remained home longer than did upper or middle-class children. However, there can be little doubt that this pattern is closely related to new developments in the educational field in the second half of the last century, which in turn were brought about by the changing socio-economic structure of Dutch society.[37] Instead of an old-fashioned training on the work-

[34] Anderson, *Family structure*, pp. 125–6.
[35] See chapter 2, page 42, concerning the opposition to factory work by women.
[36] Richard Wall also opts for the explanation in which variation in age at leaving home between the sexes is related to local employment opportunities (Wall, 'The age', pp. 194–5).
[37] A completely new type of secondary education was created in The Netherlands in 1863, the 'Hogere Burger School' (HBS), mainly aiming at children from the lower bourgeoisie, while the old Latin Schools were being transformed into 'Gymnasia'

floor, or private tutoring, many more upper-class families started to send their sons to boarding schools outside Tilburg to receive not only a modern and advanced education, but also a proper Catholic one.[38] In the second half of the century the number of private Catholic boarding schools for both boys and girls increased at a steady rate, and many of the destinations given in the registers for out-migrating girls and boys from upper-class families were communities where some of the most popular boarding schools were located.[39] This accounts for the early age of first departure from home for upper-class boys in particular. It also helps to explain overall upper and middle-class development between the two cohorts. There was another educational trend which may have lowered the age at first exit for upper-class boys even further. After about 1880 Dutch universities started to attract far more students and increasing numbers of leading industrial families seem to have begun sending their sons to universities or technical colleges, such as the one in Delft, or to foreign colleges of textile technology.[40] Modern economic development in this period required more advanced technical schooling for what was to be the next generation of the industrial elite.[41]

Most upper-class boys migrated to places outside Tilburg when they left home for the first time, further supporting the assumptions made above. Initially, sons of working-class fathers tended to remain at home until their marriage; this was true for two-thirds of all working class sons in the first cohort. The proportion of exits through marriage for working-class sons did fall below a half, however, in the

---

preparatory to an academic education. For this see: Dasberg et al., 'Het socio-culturele leven', pp. 129–44, 361–72; and Idenburg, *Schets*, pp. 156–9. The first HBS was established in Tilburg in 1866, the first gymnasium opened its doors only in 1899 (van de Put, *Volksleven*, p. 112).

[38] The case of Diepen (1846–95) can be seen as an illustration. Belonging to one of the most important industrial families of the town, he was sent to a boarding school sometime before his sixteenth birthday in Katwijk aan Zee, a gymnasium run by priests. (See van den Dam, *Arnold Leon Armand Diepen*, p. 149.) This type of intellectual training was in 1863 still considered to be somewhat unusual.

[39] Elite sons were often recorded as moving to Sint Michielsgestel, where there was a boarding school for boys after 1851. The school was related to one of the religious orders active in Tilburg. There was also a seminary in this town. Upper-class girls frequently went off at relatively young ages to Aarle-Rixtel, presumably to a boarding school which was also associated with one of the religious orders active in Tilburg, providing secondary education for girls.

[40] Dasberg et al., 'Het socioculturele leven', pp. 127–44, 359–72; J.M.A. Diepen, eldest son of one of the leading industrial families of the town had been sent to the Städtische höhere Webeschule in Muhlheim-am-Rhein when he was 16 years old. In 1859, he was the first to go, but others followed after some time (see van den Dam, *Arnold Leon Armand Diepen*, p. 148).

[41] van Tijn, 'Het sociale leven', p. 311; van den Eerenbeemt, *Ontwikkelingslijnen*, p. 127.

1880–1920 cohort. The shift over time in the reason for leaving home was greater among the working classes than it was for the sons of the elite. As in other behavioural patterns, middle-class boys in both cohorts occupied the middle position; the number of migrations also went up in the second cohort. Whereas, before, almost four in ten middle-class boys left home for reasons of marriage, this fell to one in four in the later cohort. For girls we find the same pattern: more migrations, fewer exits through marriage, the increase being largest for working and middle-class daughters. In both cohorts, however, we find upper-class girls maintaining their much lower proportion of exits from the parental household on account of marriage (see appendices 17 and 18 for tables on this topic). While upper and middle-class sons and daughters presumably left home for educational reasons, the increase in the number of migratory moves and the lower age at first exit for working-class children was most likely determined by the search for jobs. The elder children in these families were compelled to explore the labour market outside of their home town during the crisis of the late 1880s and early 1890s.[42]

Having analysed the social pattern of first exits over the course of two cohorts, it is surprising to find that the analysis of final exits in some ways suggests an opposite trend. Towards the close of the century the social differences in the timing of the final break from home for boys and girls became less, instead of differentiating further. This was largely the result of the fact that young men and women in the upper and middle classes respectively extended and shortened the time they spent living at home, while the pattern for working-class children remained more or less stable.

Even in the first cohort, class differences in the age at final break from home were not as large as for first exits. While middle-class boys and girls did not leave home permanently before the rather late age of 26 and 25, and working-class sons and daughters stayed home until the age of 25 and 24, the age at final break was really only substantially lower for the upper echelons of the elite. In the later cohort working-class sons and daughters continued to leave home at about the same age. Surprisingly, the much greater mobility in the later cohort had not resulted in earlier independence from their family of origin. In spite of the fact that increasingly they were leaving their home town in search of job opportunities, they apparently continued to be bound to parents and siblings. The industrialization process did not substantially alter this particular life-course experience of sons

---

[42] Keune, 'De industriële ontwikkeling', pp. 51–5.

Family and social change

Table 5.7 *Mean age at final exit from home of sons and daughters by initial social class of head for two age-cohorts of married couples*

Class of head	1849–1890		1880–1920	
	N	Age	N	Age
Sons				
upper upper class	23	21.0	19	23.0
lower upper class	24	22.9	25	24.4
middle class	71	26.4	141	24.9
skilled labour	340	25.8	428	25.1
unskilled labour	157	25.6	299	25.3
Daughters				
upper upper class	29	19.8	19	23.3
lower upper class	28	25.1	24	24.3
middle class	63	25.1	120	23.8
skilled labour	290	24.7	377	23.6
unskilled labour	136	24.6	304	24.1

and daughters in the working class. Moreover, there are no indications that working-class sons could achieve independence much earlier than daughters because their wage levels were higher.

For upper and middle-class sons and daughters the pattern did change, however. Although upper-class children (especially sons) experienced a first break at a very early age in the second cohort, their period of dependency actually grew longer. This is in keeping with the fact that more of them stayed at home until marriage, as we shall see in due course. Perhaps the protracted period of formal education which brought about earlier departure from home in many cases, at the same time lengthened the period of dependency on parents. Middle-class sons and daughters succeeded in hastening the timing of independence: their average age at final exit went down by about two years. This change must have been the result of migration out of Tilburg, because the timing of marriage did not change at all for this group of young adults.

Around the middle of the century children of working-class families usually stayed home until they married. This is to be seen in the high proportion of final exits by marriage for both boys and girls of the first cohort: a little over three-quarters of all final exits were caused by exits for marriage. This is in sharp contrast to the quarter or more of all upper-class boys who departed from home permanently because they married and set up establishments of their own. For girls the differences were a little less pronounced; only two-fifths of upper-class girls in the first cohort left permanently on marriage. For both boys and girls the middle classes occupied the middle position (for tables see appendices 19 and 20).

Because of the increased tendency for the working classes to migrate in adolescence or early adulthood during the second period of observation, the chances were that either these migrating young men and women would not return to their home town following their first exit from home, or that they would increasingly find marriage partners outside of Tilburg. In the latter case their final exit will also have been registered as a migratory exit. Results indicate that this is indeed what happened. We find in the first place that there was a considerable fall in the number of working-class sons and daughters in the second cohort leaving permanently on marriage. Secondly, the age at which this event occurred was no lower than it had been earlier. Thirdly, the age at marriage for those who married in their home town also did not change. (See for type of final exit appendices 19 and 20.)

While working-class sons and daughters increasingly left home to migrate definitively, there was a reverse movement at the other end of the social scale, at least for boys. During the first period a quarter or more of upper-class sons left finally on marriage. This proportion rose to 40% in the second period. Daughters from upper-class families, similar to those in the working classes, showed a decreasing number of final exits through marriage, though the difference between the cohorts was not as large as for working-class girls. Considering the rise in age at final exit for upper-class sons in the second cohort, we may safely conclude that more of them were staying at home until marriage. Apparently, towards the close of the century the town offered sufficient prospects for young men from the upper classes to prevent their moving away.

Of course, the marriage of a son or daughter was a crucial event in the lives of ageing parents, especially the poorer ones. It determined their economic well-being and their possibilities of continued independence from kin, neighbours and the Poor Relief authorities. Marriage constituted above all the final break between parents and children; it was almost always accompanied by departure from home. For working-class children marriage was also crucial, particularly for women, because it offered the only available and generally accepted opportunity for complete independence from parents. Unmarried individuals, if they wanted to leave the parental home to acquire

Family and social change

Table 5.8 *Median age at first marriage for sons and daughters by initial
social class of head for two age-cohorts of married couples*

	1849–1890		1880–1920	
Class	Age	N	Age	N
Sons				
upper upper class	28	6	29	8
lower upper class	28	12	29	17
middle class	29	49	29	94
skilled labour	26	307	26	343
unskilled labour	26	137	26	238
Daughters				
lower upper class	25	18	24	9
upper upper class	25	10	25	11
middle class	28	51	28	64
skilled labour	26	266	25	301
unskilled labour	25	134	25	240

personal independence, were generally restricted to accommodation
within a familial setting. Large lodging houses without familial supervision simply did not exist.[43] Moreover, towards the end of the
nineteenth century a young man of 20 could earn a fair wage in the
mills, as one of the Tilburg manufacturers declared in 1887, so that no
major material obstacle existed to early marriage.[44]

It is therefore of some importance to note, from table 5.8, that the
age at first marriage among the working classes between the two
cohorts did not change at all. The median age at marriage for working-class children continued to be high throughout the period. The
figures, however, do suggest that the age at marriage, and by implica-
tion the power of parents over children, increase with the socio-
economic position of the parents. The fact that this was particularly
true for sons reinforces the plausibility of such a conclusion. Girls in
the upper classes would not have been required to work for wages in
order to secure the economic basis of the household, which made the
timing of marriage for them more open to other influences. Sons,
however, were either bringing in high wages after protracted periods
of education, or they were expected and trained to continue the

[43] In Preston for instance these lodging houses provided opportunities for working-
class children who wanted to escape parental supervision. Anderson, *Family structure*, p. 125.
[44] *Enquete*, Tilburg, question 10561.

family enterprise. Elite parents, then, had a considerable interest in maintaining a great deal of influence over the timing of marriage of their sons, and they seem to have succeeded in doing so.

Economic circumstances might also help to explain the high ages at marriage in the middle classes, for whom both sons and daughters were no doubt a considerable economic asset, especially when families were running small-scale family businesses. Although, as we have seen, some of the children coming from a middle-class background succeeded in leaving, through migration, earlier than had been the case before, others stayed on until they married at relatively advanced ages, or did so even after marriage.

In the evidence examined so far we have found noticeable shifts in the life-course experience of some young men and women. But these can hardly be regarded as signs of a serious weakening of inter-generational relations under the influence of a changing economy. Although the majority of sons and daughters began leaving the parental home at earlier ages, the final break between parents and children, as reflected in the ages at final exit and at marriage, took place at largely the same age. Social differences in the extent to which parents managed to exercise control over their children have been inferred from age at marriage, especially for sons. Age at marriage may be considered to be the most important indicator of the degree of parental control over children, the higher the occupational status the stronger the parental influence.

We have yet one more indicator of divergent life courses among young men and women in the nineteenth century. The proportion of sons and daughters who had not yet left the parental home permanently by a given age, has the advantage over other figures of including those that never married, or did not leave at all. This measure is presented in figure 5.3 which graphs the proportion of sons and daughters, married or single, not yet permanently absent from the parental home.[45]

From the right-hand upper panel of figure 5.3 it is clear that in the first cohort rather large differences between social groups existed in the rate at which sons departed from home. For working-class sons the final break occurred within a relatively short time span between the ages of 20 and 30, so that only about a fifth of 30-year-olds were still living with their parents and/or siblings. Although at that age the majority of middle and upper-class sons had also left home, we find the remarkably high figure of almost 40% still resident in their par-

[45] All exits made by children, also exits by death, are included. For figures see appendix 21 and 22.

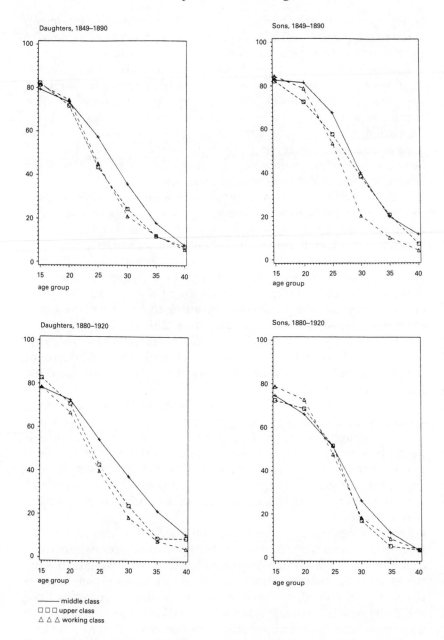

Figure 5.3. Proportion of children still at home by age group and social class for two age-cohorts of married couples

ental homes. For girls the pattern was somewhat different in this cohort. The major social difference for girls existed between lower and upper-class girls on the one hand and middle-class daughters on the other. At the age of 30, 21% of working-class daughters and 24% of those in the upper classes had not yet left permanently, whereas for those in the middle classes as many as 36% were still at home. Middle-class parents effectively managed to restrict early autonomy for daughters who were probably major economic and social assets to their households.

The left-hand lower panel of figure 5.3 suggests that middle-class parents had lost little of their hold over their daughters. Towards the end of the nineteenth century we find about 37% of middle-class daughters still living with parents at the age of 30, which was the case for only 18% of working-class women at that age and 24% of those in the upper classes. The lower panel of figure 5.3 indicates that middle-class daughters, in contrast to their brothers, had not broken free from parental authority. While middle-class sons in the second cohort were leaving home in larger proportions than before, daughters were still prevailed upon to remain at home, presumably to assist parents in old age. Like their brothers, they were marrying late when compared with other social groups. It was the middle-class daughters who payed the heavy price of delayed independence for the increased longevity of their parents, who no doubt were in their care.

Class patterns in the life-course experience for young men seem to have been less pronounced in the second cohort. Between 15 and 20, there was only a slight variation between the social groups in the proportion of sons still at home. However, at age 30 the gap was still considerable, but the linear relationship between proportion still at home and social class had disappeared. As in the case of the girls, the middle classes were most successful in delaying the moment of final break from home for their sons. About a quarter of 30-year-old sons in this group had not yet departed from the parental household, in contrast to the 17% of upper-class sons and 18% of all working-class sons who were also still at home at 30. Thus, the conclusion must be that, while in the earlier cohort middle and upper-class parents managed to persuade sons and daughters not to leave the parental household too rashly, in the second cohort only middle-class parents had maintained strict parental control, primarily over daughters, but also to a lesser extent over sons.

Figure 5.3 suggests that upper-class parents were among the big losers in the struggle for independence on the part of their children. In the second cohort larger proportions of both sons and daughters left home in almost all age groups. However, it is interesting to note that upper-class parents took leave of their sons and daughters in comparable proportions to working-class parents. Although the age at final exit from home rose for upper-class sons between the two cohorts, a substantially smaller proportion stayed at home until both parents had died. We can observe only modest shifts in working-class experience for both sexes between the two cohorts. The proportion of children still at home at the age of 30 decreased only slightly among working-class families, despite considerable increases in the level of migration and profound changes in the local economy.

Nevertheless, parents increasingly were living longer in the second cohort. At the same time the children of some categories of parents in this group were leaving home earlier than they had done before. These developments may have introduced an entirely new phase in the parental life course unknown to the majority of parents in previous generations: the phase of the 'empty nest'. Surely, it is incorrect to assume, even for the nineteenth-century period, that elderly parents living on their own were without any familial support in the confrontation with problems of old age. Their children might still be living in the same community, or even next door. Practical domestic support for parents by their children does not necessarily stop when these children marry and leave the parental household. However, it would be equally incorrect to assume that parents greeted the period of the empty nest with equanimity. The marriage of a child and his or her departure from the parental household will in all cases have involved a shift of the child's financial priority from the family of origin towards his or her newly established family of procreation. In particular, working-class parents felt the threat of approaching old age full of financial and other insecurities rather acutely. It is reasonable, therefore, that they tried to postpone the moment when they would have to face the empty nest. Parents from different social groups may have tried to counteract these developments by persuading at least one child to remain at home until the death of the last surviving parent. Table 5.9 throws some light on this question. In this table we examine household composition at the time at which parents were last observed to be heading their own household.[46] At that point, coming shortly before parents either died or moved away, we may wonder how many parents had children still living with them. In addition, the table distinguishes between parents living with married or unmarried children.

[46] Those households in which no children were born at all were excluded from this table, as well as those that could be observed for less than twenty years.

Table 5.9 *Household composition at the end of the history of the household by initial social class for two age-cohorts of married couples*

Class	Parents with children	Parents with married children	Parents without children	Parents with others only	N
Cohort 1849–1890					
upper class	94.4	5.6	0.0	0.0	18
middle class	73.5	2.9	11.8	11.8	34
lower class	66.1	6.3	25.0	2.7	224
Cohort 1880–1920					
upper class	63.2	5.3	26.3	5.3	19
middle class	60.4	15.1	22.6	1.9	53
lower class	53.0	11.6	33.6	1.9	268

In the earlier cohort all of the parents in the upper strata of Tilburg society lived with children until the end of their lives, or at least for as long as they headed their own household, while only a small proportion of these parents had only married children living with them. This is in marked contrast with middle-class families, but even more so with lower-class parents of whom as many as a quarter experienced a phase without children at the end of the history of their household. In general, co-residence with married children in this cohort was still rare, as we have already seen in the previous chapter.

The later cohort of parents increasingly saw all of their children leave while they themselves were still heading their own household. This was true for all classes, but the change was particularly noticeable for upper-class parents. While the preceding cohort of upper-class parents had not known the empty nest phase at all, almost a third of upper-class parents in the second cohort ended the history of their household without co-residing children. Although far fewer upper-class parents had unmarried children living with them, they were still unlikely to have married children living in their household. Parents in higher social circles did not respond to the empty nest phase by inviting married children into the parental household. However, upper-class parents would not have experienced the departure of the last of their children as a problem to the same extent as working or middle-class parents. The financial position of upper-class parents made other options available, such as paid services of various kinds, to solve any problems relating to old age.

While in middle-class families in the later cohort children left the parental household earlier than children from other social classes, parents did not always manage to avoid the empty nest. Nevertheless, they had quite some success: unlike the first cohort, middle-class parents now had the lowest percentage of households without any children present. In figure 5.3 we have seen that in this social group a strong appeal was made to daughters to continue to live with their parents. The lower panel of table 5.9 also indicates that lower and especially middle-class parents increasingly had married children present in their household shortly before they either died or moved away. In fact, this is the main reason why middle-class parents had a lower proportion of households without children when compared with the upper class. While upper-class parents clearly continued their stronger hold over sons and daughters so that they had at least one unmarried child living with them, they did not, or perhaps did not want to, opt for co-residence with married children.

It is clear that during our period of observation parents increasingly came to reside on their own towards the end of their lives. In the great majority of cases there was only one parent left at that point. This was so for 69% of all households without children in the 1880–1920 cohort and 77% for those in the previous one. Some of these couples or widow(er)s without children continued living in their own household until the period of observation ended, at the end of the year 1890 or 1920. What ultimately happened to them is unknown. The others gave up their households by leaving in various ways. In the earlier cohort we observed twenty-four 'known' exits of parents which brought the histories of their households to an end. In only three cases did the parent move in with one of the married children, while three others were taken in by the *gasthuis* (hospital). The remaining parents all died, although a few migrated or remarried and so moved to another household. Distinctions between social classes could not be made because there were only six cases in the middle class and none among the upper classes.

In the second cohort we again find that parents without co-residing children at the end of the histories of their households were mainly widowed: 69% of all cases. But some things have changed in the life course of this cohort. If parents gave up their own household and moved away, they moved in with their married children. In working-class households this happened in 59% of all such cases, whilst another 8% of these parents had married children come in and take over headship of the parental household. Only 33% departed in other ways, as a result of either death or migration. Unfortunately, there are only a few cases available for the middle class and upper classes, nevertheless the figures for these groups are perhaps indicative. While middle-class parents also customarily moved into the households of married children (in three out of five cases of 'known' exits) this never happened with upper-class parents. In none of the seven cases in this social class did the parent move to the household of a married child. Instead we find that on two occasions married children moved (back) into the parental household, with the son or son-in-law becoming the new head of household. The other five cases concerned parents ending the history of their household through death.

This result seems to tie in with other figures on upper-class extension patterns which principally involved co-residing brothers and sisters of the head or his wife rather than their parents. We have already established the fact that upper-class parents were not very likely ever to live with married children. Now it seems we should extend that conclusion and state that in the few cases where they did, these arrangements came about primarily because married children moved in with parents instead of the other way around. While the data seem to support the assumption that parents in all classes were trying to continue headship of their own households, even in very old age, in order to maintain independence, perhaps only upper-class parents were entirely successful. Upper-class parents possessed the means to persuade sons in particular to marry late and to have at least one unmarried child stay at home. In the event that all of their children married and left, they were able to prevail upon one of them to come and live with them. Despite the fact that subsequently the charge of the household was passed on to the son or son-in-law, this arrangement undoubtedly gave the parent the opportunity to make demands if necessary.

Complete dependency upon others, kin or non-kin, which to all appearances may have been the inevitable fate for a considerable proportion of working-class parents, was thus avoided. More or less the same may be said of middle-class parents. They had a stronger hold over their children, resulting in high proportions of adult children still at home, a late age at marriage and only a few parents who at the end of their lives had to go without the presence of co-residing children. But in their co-residence pattern in old age middle-class parents resembled the working classes because of the higher frequency of parents co-residing with married children as well as the higher frequency with which they moved into the households of married children.

5.3   *Family structure and social mobility*

In his study of middle-class family life in nineteenth-century Chicago, Richard Sennett advanced the hypothesis that the nuclear families in his research were unable to cope with the dynamics of urban-industrial life. The vast changes and the sense of dislocation created by the emergence of an industrial environment caused the heads of these families to retreat into the warm and protective haven of the family. This, however, could only work in the intensive and private atmosphere of the smaller, nuclear families. As Sennett put it: 'For men confused and scared by the new city, the family offered an intimate world with an internal binding power of its own: both the city and the nature of the family unit would lead men to become absorbed in "home".'[47] Since within their families these family heads were the only persons travelling between the world of work and the world of family life they could 'lock themselves away' from the world into the privacy of their homes. In their work patterns they held on to what they already had, instead of being competitive and mobile, out of fear of taking risks that could bring ruin to the entire family. Instead of concentrating on the pursuit of upward mobility, these fathers aimed at strengthening family life. The intensive nuclear family unit became 'a weapon of defense against, and refuge from the city'.[48]

According to Sennett the heads of extended families could not use family life as a tool for withdrawal because these families included other adult workers. This made it more difficult to prevent outside industrial values, that is achievement and universalistic values, from seeping into the family sphere. Whilst competition did not stop at the front door of these families, the fathers were stimulated to be more mobile in their occupational patterns. Moreover, the historical experience of the fathers was passed on to the sons. Heads of nuclear families transmitted the apprehension they felt about work and city life to their sons, while at the same time the protective shelter of the family had scarcely prepared the sons for the competitive world outside it. Sons from extended families on the other hand had been introduced to the dominant values of industrial city life by their fathers and other kin members at an early age. The father's success also worked as a strong incentive to encourage the sons towards

---

[47] Sennett, *Families*, p. 196.
[48] Ibid., p. 199.

occupational mobility. Thus, the very segregation between the family and other kin, and between the family and the world of work, which Parsons had thought necessary to bring about mobile individuals, had made Sennett's nuclear families unfit to perform in industrial society.

This elaborate exposition of Sennett's work should not be taken to indicate that I intend to adopt his extensive psychological interpretation of family patterns in relation to social change. On the contrary, I intend to carry on from his basic finding that the nuclear family structure was dysfunctional in terms of social or occupational mobility. Sennett's conclusion was supposed to refute the element most central to functionalist family theory, that is the more or less complete 'fit' between familial and societal structures. This also constitutes the issue I wish to explore here. I will compare two main family structures, nuclear and extended, examining the extent to which they permit or inhibit individuals from seizing the sometimes very restricted opportunities offered to them to rise on the social ladder.

At the beginning of this chapter it was shown that extended families were not common among those at the very bottom of the social scale. Perhaps there may even be a cumulative effect to the relationship between social class and extended family structures, so that extension, being frequent among middle-class families, is particularly frequent amongst those most successful within that group. Yet it may be still that the more pronounced, intensive orientation towards kinship relations, reflected in the tendency to co-reside with extended kin, prevented the individual from moving out and socially bettering himself. Or, to put it the other way around, socially mobile individuals may want to relinquish their possibly inconvenient kin ties. This approach allows us to examine the relationship between the family and the social structure from a new and more dynamic perspective on both family and social structure. In the following two paragraphs I will briefly outline the way I approached the allocation of intra- and intergenerational mobility, and in addition I will present some general observations on social mobility in the Netherlands in the nineteenth century.

Intragenerational mobility relates to the social mobility achieved by an individual within his or her lifetime, whilst intergenerational mobility looks at the extent to which improvements in social status between generations were realized. In this final part of chapter 5, I will first look at intragenerational mobility when examining the social mobility achieved by the heads of household in the two cohorts. Following that, the socio-economic status of the sons at a particular point in their lives is compared with the status of the father to produce measures of intergenerational mobility.

For all following allocations of social mobility I will again make use of the five-class social stratification model previously employed. For all male family heads I relate social and economic position at the age of 50 to their social and economic position at the beginning of each period of observation, that is in 1849 or 1880, when these household heads were around the age of 30–35. In the case of the sons belonging to both groups of households I aimed at three separate allocations: one at the age of 19 and another one at the age of 35. A last allocation at the end of each period, in 1890 and 1920, includes those sons who were by that time 40 years old or more. However, occupational entries in the national militia registers, on which data the first allocation of class were based, could not be found for all sons, for the reasons explained in chapter 3. When the age range for this allocation was somewhat expanded to include all sons for which an occupation could be found in one of the sources used here prior to their thirtieth birthday, most sons still alive could be included. Likewise, a very strict application of the 35-age norm for the second allocation would needlessly have limited absolute numbers. It often occurred, especially in the 1880–1920 cohort, that sons were absent for a short time period following a migratory move in precisely their thirty-fifth year of age. It was therefore decided to include all sons in this second allocation for whom social class and economic position could be determined between the ages of 30 and 35. For the assessment of intergenerational mobility we thus have three allocations of social class to link to the initial class of the father. On the social mobility of the household heads, tables included in this text will only summarize results. Complete mobility matrices can be consulted in the appendices, along with results for intergenerational mobility.

Opportunities for upward social mobility in nineteenth-century Dutch society are generally considered to have been very limited indeed. Only in the final decades of the century did the social structure begin to open up, offering new opportunities and new roads to social success.[49] Even then, prospects were still very unfavourable for those belonging to the working classes. When we come to examine mobility patterns of the inhabitants of Tilburg we will find a similar pattern emerging, with mobility being low for heads in the first cohort and significantly higher in the second. On the whole, the road to social success in Tilburg can be regarded as traditional, and to

[49] van Tijn, 'Het sociale leven', pp. 87–8, 311; van Dijk, *Rotterdam*, pp. 146–56; Kooij, *Groningen*, pp. 72–7.

consist in artisans' success in attaining the status of independent master. For skilled workers to rise into the group of large industrial entrepreneurs was almost impossible; nearly all large factory owners were recruited from the traditional commercial families. Towards the close of the century, however, new opportunities were created for skilled labourers in Tilburg to improve their social standing and financial situation. New higher-status and better-paid occupations were created, for example in the metallurgical sector with the arrival of the national railroad construction yard. In addition, entirely new routes for social advancement opened up, such as training schools for primary school masters. On the whole, however, social advancement within traditionally oriented industries remained the primary road to social advance. Although the mobility scores presented in this section do give an indication of the general development of social opportunities in nineteenth-century Tilburg, we should remain cautious when regarding them as indicators of the overall level of social mobility in this period. The analysis and presentation put forward in this chapter do not intend to serve that point.

Fathers heading nuclear families were certainly not more mobile than fathers heading extended families, as is evident in table 5.10.[50] This table, as well as all following tables on social mobility, presents social mobility rates by class in the upper panel while the lower panel indicates total rates of upward and downward mobility. Mobility matrices relating to intragenerational mobility are presented in appendix tables 23 to 28. Returning to table 5.10, we find that total upward mobility figures, as well as total upward mobility into the middle class, indicate that the extended family structure was the background of some quite successful careers. However, the results set out in table 5.10 are not consistent. In the earliest cohort we find, for example, that, while total upward mobility for extended households is a little higher than for nuclear households, an extended household structure among unskilled labourers was not accompanied by a very successful outcome. At the bottom of the social scale it would seem to have been more sensible not to be involved with kin beyond the immediate family. The difference in mobility rates for unskilled labourers from different household structures are enor-

---

[50] We need to consider to what extent these results may have been biased by ambiguous occupational titles in the sources that were used. In general, however, I feel that it was possible to place both heads and sons adequately in the various categories on the basis of the information available. Those recorded in the sources as factory workers may, however, in some cases have been incorrectly categorized as being unskilled (see appendix 5). Mobility scores pertaining to the latter social group should, therefore, be treated with some caution.

Table 5.10 *Upward mobility of heads by social class and total mobility scores by first-phase household structure for two age-cohorts of married couples*

Class	Nuclear families	Extended families	Extended 5-> years
Cohort 1849–1890			
I	—	—	—
II	55.6	0.0	0.0
III	17.6	45.0	40.0
IV	6.3	6.3	13.1
V	42.9	21.1	18.2
total upward mobility	18.8	19.5	21.2
unchanged	63.9	70.1	69.2
total downward mobility	17.4	10.4	9.6
from class IV–V to III–I	4.9	3.9	9.6
N	213	77	52
Cohort 1880–1920			
I	—	—	—
II	57.1	71.4	80.0
III	28.0	38.7	50.0
IV	15.2	12.9	9.1
V	50.6	56.8	63.2
total upward mobility	30.5	32.6	35.6
unchanged	60.5	56.0	50.7
total downward mobility	9.1	11.4	13.7
from class IV–V to III–I	10.9	11.1	9.6
N	220	141	73

mous. Surprisingly, this is also the case at the far end of the social ladder. Class II, containing the smaller traders and industrial entrepreneurs, also does extremely well while adhering to a nuclear family structure.

In between both ends of the social scale, however, results indicate the opposite. The social success of middle-class extended families is especially conspicuous. In addition, the results for skilled labourers co-residing with kin appear to be quite favourable. For this last figure and for the total upward mobility into the middle classes we may safely state that they involve the biggest hurdle in the model of social stratification. The first table presented in this chapter showed that in the earlier cohort extended families were particularly prevalent among those initially belonging to the middle classes. Now it also seems that, both for ambitious labourers aiming at the middle class as well as for those stemming from it, an extended family structure carried the best promise of success. It reinforces the close association between the middle strata of society and the phenomenon of kin co-residence in the middle of the nineteenth century.

In the second cohort, social success, when looked at by class, appears to be more closely related to extended family structures. In all social classes with only one exception (skilled labourers), extended families achieved higher upward mobility rates. Differences in upward mobility between the two family forms are especially large for middle and upper classes. However, upward mobility into class III in this cohort, while being generally on a higher level than before, was not exclusively achieved by extended families.

Instead of associating the extended family structure with social success, however, it is more important to emphasize that these Tilburg nuclear families clearly do not substantiate the structural fit between an industrializing economy and the nuclear family structure. The results for the first cohort could perhaps, up to a point, suggest a basis for such a fit because of the successful bourgeoisie that had severed extended family ties. But then again, so had the sub-class of unskilled factory workers and day-labourers. As the nineteenth century advanced every ground for the structuralist hypothesis is lost. Those families that had managed to make the best of the opportunities offered to them by the evolving industrial structure of Tilburg did not refrain from taking in extended kin members in the first phase of their family cycle. Or, when seen from the opposite perspective, heads of extended families were not restrained in terms of social opportunities by the fact that they were strongly embedded in their extended kin network.

To what extent is this development reflected in the social experience of the sons coming from various household structures? I will examine the results on intergenerational mobility by age group instead of by cohort group. The first measurement, concerning sons up to the age of 30, reveals the fact that the majority of young men embarked upon their careers as skilled labourers or artisanal workers. Regardless of the class position of the father, most sons under the age of 30 can be graded in class IV. This holds true for 71% of the sons from nuclear families, and for 77% of sons of fathers heading extended families in the second cohort. The previous cohort had a comparable experience in that 69% of nuclear family sons, and 71%

and 68% of the sons from extended families began their career in class IV. It may seem surprising, even astonishing, that sons of middle class and, to some extent, even upper-class fathers were to be found in artisanal work before their thirtieth birthday. This becomes understandable when we know that most middle-class family heads were heading medium to large-scale commercial enterprises. Most of the time the sons were placed in the family business, as successors, assisting their fathers and learning the business. Thus, the son of a wealthy contractor could begin his career as a carpenter in his father's company. This also helps explain the higher level of downward mobility for sons from extended families in this age group, occurring in both cohorts, as these families comprised a larger number of middle and upper-class families.

However, let us concentrate on the comparison between sons from extended families and those from nuclear families. Results presented in appendix 29 demonstrate that in both cohorts sons from extended families frequently rose socially. In the first cohort the percentage of sons from class IV rising upwards is much higher for extended families when compared with sons from nuclear families; the same may be said for total upward mobility scores as well as total upward mobility into the middle class. In the following cohort total upward mobility scores do not differ greatly, but upward mobility into class III is again higher for extended family sons; this also holds for mobility out of class V and III. It is especially remarkable to note that in the second cohort a number of middle-class sons from extended families had already risen to class II or even I before they reached the age of 30.

However, the mobility scores for sons at the age of 30–35 from different household structures are not so far apart. Results on this age group are presented in appendix 30. In this age group household structure does not seem to be in any way related in a statistical sense to social mobility. But, in so far as results do diverge between household structures in this age group, they often do so in favour of sons from nuclear families. In the first cohort nuclear families among unskilled labourers in class V and among the bourgeoisie in class II have higher mobility scores, while only middle-class sons seem to benefit a little by coming from extended households. It is a rather weak reflection of their father's mobility pattern, which suggests that middle-class fathers do not automatically pass on the ability to rise on the social ladder to their sons. Total upward mobility scores as well as total mobility into the middle class for this cohort are virtually identical between the family forms.

...hort total mobility scores are again higher for
...especially when compared with sons coming
... kin co-resided for five years or more. This
... totally by the social success of upper-class
...es. For other social classes, the nuclear family
...nguish itself by any significant degree of social success.
...he data for sons at the age of 40 or above, contained in appendix
31, further confirm the assumption that there is no consistent statistical relationship between the structure of the family and the degree of intergenerational mobility. Although in the first cohort, classes II, III and V have considerably higher mobility scores for nuclear families, resulting in a higher total upward mobility, this pattern is not repeated in the second cohort. Here again, only heads of upper-class nuclear families have successful sons, while for extended families middle-class sons seem to have done extremely well in life. No less than three-quarters of all middle-class sons from families in which kin had co-resided for five years or more managed to rise into the upper classes.

In table 5.11 I examine the position in the social hierarchy that these sons finally end up in as a result of the rates of differential mobility established above. The difference in social position between the two family groups that existed for their fathers may have been erased by the favourable careers of some of the sons. In particular, I have in mind here the relatively lower social mobility of extended family sons in the second cohort. Examining the class position achieved by sons at the age of 40 or above for both cohorts we must conclude anew that the data do not consistently suggest that one or other family structure was more functional in terms of intergenerational mobility. Table 5.11 shows that more sons from nuclear families in the first cohort ultimately joined the highest strata of Tilburg society, while exactly the opposite may be said for those in the second cohort.[51] A larger number of sons from extended families of the 1880–1920 cohort managed to get into class I and II. Moreover, assuming that these results were not the simple effect of random chance, it is also worth noting the sequence of change. As Tilburg society increasingly took on an industrial shape towards the end of the nineteenth and the beginning of the twentieth century, sons from nuclear families began to be less successful instead of the other way around.

---

[51] In order to avoid bias in favour of the sons from upper-class fathers the corrected 1880–1920 sample was used for this tabulation.

Table 5.11 *Social stratification of sons at the age of 40 or abou*
first-phase household structure for two age-cohorts of married cou

Class	Nuclear families	Extended families
Cohort 1849–1890		
upper class	7.0	3.1
middle class	14.1	17.8
skilled labour	57.9	54.3
unskilled labour	21.1	24.8
total	446	129
Cohort 1880–1920		
upper class	5.0	14.5
middle class	16.5	20.7
skilled labour	70.5	58.2
unskilled labour	9.0	6.6
total	501	227

5.4 Conclusion

Extended family households were a key feature of middle-class family life in nineteenth-century Tilburg. In both cohorts middle-class families not only had the highest level of extensions by family cycle year, but they also had the highest number of households ever extended. More than half of all first cohort middle-class households were extended at least once along their cycle, this rose to three-quarters in the second cohort. Kin co-residence was clearly not an exclusively working-class phenomenon: in the first cohort lower-class households experienced extensions about as often as did upper-class households, while they occupied a middle position in the second cohort. Nor can household extension be said to have been associated above all with higher social positions, in fact the higher social classes were the least inclined towards kin co-residence. No linear relationship between social class and family structure could be established.

The second cohort experienced a general rise towards a higher proportion of families ever becoming extended. A number of converging micro and macro-level developments were responsible for this result, affecting most of all the lives of those in the working and middle classes. First of all, parents were increasingly living longer, a development which had already set in around the middle of the nineteenth century, thereby creating a larger number of extensions at the beginning of the cycle of the families in the second cohort. Towards the close of the history of these households, problems of old age, created by increased longevity, became more serious as children either continued to leave the parental household at the same time as before or even a little earlier. A larger number of parents at the end of their lives were experiencing a short empty nest phase when all of their children had left the parental household. Furthermore, this period also witnessed a considerable increase in the mobility of married and unmarried children in and out of their parental households. In view of the growing housing shortage after 1912 this created even further problems. Married children who had migrated were forced to apply to parents and siblings for temporary accommodation. World War I in all probability only served to aggravate the situation, since the entire private house-building sector had collapsed.

Only the more affluent classes were successfully able to resist or to counterbalance the forces promoting extended households, and then only to a certain extent. Upper-class households clearly differed from all other social strata in that they did not share in the rise towards a higher level of extensions. They were the least inclined to live with kin, and, if they did, they co-resided with different types of kin compared with other social groups. During the first phase of the family cycle they only infrequently lived with grandparents but more often had co-resident unmarried brothers and sisters. This pattern repeated itself at the other end of the cycle when parents rarely co-resided with married children. The upper classes recognized a far wider circle of extended kin relations and were prepared to take them in, if need be. The second cohort in particular co-resided with a relatively large number of cousins and uncles and aunts during the middle years of the family cycle.

We would argue, therefore, that the lower level of household extensions among upper-class households is not an expression of a lesser commitment to family and kin. On the contrary, it resulted from a much larger and more cohesive kin network. To begin with, the upper classes could exercise a much stronger hold over their sons and daughters than could other social groups. In both cohorts upper-class parents showed the highest frequency of co-residence with unmarried children. This enabled parents to escape the necessity of living with married children or other kin when they became elderly. In addition, it should be stressed that some of the problems associated with this stage in an individual's life course were either non-existant or much less serious because of greater financial resources. These factors taken together reduced the number of extensions at the beginning of the family cycle as well as at the end. The much larger inclination to co-reside with more distant kin further illustrates the strength of family ties at the top of the social hierarchy. Not only unmarried siblings but also cousins, aunts and uncles, or nephews and nieces, were taken into the household when they were no longer able to reside with their own families. Upper-class household extension came about much more as the result of the needs of the individual kin member, and to a much lesser extent resulted from the needs of the receiving household. This implies that upper-class household structure was much less determined by family cycle conditions than is the case among other social classes.

Upper class parents did not, however, totally escape pressures on their parental authority and family cohesion. While none of the upper-class parents of the first cohort had to live without the support of co-residing children, upper-class parents in the second resided with children much less often towards the end of their lives. Their children left the parental household in about the same proportions as working-class children. However, this should not obscure an important difference: a much larger proportion of working-class children still at home at the age of 30 were actually married, in comparison with upper-class children. At the end of their lives upper-class parents co-resided without children as often as did working-class parents, solely because they did not live with married children to the same degree. Upper-class families demonstrated that they were taking care of lone kin members, but there was an apparent hesitation when it came to co-residence involving two nuclear families.

The upper classes were thus much more able to conform to the cultural ideal of the independence of the nuclear family. Evidently, either out of need or out of choice working and middle-class parents did not conform to this family norm. Not only did they open their households to solitary kin members, such as ageing parents or unmarried siblings, they also took in their children's families at a later stage in their lives. Working-class parents were in addition more often forced to surrender their independence and join the households of their children when reaching old age. This was directly related to the fact that they could not subordinate their children's interests to their own to the same degree as upper-class parents.

However, the middle classes in this study may be regarded as the true champions of family and kinship. The strength of family life in the middle-class milieu is not only evident from the great number of extended families, but is also clear in their strong intergenerational links. Middle-class children throughout the entire period married at very late ages, they left the parental home in much smaller proportions and, in the second cohort, often resided with parents after their marriage. The girls especially were tied to their families of origin by very strong bonds, sacrificing their independence to the interests of parents and family. Although the data available were far from perfect, I tried to test the hypothesis that the particular structure of the middle-class family is related to the presence of family property in the form of a commercial or industrial family business. However, wage-dependent middle and upper-class families appeared to be even more hospitable towards extended kin than did those who ran a family enterprise.

The results presented in this chapter certainly do not support the supposed association of extended family structures with the margins of industrial society nor do they support the supposed structural fit between the nuclear family and industrial society during the initial stages of the process of industrialization. This was further confirmed by the section on intra- and intergenerational social mobility. There were no indications that families which had been extended at some point during the first twenty years of their cycle in any way impeded the social advancement of the family head or the sons. Although the results contained some ambiguities, they may be summed up as follows. As far as intragenerational mobility is concerned, nuclear families in the first cohort showed themselves to be more upwardly mobile than the extended families in this group, while the situation was the reverse in the succeeding cohort. There was one notable exception: middle-class extended family households in both cohorts were very successful indeed in terms of social mobility. Household extension in nineteenth-century Tilburg should, therefore, primarily, though not exclusively, be associated with socially vigorous middle-class groups. The social mobility of sons, viewed in comparison with the class position of their fathers, weakly reflected mobility scores of the heads, with sons from nuclear families being a little better off in the first cohort, and sons from extended families in the second. The intergenerational mobility scores further helped to dissolve remaining doubts about the functionalist hypothesis: there was patently no such thing as a structural fit between the nuclear family and early industrial society. If anything, the social success of the extended family structure increased as the process of industrialization transformed traditional economic and social structures.

6

Family structure and geographical mobility

This chapter pursues the third of the research strategies outlined in chapter 1, namely an examination of the household structure of migrant and non-migrant households in Tilburg during the nineteenth century. After a short discussion of the relevant literature I will outline a number of general characteristics of the migrant households in the two cohorts of married couples. The next section explores household structure of migrant and non-migrant couples, while the final part of this chapter looks at the inter-relationships between household structure and geographical as well as social mobility. In this chapter analysis focuses on the traditional assumption that geographical mobility will inevitably lead to a breakdown of extended family ties, so that geographical mobility and extended families must be considered as mutually exclusive.

6.1 *Migration and family disintegration*

Conventional sociological theory has painted a rather grim picture of migrant family life in the nineteenth-century urban arena. According to the theory of social disorganization, transition from rural peasant communities to the industrial urban landscape involved abrupt discontinuities, leading to the uprooting of individuals and families. The transition to industrial work routines and the anonymities of life in towns and cities frequently resulted in stress and anomie. The nineteenth-century migrant was basically a lonely, uprooted individual cut off from the support of extensive family and community networks. R.E. Park and E.W. Burgess were major representatives in a respectable line of scholars adhering to this perspective.[1]

---

[1] Park and Burgess, *The city*.

Very much in line with the theory of social disorganization, structural-functionalist sociologists stressed the incompatibility of vigorous extended kin networks with geographical mobility. It was pointed out that large family groups would necessarily hinder the geographical mobility of individuals which was so vital to the modern economic system. Thus, the smaller nuclear-family unit emerged, facilitating not only individual social mobility but, since the two are thought to be related, geographical mobility as well. In addition to the effects of the family system on the degree of mobility, there is also the effect of migration on the family system to be considered. Once the nuclear-family unit had removed itself geographically from its extended kin members, opportunities and possibilities for mutual support and aid declined. Along with the weakening of kin ties there would also be a decline in the formation of extended family households.

A large body of historical and sociological research already exists questioning the validity of these traditional positions. Studies of nineteenth-century migration have shown that it mostly involved a chain process over short distances enabling the migrant to adjust gradually to the urban setting.[2] As in other European areas this appears also to have been the case in Tilburg and other Dutch communities.[3] Furthermore, in many instances it was found that migrants retained connections with relatives whom they had left behind.[4] Whatever the distances travelled, migrants were not suddenly stripped of their traditional culture; in fact, they actively made use of it in their process of adjustment.

The family played a key role in the process of migration itself and the subsequent processes of adjustment and acculturation. In many instances the family network functioned as an agency directing and facilitating migration.[5] The family provided communication links, while in determining their destination migrants would largely follow those kin members who had preceded them.[6] Kin assistance in migration is thought to have been particularly valuable for those groups who were socially less resourceful or powerful.[7] While many ventured to migrate together with their families of origin, individual migrants would mostly choose to reside within a familial context.[8] Family life also promoted residential stability: single migrants co-

[2] Drake, *Historical demography*, pp. 119–45; Anderson, *Family structure*, p. 37.
[3] Peters, 'De migratie', p. 155; Kooij, *Groningen*, p. 186.
[4] Hareven, *Family time*, pp. 114–16.
[5] Yans-McLaughlin, *Family*, pp. 55–81.
[6] Neuman, 'The influence'.
[7] Tilly and Brown, 'On uprooting', pp. 116–20.
[8] Glasco, 'Migration', p. 165.

residing with relatives were found to have higher permanency rates compared with those living in other arrangements.[9]

It would thus appear that extended family ties could survive migration. The assumption that geographical mobility and the extended family network would be incompatible is precisely the idea Litwak set out to refute.[10] In post-war America, widely separated kin continued to exchange help and recognize kinship relations beyond the immediate nuclear family. These 'modified extended families', Litwak argued, aided geographical mobility and retained extended family identification in spite of physical distance between them. Did Litwak thus effectively disprove Parsons' contention on family structure and geographical mobility? Harris points out that this can never be the case as these families were not forming extended family groups in the classical and Parsonian sense of a co-residing domestic group.[11] Parsons did not deny the continued existence of help patterns between dispersed nuclear families related by kinship ties. Harris concludes his discussion on this issue by saying that 'the existence of extended-family groups inhibits differential mobility and adversely affects the assimilation of immigrants'.[12] If migrants do retain extended kinship ties leading to the formation of extended family groups this will endanger a successful integration into the host society. In other words, there can be no structural fit between migrants huddled together in extended family households and modern industrial society.

In this chapter on household structure and migration I will first compare the incidence of extended kin co-residence in migrant and non-migrant families in nineteenth-century Tilburg to see to what extent geographical mobility did inhibit the formation of extended family households. In addition, I will examine the extent to which migrant extended families were bordering on the margins of society. If household extension indeed mainly did occur with migrants from more 'backward' agrarian areas, who upon arrival in the town occupied and continued to occupy the lower social positions, this would indicate one particular way in which the extended family structure was dysfunctional in an emerging industrial society.

6.2 Migrant households

Both the 1849 and the 1880 age-cohort of married couples contained migrant and non-migrant households. When speaking of migrant

[9] Jackson Jr, 'Migration'.
[10] Litwak, 'Geographic mobility'.
[11] Harris, *The family*, p. 82.
[12] Ibid., p. 84.

households we are referring to households where both husband and wife were born outside Tilburg. In non-migrant households both partners were born within the community's boundries. From chapter 2 we know that the town derived its most powerful growth potential in the nineteenth century from an excess of births over deaths. The low level of migration and the relative isolation of the town is effectively illustrated by the fact that in 1899, and even in 1919, about three-quarters of its inhabitants had been born within the town itself.[13]

However, Tilburg did experience one short period of heavy in-migration in the 1860s, when large numbers from the surrounding countryside were attracted by the town's growing economic opportunities.[14] The boom in woollen textiles of the sixties induced investments in a great many additional mills based on current technology rather than in more advanced large-scale production techniques in the existing mills. Consequently, employment opportunities expanded greatly both in textiles and the artisanal sectors such as building or shoemaking. The in-migration of the 1860s therefore may be considered to be the effect of strong pull variables attracting, for the greater part, young families with small children from the surrounding countryside, rather than the more deprived lone migrant turning up due to the effect of push variables.[15] In 1869 half of all incoming migrants were migrating with their families.

In view of the above it is no surprise to find that in 1849 few migrant families could be found among the Tilburg population. Of all couples heading a household at the time of the 1849 census only 12.7% were of migrant origin, while 31.7% were of mixed origin. The further decline in the already low level of migration during the crisis of the 1840s may help explain the fact that migrant couples in 1849 were principally to be found among those over the age of 35. Although in 1880 migrant households were still a minority group, their proportion in the total population had risen considerably. Of all households headed by married couples in 1880 26.5% were of migrant origin while 28.8% of the couples were of mixed, migrant and non-migrant, origin. In 1880 migrant households were very evenly distributed over different age categories of couples heading a household.[16]

It is unfortunate that the first age-cohort of married couples con-

---

[13] Rossen, *Het gemeentelijk volkshuisvestingsbeleid*, p. 151.
[14] See chapter 2, p. 32.
[15] Peters, 'De migratie', pp. 159, 166–7.
[16] For figures see appendix 33.

tained only fifty-one households headed by a migrant couple (see appendix 34). I have included data on these households in the present chapter, but for more significant evidence we will have to rely more heavily on the later cohort. In this latter group 169 households were of migrant origin. For some statistics in this chapter, however, I will be using the corrected sample for the 1880–1920 cohort, which reduces the number of migrant households to 156.[17]

The two cohorts of migrants were to some extent drawn from two distinct migratory streams. In the first cohort 43% of the migrant households were headed by couples where at least one originated from outside the province of Brabant. This was the case for only 29% of the migrant households in the following cohort.[18] The two groups, however, showed a similar proportion of rural migrants: only 27% of the households in the first cohort and 28% in the second were headed by a couple where either husband or wife were of urban origin.[19] The rather large proportion of rural migrants may be considered to be typical of Tilburg and was also found for all migrants coming into Tilburg in the 1860s.[20]

There were other important differences, however, in the migration pattern of the households in the two cohorts. Table 6.1 indicates that a much larger percentage of the migrant households of the first cohort had migrated together as a family.[21] Almost half of these households contained children who were not born in Tilburg. The couples in the second cohort had probably all come to Tilburg in adolescence or early adulthood, with or without their families of origin.[22] Of this cohort eight out of ten households had all of its children born in Tilburg, making them a very stable group of migrants. Only one in ten families displayed a two-step migration pattern with children born outside Tilburg in places other than the place of birth of either parent.

---

[17] See chapter 3, pages 66–68.

[18] Migration over larger distances is probably determined by different variables from short-distance migration. Perhaps the absence of strong pull variables in the first half of the century mainly affected the influx from the Brabantine province. Figures for the second cohort conform to the pattern found for all migrants to Tilburg in the 1860s (Peters, 'De migratie', p. 156) as well as for single migrants to Eindhoven in the second half of the century (van der Woude, 'De trek', p. 178).

[19] To distinguish towns and villages in the birthplaces of migrants in the two cohorts I classified those places that had 10,000 inhabitants or more at the time of the 1849 and 1879 census respectively as towns.

[20] Peters, 'De migratie', p. 156.

[21] The uncorrected sample for the 1880–1920 cohort was used.

[22] In the 1860s 50% to 60% of all incoming migrants were single individuals (see Peters, 'De migratie', p. 159).

Table 6.1 *Migration pattern of migrant families by place of birth of offspring for two age-cohorts of married couples*

Children born in	%
Cohort 1849–1890	
Tilburg	56.3
one or more in place of birth parents	12.5
one or more in another place	31.3
Cohort 1880–1920	
Tilburg	79.6
one or more in place of birth parents	9.0
one or more in another place	10.8

The fact that the migrant families of both cohorts had migrated into Tilburg and subsequently stayed could be taken to indicate that they were relatively successful socially. In fact, table 6.2 shows that these migrant families as a group were doing very well in the Tilburg community. In the earlier cohort skilled and unskilled labourers were relatively underrepresented, when compared with non-migrant families, in favour of middle-class occupations in particular and to a lesser extent also upper-class occupations. In the later cohort we find fewer skilled labourers among migrant families than among the native-born, and for migrant families a marked overrepresentation in upper-class occupations. Both sets of migrants would thus appear to be socially and economically very stable and well-integrated groups. This conclusion must be seen in light of the fact that this study deals with those who stayed, rather than with more volatile migrants. It would be incorrect to infer generalizations about nineteenth-century migration as such from the characteristics of the migrant families in the two cohorts looked at here.

6.3   Migration and family structure

The extensive literature today on the important role played by the family and wider kin relations for migrants of all sorts raises certain expectations as to family structure. If indeed migrants were actually using dispersed kin members from their family network as stepping stones in their own processes of migration, that should mean that migrant households more often saw the arrival of extended kin as temporary members of their household. We would then expect to

Table 6.2 *Initial social status of migrant and non-migrant households for two age-cohorts of married couples*

Class	Non-migrant	Migrant
Cohort 1849–1890		
upper upper class	2.3	5.9
lower upper class	3.9	3.9
middle class	11.0	29.4
skilled labour	55.5	43.1
unskilled labour	27.4	17.7
Cohort 1880–1920		
upper upper class	0.5	3.9
lower upper class	0.5	7.1
middle class	14.5	17.3
skilled labour	52.4	39.1
unskilled labour	32.1	32.7

find that families of migrant origin were extended more often over the course of their cycle than others. On the other hand, it is also true that migrant families had a smaller number of kin available locally and therefore fewer opportunities of living with them compared with native families. If the stepping stone mechanism does not outweigh the reduced opportunities for migrant households in kin assistance, the net result would then be that migrants formed extended family households less often than did the native born. This would lend some support to traditional sociological theory on family and migration.

In most research it has proved difficult to establish a clear negative or positive relationship between migration and the incidence of extended households. In mid-nineteenth-century Graz the distinction between migrants and non-migrants did not appear to be relevant in terms of household structure.[23] Natives and non-natives had extended family households in equal proportions. Late-nineteenth-century migrants to Bologna equally included a similar percentage of complex families compared with stayers.[24] Much the same situation existed in the United States for foreign and American-born migrants. Sennett in his Chicago study wondered 'Why should birthplace have counted for so little in the lives of these people?'[25] He could find no

[23] Hubbard, 'Städtische Haushaltsstruktur', p. 208.
[24] Kertzer, *Family life*, p. 121.
[25] Sennett, *Families*, p. 83.

differences in household structure between various ethnic groups in Chicago in 1880. In Buffalo, New York, however, foreign-born heads of households did co-reside with extended kin considerably less often than the native born. In 1855, for instance, only 15% of the Irish households were taking in relatives compared with 25% of the native households.[26] Similarly, family life among Irish immigrants in London was clearly characterized by nuclear family living, despite the strong inclination of Irish immigrants to seek the support of friends and family members upon arrival in the city, and also despite the fact that extended family links dominated Irish peasant culture at the time.[27] Although Irish households included more extended kin members than did English working-class households, the percentage of Irish extended households did not exceed that of the middle-class areas in London. In Preston migrant couples were less likely to be living with kin than were non-migrant couples.[28] Anderson presumed that this was because they were less likely to have kin in town with whom to live. Thus, international research indicates that migrant households could contain kin as often as those of non-migrants, or even significantly less.

The static data on migration and family structure in Tilburg in 1849 and 1880 only complicate things further. As table 6.3 indicates, migrant couples in 1849 were co-residing with kin more often than were those where both husband and wife were born in Tilburg. This was the case for all couples regardless of their age. In 1880 the situation had been reversed. Migrant couples of all ages were living in extended family households less often than were native couples of any age. Such an outcome is all the more surprising given the fact that half of the 1849 cohort migrants were composed of adult migrants. These might be expected to have had fewer kin available in Tilburg to co-reside with than the cohort-migrants of 1880, of whom a substantial proportion had probably migrated as children together with parents and siblings. Results for the 1849 cohort could be the effect of small numbers, but figures for all married couples do support the cohort results.

We assumed the effect of migration to have been relevant primarily, if at all, during the first half of the family cycle. The previous two chapters have shown that in general, after the first

---

[26] Glasco, 'The life cycles', p. 129; on a higher level of aggregation American migrant families also live with kin less often than do non-migrant families, see Seward, *The American family*, p. 109.

[27] Lees, 'Patterns', pp. 375–80.

[28] Anderson, *Family structure*, p. 52.

Table 6.3 *Proportion of extended households for migrant and non-migrant couples in 1849 and 1880 for total population and two age-cohorts of married couples*

	Non-migrant %	Migrant %
total population in 1849	10.0	12.1
1849–1890 cohort in 1849	13.2	19.6
total population in 1880	10.0	7.8
1880–1920 cohort in 1880	15.0	8.3

twenty years of the family cycle, household extension occurs through the addition to the household of married children and grandchildren. There is no immediate reason why the geographical origin of the couple should affect the occurrence of co-residence with married children in their later lives, except of course when migrants originate from widely different cultural backgrounds. In the case of Tilburg the occurrence of kin co-residence in the second half of the family cycle proved to be unrelated to the place of birth of the couple heading the household.[29] In the following section I will therefore concentrate on household structure during the first twenty years of the family cycle of migrant and non-migrant households.

When kin co-residence is looked at from a dynamic point of view it is clear that migration and extended family households were certainly not mutually exclusive in nineteenth-century Tilburg. In the first twenty years of the family cycle a larger proportion of migrant households experienced a transition from a simple family structure towards the more complex structure of the extended family than did non-migrants. Kin co-residence was evidently a more frequent experience for migrant families. This was so for both cohorts of households, although they had moved into Tilburg from very different areas. Table 6.4 therefore refutes the proposition that geographical mobility diminishes the extent to which family members keep in contact and form co-residential arrangements.

Table 6.4 is a good illustration of the way in which static data on households may lead one astray. It indicates that, whatever percentage of extensions a static approach may yield, it is not necessarily representative of family experience over time. In particular in the case

---

[29] See appendix 35.

Table 6.4 *Proportion of extended households during first-phase of family cycle for migrant and non-migrant families for two age-cohorts of married couples*

Cohort	Non-migrant %	Migrant %
1849–1890	24.5	27.5
1880–1920	30.5	34.0

of the second cohort of migrant households it was more likely that kin members would be added to the household more evenly over the entire span of the first twenty years of the family cycle. However, as we shall see, co-resident kin in the households of the second cohort would remain for only short periods of time. A static approach is, therefore, unable to capture the full dimension of the household dynamics of this section of the population. It would have led us inevitably to the incorrect suggestion that geographical mobility and extended family households were incompatible, despite the findings for the first cohort. This very constraint may have undermined other results, cited above, which indicated a lower frequency of extended family households among migrants compared with non-migrants. Of course, it is clear that a static approach may equally well suggest incorrectly that migrants live with kin more often than natives.

Where migrants are frequently found to co-reside with kin it has been suggested that this is because migrants make use of the households of their kin as stepping stones in their process of migration. Kin related households are then either used as an intermediary stage on the way to a more distant final destination, or serve as a base from which to prepare for independent living after arrival in town. This was often the case with the French-Canadians in Manchester, the United States, as well as with migrants to Preston.[30] Migrant households in Tilburg may well have served similar purposes in which case we may expect co-residence patterns to be clearly shaped by the demands and exigencies of the migration process. Migrants in most studies have been found to be young and still unattached adults looking for opportunities at the start of a career. This was also the case in Tilburg where at the beginning of the 1860s, shortly before powerful pull variables changed the pattern of migration, two-thirds

---

[30] Hareven, *Family time*, pp. 114–16; Anderson, *Family structure*, p. 155.

Family and social change

Table 6.5 *Relationship to head of household of extended kin present during first phase of family cycle in migrant and non-migrant households for two age-cohorts of married couples*

Relationship	non-migrant			migrant		
	Female	Male	All	Female	Male	All
Cohort 1849–1890						
parents	50.0	50.0	32.2	66.7	33.3	27.3
siblings	31.7	68.3	47.1	40.0	60.0	68.2
uncles/aunts	60.0	40.0	5.7	—	—	—
cousins	0.0	100.0	2.3	—	—	—
others	45.5	54.6	12.6	100.0	0.0	4.6
N	35	52	87	11	11	22
Cohort 1880–1920						
parents	58.5	41.5	36.6	79.3	20.7	31.9
siblings	45.1	54.9	45.5	38.9	61.1	39.6
uncles/aunts	75.0	25.0	3.6	75.0	25.0	4.4
cousins	33.3	66.7	2.7	40.0	60.0	5.5
others	69.2	30.8	11.6	41.2	58.8	18.7
N	60	52	112	49	42	91

of all migrants were lone individuals aged 20–29.[31] The existing literature suggests that while male migrants generally had some additional options for accommodation at their disposal, in particular by boarding or lodging with other unrelated families, women are most likely to be found living in households headed by kin.[32]

Thus, in an attempt to understand the nature of co-residence in migrant families we will first seek to identify the characteristics of these co-resident kin members. Table 6.5 describes the relationship of co-resident kin to the head of the household for non-migrant and migrant households of both cohorts.[33] Included are only those kin members who were present during the first twenty years of the family cycle with the exception of a few married children who had already entered some households in this period. In order to increase absolute numbers the uncorrected sample was used for the second cohort.

[31] Peters, 'De migratie', pp. 159–60.
[32] Glasco, 'Migration', p. 177.
[33] The uncorrected sample was used for the 1880–1920 cohort.

The migrant households in the earlier cohort were clearly receiving only their nearest kin relations into their homes: parents and siblings. Siblings, who were all young and unmarried, constituted the most important group of kin living with migrant families of the earlier cohort. In the following cohort migrant households attracted a wider range of kin, while the predominance of brothers and sisters disappeared. However, compared with non-migrants in this cohort they accommodated a larger proportion of cousins and 'others', the latter being principally nephews and nieces. These two categories are residual catch-alls and include all young and single individuals. Still, the differences between the two cohorts are by no means overwhelming. The data suggest that while migrant households were to some extent offering opportunities to young kin to adjust to a new environment, they were also doing the same as non-migrant households, and providing care and relief for elderly people. The same set of services may thus have been provided by migrant and non-migrant households alike, only in different proportions. Non-migrant households may, to a lesser degree perhaps, also have aided relatives in processes of migration, offering them a place to recuperate when things were too rough.

Table 6.5, also, reveals some interesting information where the sex of co-resident kin is considered. In both cohorts a co-resident parent in a migrant household appeared most likely to be the mother of the head or his wife, while in the case of siblings a brother more often than a sister was found to be present in the household.[34] In addition, male relatives predominated among cousins in the later cohort of migrants. For the sake of accuracy, however, we should add that much the same applies to non-migrants. There does not appear to be any preference for mothers over fathers in non-migrant households, but as far as cousins or siblings are concerned, the same preponderance of male relatives comes out.

How do we explain these patterns? Why should co-resident fathers be so evidently absent from migrant households, while in many other kin categories men are clearly overrepresented? Taking the latter point first, we have to bear in mind that most young migrating women were taking on positions in town as domestic servants. Given the fact that domestic servants were expected to reside in their master's household, young migrating women were less likely to need to appeal to relatives for board and lodgings. This may explain their

---

[34] Similarly, when Irish immigrant families in London became extended this was most likely to happen through the addition to the household of the widowed mother of the household head. See Lees, 'Patterns', p. 380.

relative underrepresentation not only in the households of migrant couples, but also in those of non-migrants.

On the issue of the pattern for co-resident parents we may advance the hypothesis that widowed women, in contrast to men, in general experienced more difficulty in maintaining independence in old age after the departure of the last of their children. The economic basis of such a household structure would have become very weak indeed.[35] Elderly women would consequently more frequently be faced by the need to move into other people's households, or to migrate to move in with their married children in the absence of local options. Richard Wall indicated a more or less similar situation to have been the case in nineteenth-century England: co-residential kinship ties for elderly women more often crossed generations while for elderly men ties within generations were the critical ones. Elderly women more often co-resided with unmarried or ever-married children whereas elderly men were more likely to be living with a spouse.[36] Widowhood is one of these critical life situations considered by Anderson to have had more severe effects on women than on men, making for strong bonds especially between female kin.[37]

An additional factor reinforcing this trend is the tendency for women to outlive their husbands, that is once they had survived the dangers of childbirth, thereby increasing the numbers of widowed grandmothers in need of co-residential support.[38] Another important factor in this connection may be that elderly widowed women were less likely than were men to opt for remarriage in order to ensure residential independence and stability in comparison to men. In both cohorts about a quarter of the male heads of household remarried after they had become widowers, while few women remarried after their husband's death.

Indeed, it may be considered surprising that these influences did not result in even larger proportions of co-resident grandmothers

---

[35] This may also be largely responsible for George Alter's finding that in nineteenth-century Verviers, Belgium, co-residence with a widowed mother made a daughter's marriage less likely when compared with co-residence with a widowed father. See Alter, *Family life*, p. 138. Female headed households were much more vulnerable in the past just as they are today. Even in a place culturally and geographically as far removed as China, female-headed households experienced greater instability than male-headed households. See Wolf, 'Family life', p. 289.

[36] Wall, *Relationships*, p. 10.

[37] Anderson, *Family structure*, p. 169.

[38] Figures on age-specific survival rates of the couples in the two cohorts do, however, not at all support this idea strongly. For all heads and wives who had reached the age of 50, 69.3% and 64.0% survived until the age of 65 in the first cohort. For the second cohort these percentages were 71.6 and 73.1 respectively.

relative to the proportion of co-resident grandfathers. Perhaps one factor may have curbed the effects of the influences creating a larger reservoir of potential grandmothers for families to co-reside with. In his work on Verviers, George Alter demonstrated that daughters were more likely to postpone marriage and continue co-residence with a widowed mother than with a widowed father.[39] Alter explicitly relates this result to the tendency for widowers to remarry and thereby to release daughters of their obligations to him. but it is also clear that the greater earning power of fathers over mothers will have made it easier for daughters to marry and leave their widowed father behind. Ultimately, the widower may have felt it necessary to move into the household of a married child to seek domestic support. Nevertheless, whatever the precise influences may have been it did result, for the Netherlands as a whole throughout the nineteenth and twentieth centuries, in a much larger proportion of widowed women at age 50 and over compared with men of the same age.[40]

Of course, all of the above considerations would also apply to the families of non-migrants. The latter would then also have to display a similar preponderance of mothers over fathers. There is, however, one important difference in the relative position of the 'native' and the 'migrant' father. The 'native' father would not have to migrate in order to live with his married children. For the 'migrant' father the balance of pros and cons in this decision would be quite different and he may have found problems not pressing enough to justify the upheavals involved in migration. Admittedly, we cannot at present substantiate this argument. However, it seems likely that the above results demonstrate that in old age men were not forced or perhaps prepared to accept the anxieties of migration in order to procure some additional domestic support. Finally, the higher age-specific life expectancy of women and their residential vulnerability in old age may also explain the less prominent, but still clear, overrepresentation of women among co-resident parents in non-migrant households of the later cohort as well as the preponderance of aunts over uncles found in all households.

Other evidence suggesting that kin co-residence in migrant households served in some cases to facilitate migration is provided by the length of time kin members remained in the households of their relatives. All categories of kin in the migrant households of both cohorts co-resided for shorter time periods than did comparable kin

[39] Alter, *Family life*, p. 159.
[40] Hofstee, *Korte demografische geschiedenis*, pp. 126–7; Hofstee, 'Demografische', pp. 66–7.

in non-migrant households.[41] The differences between migrants and non-migrants were especially distinct where it concerned co-resident sisters of the head or his wife in the second cohort. While in non-migrant households sisters resided on average for 7.1 years in the households of their brothers, this duration was only 2.5 years for sisters in migrant households. These figures would suggest that female siblings in migrant households were merely passing by in the process of looking for a job in Tilburg or some other town. Their male counterparts likewise stayed for only a short time, although here the difference with those in non-migrant households were minor. Finally, we should note the fact that in non-migrant households of both cohorts male kin members, i.e. fathers and brothers, co-resided for shorter time periods than female kin within the same kin category. This implies that non-migrant households were also used as transitional stages or interludes in the process of migration by male kin members, particularly brothers, while female kin in these households often appear to have been in want of a home to stay.[42]

Additional evidence on the migratory aspects of co-residence in migrant households is provided by the fact that nearly all (more than 90%) of co-resident kin moved into the household from locations outside Tilburg. Kin members in non-migrant households more often (25% to 40%) entered by way of migration from within the town itself. Between 40% and 60% of young co-resident relatives living in households of migrant origin would eventually migrate again to other places, while a minority, varying from 10% to 30%, moved to other households in Tilburg. In native households similar co-resident relatives more frequently moved over to other households in town, or married and moved to their own homes, rather than emigrate. Out-migration of the extended kin member did not occur at all in the first cohort, and in only 10% of all cases in the second cohort. Elderly kin, however, as a rule remained in the household until they died, in both native and migrant households. Finally, nearly all of the co-resident kin in migrant households in-migrated individually, sometimes in chains of kin entering one after the other. As many as 40% of migrant extended households in the second cohort had more than one kin member present at some time. Judging by the timing and the type of co-residential configuration involved, it does not seem plausible to assume that extended households among some of these migrants came about as a result of the reconstruction of the rural extended family that had existed prior to migration to Tilburg.

---

[41] With the exception of the categories of married children and grandchildren.
[42] For further details on length of co-residence see appendix 6.4.

Some of the research describing the continuation of intensive family networks of migrants to an urban industrial context principally deals with rural migrants. In these cases the area or place of origin is known to have been characterized by strong normative family ties and household formations extending beyond the nuclear family unit. Two typical examples of this type of study are Hareven's research of kinship patterns among French-Canadians in Manchester, United States, and the study carried out by Virginia Yans-McLaughlin of the Italian immigrant families in Buffalo, also in the United States.[43] Both studies demonstrate how immigrant families adapted their pre-migration or 'traditional' family patterns to meet new industrial conditions. In the course of this process specific family practices might be eroded, but they were succeeded by new ones making for the continuation of cohesive family networks while in some ways even reinforcing family ties.[44]

Studies such as these create certain expectations concerning household structure among migrant families in Tilburg. In particular, in the second cohort most migrant households had moved in from rural areas in the province of Noord-Brabant, which, rightly or not, is frequently associated with a traditional familistic culture.[45] Indeed, we do have some modest evidence indicating that extended family households were very frequent for farmers and domestic workers in the Brabantine countryside.[46] In some villages in the eastern part of the province 16% to 19% of the households had co-resident kin present in the second half of the nineteenth century.[47] Clearly, within the province of Noord-Brabant variation existed in the occurrence of kin co-residence, due to differences in the socio-economic structure of the area.[48] The higher the proportion of farmers in the total population, the higher the proportion of extended households. Nevertheless, it does give us some reason to assume that kinship ties in the Brabantine countryside in general were strong and dominated many aspects of everyday life. Therefore the migrant families in Tilburg offer an excellent opportunity to assess the extent to which rural migrants adapted their family patterns to fit the industrial context as expected by Parsonian theory. The Tilburg situation may have been

[43] Hareven, *Family time*; Yans-McLaughlin, *Family*.
[44] Hareven, *Family time*, p. 117.
[45] Even in more modern times, the 1960s, sociologists claimed remnants of the extended family system to be still alive in the east and the south, areas described as 'under-developed'. See Ishwaran, *Family life*, p. 40.
[46] van der Heijden, 'Gezin'.
[47] Meurkens, *Bevolking*, p. 164.
[48] Klep, 'Het huishouden', p. 84.

similar to that found by Hareven in Manchester, where kin co-residence was above all a feature of the family life of rural migrants who kept in touch with the family network in their place of origin. With this in mind we turn to an examination of household structure in relation to geographical origin of migrant households.

Table 6.6 presents data on the proportions of migrant nuclear and extended households during the first twenty years of the family cycle by geographical origin of the couple.[49] The outcome is somewhat surprising. Unfortunately, the data on the first cohort are too scanty to draw any conclusions and are principally presented by way of illustration. For the second cohort, however, somewhat larger absolute numbers are available. The first notable feature of table 6.6 is that it is not only families with roots in the province of Noord-Brabant that co-resided with kin in the first half of the family cycle. There even seems to be a slightly larger preference for extended family living on the part of families coming from other provinces of The Netherlands. However, the differences are more marked when the rural-urban distinction is considered, yielding the surprising result that couples coming from an urban background were more likely to receive extended kin into their homes than were rural migrants. Although here numbers become very small again, the impression is left that families and individuals moving between towns, in particular within Brabant, made most use of kin links. The link between urban origin and extended households is also suggested in the case of households classified as coming from outside of the province of Noord-Brabant. However, although the urban background in general appears to pro-mote family ties and contacts, we should also stress that rural migrants, from Brabant or elsewhere, did not seem to relinquish their family ties to any considerable degree. Compared with the native population of Tilburg, who may be expected to have many more kin locally available, a considerable proportion of these rural migrants had kin present in the household at some point.

Although based on small numbers, the first cohort does not provide any confirmation of the urban-extended connection. It would

[49] This table has been constructed in the following way: in the case of couples, where one of the two partners was born outside of Noord-Brabant they were both assigned to the category 'other areas'. If either of them was born in an urban community they were classified as 'urban'. This implies that when either husband or wife was born in a town outside Noord-Brabant the couple was classified as 'other urban areas'. The criterion used to distinguish between rural and urban migrants for the two cohorts was derived from the 1849 and 1879 census respectively, ranking communities of 10,000 inhabitants or more as urban. See *Uitkomsten der derde* and *Uitkomsten der zesde*. For this table the uncorrected sample was used for the 1880–1920 cohort.

Table 6.6 *First-phase household structure for migrant households by geographical origin of couple for two age-cohorts of married couples*[a]

	Nuclear families %	Extended families %	N
Cohort 1849–1890			
Noord-Brabant	65.5	34.5	29
other areas	81.8	18.2	22
villages	70.3	29.7	37
towns	78.6	21.4	14
rural Noord-Brabant	68.0	32.0	25
urban Noord-Brabant	50.0	50.0	4
rural other areas	75.0	25.0	12
urban other areas	90.0	10.0	10
all	72.6	27.5	51
Cohort 1880–1920			
Noord-Brabant	62.2	37.8	119
other areas	58.0	42.0	50
villages	66.1	33.9	121
towns	47.9	52.1	48
rural Noord-Brabant	66.4	33.6	104
urban Noord-Brabant	33.3	66.7	15
rural other areas	64.7	35.3	17
urban other areas	54.6	45.5	33
all	61.0	39.1	169

[a] Uncorrected sample was used for 1880–1920 cohort. The total percentage of extensions in this group is therefore somewhat higher than the figure mentioned in table 6.4.

seem as if in this cohort people from outside the province of Noord-Brabant were less frequently in contact with relatives elsewhere than were other migrants. Perhaps this reflects the rather isolated position of the entire province at the time. This was true in terms of transportation networks as well as in other respects, diminishing the attractiveness for mobile kin of migrant families already established in Tilburg.[50] However, it remains difficult to advance anything other

[50] See van de Weijer, *De religieuse practijk*, pp. 122—9.

than mere speculation where the 1849 cohort is concerned given the small numbers involved.

We may conclude this section on migration and family structure by stating that geographical mobility and extended household formation were not mutually exclusive in nineteenth-century Tilburg. Families apparently kept in close contact with geographically dispersed kin members which produced extended family households among migrant couples as often as among non-migrants. Migrant families already established in the town appear to have provided not only stepping stones in migration processes for young relations, they also opened their homes to elderly kin in search of relief and care. In this they showed a marked preference for their female relatives. Somewhat surprisingly, it appeared that in the second cohort more intensive networks of exchange of household members existed between towns than between town and countryside. In this respect results went against expectations as based on recent historical research in this field. This is, however, not to say that rural migrants were out of touch with their kin 'back home'. Although we do not know much about kin patterns in the rural communities of origin, the data do imply a strong sense of continuity in exchanges between extended kin even after migration.

This continuity, it must be stressed, was not necessarily based on a continuity in the mechanisms that produce extended family households or the reciprocal functions that kin may have had. A reasonable assumption is that in the countryside, compared with urban areas, economic considerations will more often have prevailed over others in the decisions to co-reside with kin. The peasant family may have attracted kin members at times because it needed the additional labour to work the farm. The ageing farmer and his wife may have decided to co-reside with one of their married sons and the latter's family as part of the process of handing over the family farm to the next cohort and because they could no longer work the farm on their own. Kin co-residence in the households of Tilburg migrants clearly was not exclusively related to the labour needs of the household as a work group. Rather it served to facilitate migration of young adults and to offer domestic support to widowed parents. As Hareven put it when describing the family life of rural migrants in Manchester: 'Life in the industrial town added new functions to an already long repertory of kin interaction.'[51] For nineteenth-century migrant families in Tilburg assistance in the labour mobility of young adults

[51] Hareven, *Family time*, p. 118.

was probably one of these new kin functions that were added to other, more traditional, social functions such as domestic assistance for the old and the sick. Discontinuity was thus as much part and parcel of nineteenth-century family life as was continuity.

6.4   *Migration, family structure and social success*

Earlier in this chapter it was pointed out that migrant families generally occupied strong social and economic positions in town. Migrant families in both cohorts of households were found first and foremost among the solid middle-class section of society, and to a lesser extent among the elite. In the remaining part of this chapter I will examine the interrelationships between migration, household structure, economic position and social success.[52] The main question that needs answering is to what extent were the migrant families who received extended kin members into their homes socially successful in the town to which they had migrated. Did the retention of kinship practices considered to be 'traditional' by modernization theorists inhibit their successful integration into the social structure of Tilburg? Was the nineteenth-century extended household for migrants an expression of their economic and social marginality?

For these purposes we again look at the structure of the household during the first phase of the family cycle in relation to the social mobility of the family head. Total mobility scores by migration status and household structure, as presented in table 6.7, indicate that migrant families, while initially occupying a relatively high position in the social hierarchy nevertheless managed to improve their position further substantially over time. Migrant families had consistently higher upward mobility scores compared with the native population of Tilburg. However, while household structure made less difference to the social success of non-migrants, it had clear repercussions for migrant families. Extended family households among migrants had the highest total upward mobility scores of all, while in addition they tended to have a higher upward mobility into class III. Socially successful migrants clearly received extended kin into their homes more often than did those who were socially stable or downwardly mobile.

Clearly, these conclusions can only be regarded as firmly based for the second cohort. Given their small numbers, the data of the first cohort of migrants are too uncertain when taken separately. When viewed in light of the results for the later cohort, however, they serve

[52] All following statistics make use of the uncorrected sample for the 1880–1920 cohort.

Table 6.7 *Social mobility of heads of household by first-phase household structure and migration status for two age-cohorts of married couples*

	Non-migrant		Migrant	
	Nuclear	Extended	Nuclear	Extended
Cohort 1849–1890				
total upward mobility	18.0	17.7	26.3	33.4
unchanged	65.5	72.1	47.4	55.6
total downward mobility	16.5	10.3	26.3	11.1
from class IV–V to I–III	5.0	2.0	6.3	50.0
N	194	68	19	9
Cohort 1880–1920				
total upward mobility	27.8	27.4	34.0	40.4
unchanged	63.5	61.9	56.4	47.4
total downward mobility	8.7	10.7	9.6	12.3
from class IV–V to I–III	10.9	9.5	10.8	13.9
N	126	84	94	57

as a tentative support of the relationship between migration, extended households and social success.

Class-specific mobility scores, for which figures are presented in appendix 37, indicate that the higher upward mobility of the migrant extended families principally came about through the higher upward mobility of the unskilled workers and the middle classes; the remaining social groups having comparable mobility scores between the two family types. For non-migrants of the later cohort upward mobility did not differ greatly nor consistently between the various social groups, thereby affirming the idea that family structure and relative social success were not related in the case of the native population. Class-specific results for non-migrants in the first cohort, however, convey a much greater diversity of experience between the two household structures, but unfortunately no regular pattern emerges from this. Nuclear families among unskilled workers as well as among the lower-upper class in this group achieved much greater upward mobility than did extended families. This effect was offset by the higher mobility score for extended families in the middle classes, producing a total upward mobility score comparable to that for nuclear families. It is again difficult to make any definite statement

Table 6.8. *Final position of heads of household by first-phase household structure and migration status for two age-cohorts of married couples*

	Non-migrant		Migrant	
	Nuclear	Extended	Nuclear	Extended
Cohort 1849–1890				
upper classes	8.2	17.6	10.5	22.2
middle class	7.7	10.3	10.5	66.7
skilled labour	54.1	41.2	42.1	11.1
unskilled labour	29.9	30.9	36.8	0.0
N	194	68	19	9
Cohort 1880–1920				
upper classes	4.0	13.1	12.8	19.3
middle class	15.1	16.7	14.9	24.6
skilled labour	57.1	47.6	47.9	38.6
unskilled labour	23.8	22.6	24.5	17.5
N	126	84	94	57

concerning the migrant families of the first cohort due to very small numbers.

The greater upward social mobility of migrant extended families effectively secured them a place in the upper strata of Tilburg society. As table 6.8 demonstrates, at the age of 50 migrant family heads of first-phase extended households were largely found among the middle classes and the elite. Only relatively few households in the second cohort had not succeeded in escaping from blue-collar jobs in general and unskilled labour in particular. Social success was not, of course, restricted to those with extended kin present in the household. Table 6.8 illustrates again the economic strength of most migrant households of the later cohort.

When discussing the data presented in table 6.7 we stated that social success and type of family were not related among the native population. In both cohorts non-migrant and migrant households, whether nuclear or extended, obtained comparable total upward mobility scores. However, in a less dynamic fashion the same relationship between social success and extended family households exists for non-migrants as well. Native-born heads of extended households embarked upon their social career from a more advantageous position. In both cohorts only about three-quarters of the native extended households began their careers as part of class IV or V, while this was the case for almost nine out of every ten of native nuclear families in the two cohorts. (Figures on this topic are shown in appendix 38.) With a similar mobility rate native extended households consequently ended up far higher on the social scale than did nuclear households, which may be seen from table 6.8. In both cohorts a larger number of the native extended families succeeded in climbing into the upper strata by the time the heads turned 50. Apparently, mobile middle-class families rising up into the elite did not discard the strong tendency towards extended family living which was so characteristic of their original social group. Social mobility would thus seem to be more important in changing the shape and form of family life between generations than within generations.

It is time to turn once again to the migrant families in our two samples and attempt to answer the following questions. How do we explain the apparent relationship between migration, extended household structure and social success? Why should successful migrants co-reside with extended kin, or vice versa, why should those migrants who co-reside with their kin be more successful than those who do not? What hypotheses or theoretical constructions are available that could help us understand the nature of this relationship? Obviously, structural-functionalism is extremely uninformative in this respect: co-residential domestic family groups, probably in particular among migrants, are only expected to inhibit differential social mobility. In opposition to this view a great deal of the literature already cited earlier in this chapter suggests that kin are of value during processes of migration in obtaining jobs and housing facilities. This was established, just to mention briefly two examples, for nineteenth-century Preston and for early twentieth-century Manchester, USA. Newcomers to town were effectively helped out by kin members who had preceded them. Recent migrants to Preston, for instance, who upon arrival stayed wth kin acquired steady jobs more quickly than did those migrants who had no kin to come to.[53] Our case, however, is entirely different. These successful migrant families in Tilburg were certainly not new arrivals. They had arrived some time before 1849 and 1880 respectively and continued to reside for many years after that. The relatives who followed them would sometimes stay only short periods of time. They were hardly in a

[53] Anderson, *Family structure*, pp. 157–8.

position to help the head of the receiving household advance socially. Rather, the visiting kin member was the one in need of help and benefiting from it when given.

Richard Sennett explained the high social mobility of extended families in Chicago by arguing that extended families displayed a more 'open' character and were consequently more oriented towards the competitive values of modern industrial society.[54] Apart from the fact that it would be impossible to substantiate such a relationship for the Tilburg households in this study, it would also be ineffective. After all, Sennett's psychological explanation is unable to explain the diverging mobility patterns between different types of families of migrants and non-migrants. In Chicago the extended family offered the best opportunities for success for all ethnic groups alike.

Perhaps other intervening variables were at work producing these results. One of them may perhaps be labelled the 'urban experience'. Charles Tilly and C.H. Brown suggested that kin links were more valuable for those migrants occupying a weak social position accompanied by an insufficient knowledge and skill for dealing with the urban context.[55] The data presented in the previous section indicated that extended family households were more frequent among urban migrants than among rural migrants. Following Tilly's reasoning, these families with an urban background may have been those responsible for the high mobility patterns in this group. Undoubtedly, migrants with a larger 'urban experience' may have had a considerable headstart compared with their rural counterparts. However, the data do not substantiate such a relationship. Although urban migrants in the second cohort were in general a little higher up in the social hierarchy, they were not more upwardly mobile than were those from rural origins.[56]

Elaborating a little further on the same theme we might assume that the 'combined urban experience' in extended migrant families was increased by the contribution of geographically mobile kin members. Table 6.6 suggested a relatively intensive exchange of related individuals between urban households. In this way migrant households were possibly accumulating the urban skills and knowledge of several individuals which may greatly have enhanced the chances of success for the individual members belonging to those households. Unfortunately, providing the evidence for such a hypothesis would

[54] Sennett, *Families*.
[55] Tilly and Brown, 'On uprooting', p. 115.
[56] For the first cohort numbers were too scarce to make such a comparison meaningful even at the illustrative level.

clearly fall outside the scope of the present research. To begin with, one would need more precise information on the life-course experience of the kin members in migrant households prior to their arrival in the household concerned. In addition, our reliance on places of birth to determine the urban origin of the members of the household is far too shaky a foundation for such an undertaking.

At this stage I prefer to advance a more probable and obvious hypothesis concerning the relationship between migration, family structure and social success. This hypothesis is based on the assumption that the migrant families captured by this study were endowed with a relatively large share of the qualities of enterprise and initiative. The very fact that they had migrated to Tilburg at some point in time, in all probability in order to improve themselves socially and economically, may be seen as supporting this assumption. Considering their persistence in the town and the subsequent rise of many of the migrant families on the social ladder we may safely assume that they had achieved some of the goals that had prompted their migration. The relative social and economic success of these families may be responsible for the presence in the household of extended kin (co-resident brothers and sisters) who were likewise migrating to Tilburg to 'try their luck', or those who were in want of care and assistance (co-resident mothers). For both categories of kin it seems likely that they would sooner turn towards those relations best able to provide support. In addition, this line of argument would conveniently explain why urban migrants more often received kin into their household than did rural migrants. The higher social position of urban migrants may have increased the attractiveness of their household to kin contemplating co-residence with them. However, this argument can only partially explain why migrants coming in from urban areas were more likely to extend their households to include extra-kin members. When the relationship was examined by social group the urban factor lost most of its strength in the case of working-class families. For middle and upper-class families, on the other hand, the fact that the family had originally come from another urban area continued to exert a most powerful influence on family structure.[57]

Following Goode's line of reasoning concerning the relationship between family and social class I assume that extended kin relations over physical distances were maintained principally when relatives had something to offer to each other.[58] This point of view also paral-

[57] Figures on this issue are shown in appendix 41.
[58] Goode, *World revolution*, pp. 12–13.

lels Anderson's perspective on the relative instrumentality of kin relations.[59] One objection to the argument advanced above could be that if kin relations were instrumental for migrant families why was this not also true for the mobile native families when compared with the less successful native families? Clearly, it would be foolish to claim that such an instrumentality was absent from non-migrant households. However, this aspect was simply more crucial to the decision to co-reside with kin when it involved at the same time the drastic step of migration and a radical change of social environment. We might say that the element of rational calculation in the attitude of the co-resident kin member in migrant households was in general stronger than in other cases. Obviously, this does not explain what was in the bargain for the receiving household. As Anderson pointed out, assistance between kin was often given without needing an immediate compensation in return.[60] To some extent people kept 'in mind' the obligation specific kin members owed them until the appropriate moment or more distressing times came along, making it difficult for us to discover such patterns in the households under study here.

This interpretation of the data on Tilburg in fact completely reverses the causal relationship posed by Sennett between upward social mobility and extended families. From Sennett's point of view social skill and social mobility were the result of the 'open', competitive climate in extended families. Here it is suggested that families became extended because of the promise of success or material well-being offered to their migrating relatives. These successful migrant families may serve as a good example of the pull which family relations may exercise on migration.[61] Finally, in partial support of Sennett's hypothesis and contrary to the structural-functionalist point of view, we should note that the decision to take kin into the household did not apparently hinder the heads of these families in their realization of further upward mobility.

The functionality of the nuclear family in industrial society in Parsonian theory extends itself to the social careers of the children stemming from these families. To conclude this section on the interrelationships between family structure, migration and social success I will, therefore, briefly deal with the social mobility scores achieved by the sons in the two cohorts. First, I will examine the extent to which

[59] Anderson, *Family structure*, pp. 170–9.
[60] Ibid., p. 158.
[61] Kooij could find no evidence of this in his research on migration patterns in Groningen in the nineteenth century, see Kooij, *Groningen*, p. 177.

migrant sons continued their father's success, and secondly, I will discuss the question of whether the close contact of the family with its extended kin constituted an impediment to the sons' successful integration into society.

In both cohorts migrant family heads had profitable social careers compared with their native-born counterparts. Naturally, we would expect their sons to derive at least some advantage from their fathers' success when embarking upon their own career. This indeed proved to be the case for migrant sons from the later cohort.[62] Apparently, fathers were not always able to transmit further mobility to their children. In the later cohort the higher mobility scores for migrants were mainly the result of the considerable success of sons from working-class families. Compared with the native born, many more sons from migrant working-class fathers managed to reach respectable middle-class or sometimes even upper-class positions. Why should results for the two cohorts diverge? Probably small numbers are confusing the issue for the first cohort. However, it seems plausible to assume that migrant sons in the later cohort were in some ways in a better position than sons from native-born families to make the most of new opportunities offered by the developing economy of the town. Towards the end of the nineteenth century and the beginning of the twentieth the process of industrialization created more medium and high skilled jobs in industry than it had done before. In addition, the intensification of the process of industrialization after the 1880s generated greater purchasing power, enabling shopkeepers, traders, builders and other servicing industries to benefit greatly. Sons of migrant fathers were in a better position to profit from these developments thanks to their fathers' strong initial positions in the social hierarchy and subsequent high rates of mobility. The jobs registered by migrant heads and their sons in the later cohort do indeed demonstrate the growing opportunities for migrant middle-class families. Quite a few heads managed to establish their own firms in carpentry or metal works, having first worked as labourers for some years. Others rose from unskilled day-labourer to blacksmith or fitter. Some of their sons entered the higher skilled trades, above all in the metallurgical sector, or even white-collar jobs in teaching or clerical work, while others took over the family enterprise and embarked on major expansion. These migrant heads and their sons were clearly seizing the new opportunities for upward mobility that were offered by a developing and diversifying economy in this period. By contrast,

---

[62] For figures on this topic appendix 39 may be consulted.

Table 6.9 *Total upward intergenerational mobility by age group,*
first-phase household structure and migration status for two age-cohorts of
married couples[a]

Age group Sons	Non-migrant		Migrant	
	Nuclear	Extended	Nuclear	Extended
Cohort 1849–1890				
< 30	13.7 (561)	21.5 (172)	8.2 (49)	8.3 (24)
30–35	18.3 (498)	21.0 (143)	17.1 (41)	10.0 (20)
40 >	28.2 (418)	25.0 (116)	21.4 (28)	23.1 (13)
Cohort 1880–1920				
< 30	22.7 (409)	24.8 (172)	34.1 (229)	27.4 (135)
30–35	33.2 (401)	30.9 (249)	45.7 (221)	34.4 (128)
40 >	43.2 (343)	44.4 (223)	57.0 (158)	42.9 (84)

[a] Absolute numbers of observation given in parentheses.

sons from native families seemed much more inclined to stick to
careers in the textile sector where career prospects and financial
remuneration were far less favourable.

Finally, table 6.9 introduces the element of family structure into the
discussion. The table may at first sight present a somewhat confusing
picture, but I would argue that the data indicate that, on the whole,
family structure was not decisive in determining a young man's social
advancement. In both cohorts mobility scores for non-migrants differed little between the two family types; in some categories extended
families registered higher percentages of upward mobility while in
others nuclear families did so. Numbers of migrant families in the
earlier cohort become perilously small again, making it impossible to
say anything other than that differences between family structures in
this cohort were slight.

In the later cohort, surprisingly enough, migrant sons from nuclear
families were extremely successful, especially in the higher age
groups. This may be viewed as a sign of the greater adaptability of the
nuclear family to industrial society. But, if this is so, why is the effect
totally absent for non-migrants? Let us suppose for a moment that a
heavy involvement in kin networks, producing a higher incidence of
extended families, only influenced the social mobility of migrants.
The results we see would then be the effect of the much stronger
orientation of migrant extended families to their extended kin net-

work which impeded their ability to integrate into the new society they had moved to. This relationship in fact was implied by Harris when referring to the problem of the integration of migrants crowding together in extended families.[63] Tilly and Brown tested a similar hypothesis on twentieth-century material but were unable to establish definite links.[64] However, if this assumption carries any truth, it would surely follow that sons from migrant extended families should have much lower mobility scores than all other groups, while sons from migrant nuclear families enjoyed comparable success to native-born sons regardless of their family type? As we can see from table 6.9 migrant extended family sons did not do badly at all when compared with native-born sons, thereby leaving the explanation for the much higher upward mobility achieved by migrant sons from nuclear families unresolved. To complicate the issue further, it should also be noted that the higher upward mobility of migrant nuclear family sons mainly applied to the upper classes. Working and middle-class sons on the whole produced better mobility results when they came from extended families. Moreover, the social stratification of migrant sons in the age groups 30–35, and 40 and over, indicates that sons from extended families were overrepresented in the middle and upper classes compared with those from nuclear families. Perhaps in relation to their fathers they had not been so successful, but when their careers are considered on their own, they certainly cannot be looked upon as social failures.[65]

However, this line of reasoning still does not explain the higher mobility of sons from migrant nuclear families. The observations advanced above only have the effect of adding some nuances to the greater relative success of migrant nuclear family sons. We might, however, consider the following speculation as a possible explanation for the successful careers of these sons. I have already argued that most migrant family heads were ambitious and successful. The main road towards success for these migrant heads consisted in the setting up and expanding of medium-scale enterprises within the service sector of the economy. The extended family heads in the lower-upper classes may only have been able to do so at the expense of the future fortunes of some or most of their sons. Perhaps the extended family heads not only neglected to invest in their sons' education and training, but they may also have been unwilling to make family capital

[63] See note 12 (above).
[64] Tilly and Brown, 'On uprooting', pp. 128–9.
[65] Appendix 40 presents detailed figures on class specific social mobility as well as the social stratification of migrant sons in the 1880–1920 cohort.

available for sons other than the heir and successor in the family enterprise. All resources would then benefit only the one son who was to succeed the father. These considerations are speculative but they rightly reflect the importance of family support in the achievement of further social mobility for elite sons. They also indicate one way in which in elite circles individual interests could be made subordinate to those of the family group. However, the somewhat lower rate of mobility of lower-upper-class sons did not prevent the migrant extended family sons moving further up the social ladder eventually. Even in the second cohort, migrant extended families retained their prominent position within society.

In summing up this section, I would like to stress again that, given the absence of any consistency in the data, it seems incorrect to see any particular value in the idea of the functionality of the nuclear family in terms of intra- and intergenerational mobility. Extended families quite frequently were successful and sometimes even notably so. Extended family heads and their sons often came to occupy leading positions in the local social hierarchy. For working and middle-class families the retention of extended family ties also did not in any way inhibit the social success of fathers and sons. Quite the contrary, social success and extended family living appeared to be strongly related in the case of migrant families whose strong economic position probably attracted extended kin members.

6.5 Conclusion

Nineteenth-century migration did not necessarily lead to the breakdown of extended family relations as suggested by the proponents of structural-functionalism. Both cohorts of migrants were found to have received extended kin members into their homes slightly more often than native-born families. This fact is all the more surprising in the case of the first cohort of migrants which contained a large proportion of adult migrants. In trying to establish links between migration and family structure the longitudinal approach followed in this study proved indispensable to capture the full dynamics of the extended families of migrants in the second cohort. These results pinpointed a serious shortcoming in the existing literature on the historical relationships between family and migration. Migrant families co-resided with their nearest relatives at various times throughout the first half of the family cycle: co-residence in this group was therefore less life-cycle specific than for native families. Migrant families were usually extended for only short stretches of time with some relatives moving in and out quickly, mostly in the course of their search for jobs.

To some extent the distinction between migrants and non-migrants proved illusive. In both groups extended households occurring during the first twenty years of the family cycle functioned as places for the relief and care of elderly people, while at the same time offering young people engaged in the risky business of migration a stepping stone into Tilburg society or a home to fall back on. The latter aspect, however, proved to be somewhat more important to household heads and their wives who at one time had been migrants themselves. They co-resided more often with 'relatives-on-the-move': mainly young and unattached siblings, nephews and nieces or cousins. Quite remarkably, the elderly people taken care of by migrant households turned out to be nearly all widowed mothers or aunts of the couple heading the household. It was argued that this resulted from the greater residential instability and more precarious economic basis of households headed by single elderly women, possibly reinforced by the higher life-expectancy of women and a lesser propensity for women than men to remarry. More elderly women will therefore have been at risk of moving in with relatives or of migrating in order to do so. Extended household structures were thus more important for women than for men in the final phase of the life course.

Recent historical writing on family and migration has connected the persistence of extended family networks in an urban context to the rural origins of the migrant population concerned. At the outset of this study we therefore expected extended households to occur first of all among those who had originally come from the rural areas of Brabant. These rural migrants provided an opportunity to study the survival of their extended kin network after their arrival in the urban context. The data indicated that rural migrants did not appear to be losing touch with their extended kin members. Parents and siblings might often follow them to Tilburg or at least pass through on their way to other destinations. By facilitating labour mobility these rural migrant families had come to be engaged in a new type of kin function, additional to the pre-existing ones, such as taking care of widowed parents. However, contrary to expectation, migrants coming from an urban background were far more likely to receive kin into their homes than were rural migrants. It appeared that the more intensive networks of communication and interchange between towns were also facilitating a more frequent exchange of extended kin members between households.

An additional explanation for the urban connection was offered after examination of the relationship between family structure, migration and social success. A relationship between social success and extended family structure was established in the case of the migrant families in the two cohorts. Migrant families who had co-resided with their extended kin at some time during the first twenty years of their family cycle, were far more successful socially, not only in comparison with other migrant households but also when contrasted with all other native-born families irrespective of their household structure. This result was particularly associated with the working and middle-class families within this group of migrant households, which further supports the assumption of the enormous importance of kin relations to the non-elite in processes of migration. After a discussion of possible explanations for the relationship it was suggested that these migrant families had become extended precisely because of their good fortune. Their relative prosperity, or perhaps even only a promise for the future, attracted kin who were looking either for a home or a place from which to venture out into Tilburg society. I believe these kin members acted in a very straightforward but rational way. In weighing the pros and cons of migrating, and subsequently in choosing a particular destination, they also took into account the relative social position of the potential host household. Moreover, the success of their kinsmen may have prompted some individuals to move, who would otherwise not have done so. Thus, we have at least a partial explanation of why families from an urban background were more likely to become extended more often than those from rural parts of the country. Urban migrants more often belonged to the middle and upper social classes, which increased the attractiveness of their household to kin. Nevertheless, the urban factor still proved to have an independent influence of its own mainly for those at the top of the social scales.

In this reasoning I assume that a fair amount of 'rational' economic calculation influenced the way extended households were formed when geographical distances had to be bridged. This is in line with the position taken by Michael Anderson and William Goode. To a certain extent kinship relations were entered into and maintained when relatives had something to offer to each other. While economic considerations may have played a minor or lesser role in the decision to co-reside with kin who either lived in the same or their native town, these aspects will certainly have been given more elaborate thought when it involved a move to an entirely new social context. For migrating individuals in the lower and middle social classes of society the social and economic resources of their kinsmen are likely to have had relatively far-reaching consequences.

Finally, the smooth careers of the heads of the migrant extended families in our study testify to the lack of any structural fit between the nuclear family and industrial society. As Tilburg industrialized in the course of the period under investigation, contacts were kept and maintained by geographically dispersed kin, while such links may even have been highly functional to some in economic terms. Moreover, the interaction between the family and the occupational system, of great importance to most social classes in a context in which few other sources were available, expressly worked towards the creation of extended family structures in the case of migrants. In addition, it is important to stress that involvement in extended family structures did not in any way impede the further social mobility and the successful integration of these families into Tilburg society, neither for migrant families nor for the native born. Kin assistance is likely to have been crucial in many cases, and not only for working-class families. Finally, in this chapter I have also suggested one particular way in which the withholding of family support may have decisively affected the lives of those in the elite groups of society.

7

Family and work: the effect of the family economy on the structural characteristics of the household

The final issue to be considered in this study concerns an examination of the relationship between changes in family dynamics and the transformation of the household from a productive unit into the type of household exclusively directed towards consumption and wage-pooling. Structural-functionalist theory considered this segregation between the family and the economy to be crucial to the emergence of the nuclear family in industrial society. In addition, a large number of writers in the field of family history have attached great importance to what is generally referred to as the family's 'loss of productive functions'. The present chapter deals with the effect of this structural process of transformation of labour on the working-class family in nineteenth-century Tilburg.

7.1 Family and factory

In the previous chapters family characteristics were examined for a number of socio-economic groups in what we might call the 'industrializing context' of nineteenth-century Tilburg. However, not all of the households we have studied so far experienced in equal degrees the influence of this transformation of economic structures. Some of them were clearly positioned in more traditional artisanal sectors of society, escaping the influence of mechanization and centralization of production until well into the twentieth century. Late-nineteenth-century carpenters, butchers and bakers, bricklayers and shoemakers in Tilburg may have lived their working lives very much along the lines followed by preceding generations. They were the least involved in the process of differentiation of their social and economic context. For those employed in the textile industry, however, the spinners and weavers, the fullers, piecers and wool-shearers the nature and organization of work changed radically. The timing and tempo of these structural changes, however, differed greatly for some of these occupations. While the spinners were among the first to undertake the transition from home into factory, the weavers were clearly the last to do so.

In the present chapter I will explore the effect of the loss of the household's productive functions on the strength of family relations by comparing the family cycle of households headed by domestic weavers and those headed by factory workers. By concentrating explicitly on those workers who had already made the transition to the factory in comparison to those who were still employed within a household-based production process we hope to add more analytical sharpness to our study of the relationships between the family and industrialization and, more generally, to contribute to the study of the working-class family in this period. The main questions addressed in this chapter focus on the consequences of these structural shifts in the economic basis of the household for extended family relations and the ties between parents and children.

One of the central arguments in the evolutionary perspective of structural-functionalist family theory pertains to the loss of economic functions of the household and the resulting segregation of the family from the economic system.[1] In preindustrial society the family and economy largely overlapped in the form of the peasant household or the artisan's workshop, forging strong bonds between family members through common interests in the productive unit of the household, reinforced by the presence of family property. Totally disregarding the fact that wage labour was not exclusively related to industrial production, Parsons assumed that the family and the economy became separated under the influence of the rise of industrial society. More specifically, the industrialization process was thought to involve the separation of the family from the economy without which the nuclear family could not have emerged.[2] After economic activity was removed from the household, the nuclear family as a unit, isolated from extended kinship and neighbourhood ties, came into being.

Other writers on the history of the family have followed in different ways and degrees this functionalist scheme of increased specialization or differentiation of the family without necessarily adopting the larger functionalist world view. Historians such as Ariès and Stone make use of the concept of specialization to explain the development

---

[1] See also chapter 1, pp. 4–6.
[2] See e.g. Smelser, 'The modernization', p. 124.

of other, mostly emotional, aspects of the family.[3] John Demos proclaimed the loss of functions to be the central theme in the history of the family.[4] In his account of seventeenth and eighteenth-century family life in the Dutch Republic, Donald Haks writes that the concept of the specialization process of society may be usefully applied in family history. He argues that the loss of the family's economic-productive and social-educational functions produced a highly specialized type of family, reducing the need for extended households and family cooperation.[5] These writers, however, do not exclusively associate specialization with the process of industrialization.

The transition from the home to the factory, and the separation between work and family, has for a long time been a central theme of family historians.[6] Despite a recognition of the fact that wage labour, and with it the separation between home and work, had already made its appearance many centuries before, it is still felt that it was 'the progress of industrialization that relieved the family of its productive functions'.[7] Many consequences have been attributed to the separation of work and family taking place in the industrial era, 'including the decline of kinship as the basis of work organization, the loss of power for mothers and children, the revolt of youth against their parents, the emergence of adolescence as a separate life stage, and greater sexual freedom for young women'.[8] The decline of parental authority is perhaps most often mentioned by both contemporaries and social scientists alike.[9] The Marxist historian E.P. Thompson effectively dramatized the effects of the specialization of the family under the influence of the industrialization process, as is well illustrated by the following quotation:

Each stage in industrial differentiation and specialization struck also at the family economy, disturbing customary relations between man and wife, parents and children, and differentiating more sharply between 'work' and 'life' . . . Meanwhile, the family was roughly torn apart each morning by the factory bell.[10]

In their analysis of the historical development of women's work Louise Tilly and Joan Scott offer an interpretation in which a close

---

[3] Ariès, *L'Enfant*, p. 268; Stone, *The family*, p. 23.
[4] Demos, *A little commonwealth*, p. 183.
[5] Haks, *Huwelijk*, p. 3.
[6] Kloek, *Gezinshistorici*, pp. 32–50; Anderson, *Approaches*, pp. 75–84.
[7] Mitterauer and Sieder, *The European family*, p. 79.
[8] Pleck, 'Two worlds', p. 179.
[9] For example: Smelser, 'The modernization', p. 125; Mitterauer and Sieder, *The European family*, p. 87; de Regt, *Arbeidersgezinnen*, p. 130.
[10] Thompson, *The making*, p. 416.

relation is assumed between the organization of the family and the mode of production the family was engaged in.[11] The productive unit of the peasant or proto-industrial household created a 'family economy' in which family life and the productive needs of the household were inseparably intertwined. The domestic mode of production, to which all family members were expected to contribute, had important consequences for family organization. The labour requirements of the household defined the work roles of its members while in addition family members were expelled or attracted in accordance with the needs of production. Where families became dependent upon wage labour, consumption and production came to be separated: the household no longer functioned as a unit of production. In the 'family wage economy' the need for family members to work together disappeared and work roles became increasingly individualized. In contrast with the family economy system no maximum household size, as defined by the peasant holding or the artisan's shop, set any constraints on the number of family members the household could contain at any one moment as long as the number of wage earners and consumers was kept in balance. However, Scott and Tilly also state that inherent in this process of change there was at the same time a certain amount of continuity in that family members continued to be guided by the interests of the family unit on which the individual depended for survival.

In addition, as Tilly and Scott rightly indicate, it is incorrect to assume that the domestic mode of production was typical of all households before industrialization. This is also Peter Laslett's main point when he discusses the family and household as work and kin group in what he refers to as 'traditional Europe'.[12] Laslett disclaims a necessary relationship between family organization and the status of the household as a work group, but on the other hand he does assume that the proletarian household, since it was not determined by the imperatives of production, more often tended towards Western family characteristics such as neo-locality, a simple family structure and few resident relatives.

Following Scott and Tilly's model, Paul Klep in his article on the decline of proto-industrial production in Brabant also writes that the transition of a family economy to a family wage economy is essential to the history of the household.[13] The transition is assumed to have had important consequences for the structure of the household and

[11] Tilly and Scott, *Women*.
[12] Laslett, 'Family and household'.
[13] Klep, 'Over de achteruitgang', p. 30.

intergenerational relations. Klep asserts that the proto-industrial household should be regarded as an attempt to continue the 'head-strong familial economy' of the peasant household which will try to maintain its economic autonomy as long as possible.[14] The Tilburg domestic weavers are indeed reported to have been quite reluctant to switch over to factory work. They preferred their independence and the freedom to work irregular hours, to cultivate their small plots of land or to do other odd jobs around the house.[15] This implies that a simple transition of the household from home to factory is in most cases very unlikely. More often there would be transitional stages in which household-based production is supplemented with wage labour outside the household in an attempt to secure the continuation of the domestic production unit.

Thus, in different ways and from different perspectives, socio-logists and historians assume that the family organization of a wage labourer's household will vary considerably from those households engaged in household-based production. Most writers on the subject tend to take the view that the proletarian household was charac-terized by less family solidarity and hence by a lesser degree of house-hold complexity. In the present chapter I will look into the degree of household complexity and family cohesion for households headed by domestic weavers and those headed by factory workers. The analysis will focus specifically on the effect of economic differentiation upon the structural evolution of these households.

It would seem entirely fair to assume that the degree of economic differentiation in the households of factory workers was considerably greater than in those headed by domestic weavers, even as late as the period considered in this study. Most of the domestic weavers in Tilburg, who usually lived on the outskirts of the town, owned their own looms and worked a small plot of land which provided the household with some basic agricultural commodities. It is likely that a large proportion also owned the family home. The production unit of the domestic weaving economy would be run by the head of the household and his wife, with perhaps the help of some of the younger children. In all probability this was not the case for most factory workers whose households will consequently have been far more differentiated and proletarianized. The combined effects of shared productive interests and the presence of family property in the form of house, land and looms on extended family relations and the bonds between parents and children may have worked to produce

[14] Cf. Sheridan, Jr, 'Family', p. 56.
[15] Klep, 'Over de achteruitgang', p. 36; see also chapter 2, p. 39.

quite distinctive family cycles. This is the main theme of this chapter with which we conclude the analysis of the relationships between the family and the process of industrialization.

Unfortunately, the available sources do not enable us to pinpoint precisely which of the families discussed here were actually in possession of their own homes and plots of land. We are left with no choice but to rely on the assertions of contemporaries stating that, by comparison with factory labourers, most domestic weavers did own land.[16] We will, however, attempt to measure explicitly the extent to which members in the respective households were indeed sharing productive interests.

Before we embark upon the comparative analysis of the households of factory workers and domestic weavers I will discuss briefly the method of data acquisition and some general characteristics of the samples involved. The next section will discuss and analyse the degree of differentiation in the economic basis of the households under study, after which I proceed to an examination of household structure. A separate section on intergenerational relations concludes the chapter.

Unless one focuses upon small communities in which centralized mechanical production is known to have been totally absent, it is no small task to isolate individual proto-industrial households for micro-level analysis. Traditional sources used by historians to gather occupational information on individuals generally do not make the distinction between workers inside or outside factories. In the Tilburg population registers and taxation listings, for instance, domestic weavers and power-loom weavers alike were registered simply as 'weavers'. This called for a somewhat unusual method to help identify a sample of Tilburg domestic weavers. This method is based on a careful analysis of a series of so-called 'weavers' books' contained in the nineteenth-century archives of the Tilburg textile factories of 'Diepen', 'Brouwers', and 'Van Dooren en Dams'. These weavers' books, roughly covering the period 1875–1900, listed every single finished piece of cloth produced in the weaving mill together with the name of the weaver who had produced it. After an extensive treatment of a number of weavers' books and with the help of the town's population registers and taxation listings, eighty-nine domestic weavers could be isolated and identified as well as twenty-three power-loom weavers working inside the factory walls. The latter group was further complemented by adding to it households from

---

[16] See chapter 2, p. 43.

the 1880–1920 cohort of which the head was consistently listed in the population registers and taxation listings as being a 'factory worker'. This produced a group of ninety-five factory workers of various types which for reasons connected with sampling procedures had to be corrected and restricted to eighty-five for some parts of the analysis.[17] A more elaborate discussion of sources and procedures involved in this part of the study is presented in appendix 42.

For both groups of workers the entire family cycle of the household they headed was reconstructed from the beginning of the history of the household until the end, if possible, and if not, until the end of 1920. This date marks the end of the traditional nineteenth-century series of population registers. As was explained in chapter 3, we take the history of a household to begin with the independent establishment of its primary marital unit. A domestic weaver's household may for instance begin at the time of his marriage and move to a household of his own, or alternatively it may begin some time after the weaver's marriage into the parental household when his parents die or he decides to move out together with his wife to a household of his own. The family cycles presented here therefore deviate from those discussed in previous chapters in the sense that the actual beginning of the cycle is included.

The family cycles of the two samples cover the period 1845–1920.[18] The group of households headed by domestic weavers is in two different ways somewhat older than the group of households headed by factory workers. The domestic weavers set off on the history of their household a little earlier on in the period of observation, while the weavers themselves were also a little older at that point in time compared with the factory workers. The bulk of the factory workers were 25–29 years old at the beginning of the history of their household, while a considerable number of the domestic weavers were already past the age of 30. Most of the household histories of the domestic weavers pertain to the period 1865–1900, while most of the

[17] These ninety-five households could not be used for all analytical procedures on account of the bias towards those households which were extended at the beginning of 1880 in the 1880–1920 cohort. See the discussion in chapter 3, pp. 66–68. A similar correction, as was applied earlier to the entire 1880–1920 cohort, brought the group of factory workers down to the total number of eighty-five.

[18] One of the domestic weavers actually began his household's history in 1845 before the beginning of the continuous population registers at the end of 1849. To bridge the gap the civil registers were used to check for births and deaths, while the taxation listings were consulted for the co-residential situation. This made possible at the very least a decision on the question whether the weaver came to head his own household upon marriage. On the use of the taxation listings for these purposes see appendix 16.

factory workers' households belong roughly to the period 1875–1905. Appendices 43 and 44 present tables on these issues. Almost all factory workers and domestic weavers followed the principle of neolocality, so typical of the Western European family system. Only 2.5% of the factory workers and 6.8% of the domestic weavers married into his own or his wife's parental household. In a minority of cases this accompanied the handing over of the headship of the household to the younger generation.[19] In the remaining cases the weaver or factory worker concerned co-resided in the parental household for a short number of years only to leave for a household of his own after the parents had died or left.

7.2   Economic differentiation of the household

Before rushing into a discussion of the structural development of the household in the two samples, the issue of the degree of differentiation in the economic organization of the households in both groups needs to be dealt with. This can be done by examining the occupational diversification of the household, giving us at least some idea of the extent to which the productive unit of the domestic weaver and his household coincided. If proto-industrial activities were marginal to the family economy of these households and household members were dispersed over a great number of economic sectors, these activities are unlikely to have had a powerful influence on its family organization. In his reaction to the Tilly–Scott model of the family economy and family wage economy, Richard Wall argued that indeed most households would try to diversify their sources of income in order to reduce economic hazards.[20] Households engaged in proto-industrial activities, for instance, would send out some of their members into wage labour outside the household in different sectors of the economy. Vice versa, households headed by wage labourers might

---

[19] In the sample of households of factory workers, one of the two young couples married into the parental household of the bride after which they took over the household. The other case is similar except that the couple did not immediately take over the headship of the household. In this group there were also four households migrating into Tilburg after marriage, which makes it impossible to determine the way they started their own household.

   In the group of domestic weavers, five couples married into their parents' households, three of them without taking over the household, while in the other two cases the weaver and his wife became the new heads of household. All five concerned the parental household of the bride. A sixth couple married into the household of other kin while taking over headship of the household. The single case of a migrant household in this group could not be included.

[20] Wall, 'Work'.

supplement the family budget by having women and children employed at home in proto-industrial production. This tendency, Wall suggests, would turn the household of the family economy into a Weberian ideal-type lacking firm ground in historical reality.

It is highly probable that towards the final decades of the nineteenth century the Tilburg domestic weavers came to resemble Wall's model of the 'adaptive family economy'. In particular, after the 1880s, employment opportunities in the proto-industrial sector declined rapidly due to an accelerated pace in the mechanization of weaving.[21] Moreover, the low wage levels in home weaving after 1890 certainly made this line of work unattractive to the younger generation. In addition, expanded opportunities in industrial and artisanal wage labour enabled sons and daughters of proto-industrial producers to acquire incomes outside the household's productive unit. An illuminating comment on the status of domestic weaving around the turn of the century was given by the Tilburg weaver Jaonneke Janssens. When asked why he had not wanted to weave at home, he said that domestic textile work had become appropriate only for young girls, widows and old men.[22]

Thus, nearly all of the domestic weaving economies studied in this chapter may have encountered great economic difficulties towards the end of the history of their household as a result of the sharp decline of their trade after 1890. In chapter 2 we discussed the tendency of the Tilburg domestic weavers to hang on to their freedom and independence; but the extent to which the weavers in our sample managed to keep themselves in domestic weaving after the early 1890s is beyond our knowledge. Nevertheless, it is very likely that the final stages of the history of the household were increasingly periods of distress for the domestic weavers, in particular because the economic decline of the domestic sector coincided with advancing age and declining ability to work in the individual life course of the weaver and his wife. All this may have drastically influenced the development and composition of the household, so that the family cycles of the present sample may not be totally representative of earlier generations of domestic weavers.

However, we will first attempt to determine the degree of occupational diversification within the households of domestic weavers and factory workers. To this end, all of the occupational information concerning the heads and their sons and daughters found in the population registers and taxation listings was used to classify households

---

[21] See also chapter 2, pp. 36–37.
[22] See: Wagemakers, 'Excellente arbeiderscultuur', p. 60.

into three separate categories: households containing a son or daughter having the same occupation as the father, those with sons or daughters holding an occupation which was complementary to the head's occupation, while the last category contained households in which sons or daughters all held occupations which were dissimilar from the head's.[23] This procedure produced some striking results which are presented in table 7.1.

The majority of the domestic weavers appear to have had one or more sons who were themselves registered as weavers. In addition, a considerable proportion of them had at least one daughter at home registered as a weaver. Apart from this many of the domestic weavers had sons or daughters employed in textile occupations which were complementary to their own. These sons were in occupations such as sizers, piecers or raisers, while the daughters were registered as dressers, burlers or darners. The position of domestic weaving in Tilburg in the second half of the nineteenth century would thus appear to be quite different, more viable perhaps, than the situation which existed in the much more advanced industrial town of Preston where the sons of hand-loom weavers were not very likely to follow in their father's trade.[24] It seems the higher wage level in the textile mills in Preston was the main reason why the younger generation had abandoned home weaving.

The households headed by factory workers on the other hand are characterized by a remarkably high level of occupational diversification. The majority of family heads in this group had no son sharing the father's occupation. Surprisingly often the sons of these factory workers were employed, not in industrial work like their fathers, but in skilled trades such as shoemaking and carpentry. For daughters the level of occupational diversification does not vary greatly between the two groups of households. In both samples we found most of the daughters contributing to the family budget as domestic servants. What remains hidden, however, in table 7.1 is the fact that the factory workers reported to have had at least one son in the same occupation

---

[23] Generally the occupational entries in the population registers are regarded as potentially unreliable or ambiguous. For the heads and most of their sons, however, we also have entries in the far more accurate municipal taxation listings, the Kohieren van de hoofdelijke omslag'. For description of this source see appendix 16. Unfortunately, for the daughters there was no choice but to rely on the entries in the population registers. For almost all of the sons and most of the daughters several entries over a number of years were available making classification feasible in all cases.

[24] Anderson, *Family structure*, p. 122. However, it is unclear whether some of the sons of hand-loom weavers had become power-loom weavers in the mill.

Table 7.1 *Occupational diversification in households of domestic weavers and factory workers: sons and daughters with same occupation as father*[a]

Households with	Domestic weavers	Factory workers
sons with same occupation	66.7	19.8
sons with complementary occupations	20.0	15.1
only sons with other occupations	24.7	70.9
N	81	86
daughters with same occupation	29.2	1.4
daughters with complementary occupations	38.5	27.5
only daughters with other occupations	43.1	71.0
N	65	69

[a] Measured as the number of households with sons and daughters having the same occupation as the father or a complementary occupation, mostly textiles.

were nearly all weavers. This was so for fifteen out of the seventeen cases in this category. It would therefore seem that the occupational homogeneity of the domestic weaver's household was not exclusively related to its status as a unit of production.

The tendency towards occupational homogeneity among weavers was reproduced again, albeit in a somewhat weakened version, in tables on the occupational diversification of their fathers and fathers-in-law.[25] More than half of the domestic weavers appeared to be themselves sons of weavers, while all of the factory workers had different occupations from their father's, except for the power-loom weavers whose fathers were all weavers. The same result, though less marked, was produced when the focus was shifted towards the occupations held by the heads' fathers-in-law. The occupations of the spouses, as listed in the marriage registers, indicated that a larger proportion of factory workers' wives had been engaged in (industrial) textile work prior to their marriage, while a relatively high percentage of the domestic weavers' wives were reported as having had 'no occupation'. It is difficult to say what these latter wives were really doing before marriage, but it would seem most plausible to suggest that they were engaged in textile production within the household

[25] Information on father's and father-in-law's occupation, as well as the wife's occupation, was gathered from the marriage registers.

and/or domestic service. For both groups of households the largest single category of employment of spouses concerned 'textiles, including factory workers'. This category will most likely have been almost entirely composed of textile occupations considering the fact that there were few opportunities for female industrial labour outside this particular sector of the economy.[26]

What do the figures summed up above tell us about the occupational diversification in the two groups of households? First of all, I think it is important to say that they reflect the extent to which the weavers managed to monopolize production and restrict participation, both inside and outside the factory walls, to members of their own families. The importance of kinship for obtaining employment in weaving was indicated by the frequency with which the analysis of the weavers' books showed these weavers to be kin-related. It is also reported by the Tilburg weaver Jaonneke Janssens in his account of his work experience as a power-loom weaver during the period 1907–14.[27] The informal work culture in the weaving mills which existed right up to this period may have enabled the weavers to continue their (partial) control over production.[28] What I believe these weaving families in fact managed to do was to transfer their family economy over to the factory while at the same time extending its connections to include other more remotely related households.

It is difficult to decide whether the occupational homogeneity among weavers is a typically Tilburg phenomenon, even though we do have some evidence from the French textile industry indicating that at the beginning of the twentieth century kinship relations were far more frequent in the weaving mills than among other textile workers.[29] The fact that traditionally one was educated in the weaving trade at home at an early age will have stimulated the continuation of the trade down successive generations.[30]

---

[26] Appendix 45 presents tables on these issues.

[27] Wagemakers, 'Excellente arbeiderscultuur'.

[28] This is very similar to the situation described by Tamara Hareven in her book on the workers of the Amoskeag Company in Manchester, USA (Hareven, *Family time*). The paternalistic policies of the Amoskeag mill allowed its overseers, who were often related by blood to the workers they were supervising, considerable freedom to decide on such issues as the hiring of new recruits, in what workroom a worker would be placed or the quality and quantity of the work to be allocated. Under these conditions kinship ties could be used to control the labour process.

[29] Reddy, 'Family'.

[30] The proto-industrial iron workers of the Liégeoise Basse-Meuse (Belgium) in the second half of the nineteenth century similarly displayed a lower level of occupational diversification compared with the coalminers engaged in industrial wage work (see Leboutte, 'Household dynamics', p. 12). Here too the sons of gunsmiths used to adopt their father's occupation to which they were probably also introduced at early ages within the home.

Despite the low level of occupational diversification of the domestic weaver's household, the data presented in table 7.1 obviously offer no direct evidence of a commensurately high level of overlap between the productive unit of the household and the family of the domestic weaver. Almost all households combined their proto-industrial activities with wage labour, which was primarily regarded as a task for the sons and daughters. In 60.5% of all families with sons of working age one or more of these sons was sent out to acquire an income in occupations which were different from their fathers. Also, it is unclear whether the sons recorded as weavers were actually working within the productive unit of their parental household, or were employed within the factory. The same applies to those sons and daughters holding complementary occupations. It is generally assumed that unmarried women employed as dressers, burlers or darners were at work inside the factory, while married women by contrast would be at work within the home. But even then, these sons and daughters may have combined their factory work with proto-industrial labour at home in busy times. However, the presence of female weavers in the domestic weaving economy is unmistakably proof of proto-industrial activities which household members shared together; female weavers, as was mentioned in chapter 2, were not allowed to enter the weaving mill. Apart from households with one or more daughters working as weavers, there were also a few households of domestic weavers in which the wife appeared to be weaving as well, or was recorded as having a complementary occupation.

The factory workers' families on the other hand were undeniably highly differentiated in their sources of income. In 89.5% of all families with sons there was at least one son holding a different occupation from his father, while for as many as 70.9% not one of the sons appeared to be within his father's line of work. Considering the nature of the occupations recorded for these families, there may have been only one or two cases in which proto-industrial activities went on in the home. Only two households contained a female weaver, while there were hardly any women recorded as fluffers, burlers or darners present. A little restraint is called for here though, because it may be quite possible that in a number of these households the wives and the younger daughters were engaged in domestic textile production. For a long time some of the mill workers continued to bring home domestic textile work for their wives to do.

It seems evident that the households of factory workers in this sample should almost all be regarded as income pooling, highly differentiated economic units. Kinship clearly did not constitute the basis of work organization in these families. Although the individualization of work roles and the dispersal over different sectors of the economy probably acted to lessen the interdependance of family members, it also reduced opportunities for mutual assistance in times of economic crisis. This discontinuity in the households of industrial wage labourers may well have severed the ties between successive generations and broken the bonds uniting parents and children. However, it should not be overlooked that factory workers did in some cases have the opportunity to procure employment for family members within the same mill.[31] Fathers may not have been able to work side by side with their sons and daughters anymore, but some of them may still have been united in their bond with one particular company. This may have cushioned the break between the generations.

The households of domestic weavers by contrast showed a tremendous amount of occupational continuity over successive generations. Undoubtedly, not all family members shared in the productive tasks of the household all of the time. This would have exceeded the limits of the family economy of the average Tilburg domestic weaver, who mostly operated only one loom. But, it is difficult to see how successive children would not be set to work within the home in their teens, to be taught the trade, and also to provide extra labour when needed by the household.[32] Some or most of these children would eventually enter the factory, but perhaps one or more of the adult sons would succeed his father on the loom when, with increasing age, the father's working abilities declined. Thus, during the early stages in the history of these households the family economy of the weaver and his wife and their household will have coincided. In addition, the domestic weaving economy allowed time for other home-based productive activities in which the family shared, such as growing vegetables and raising a few cattle, or perhaps running a small shop. During the later stages in the history of the household, with an increasing number of adult children still residing at home, the household came to function as a combination of family economy and family wage economy,[33] only to return to its initial position with the departure of most or all of the children.

---

[31] Wagemakers, 'Excellente arbeiderscultuur', pp. 64–6.

[32] In the labour inquiry of 1887 contemporaries indicated that children of domestic weavers would start working at the loom at the age of 11 to 12 (*Enquete*, Tilburg, question 10603). It is also mentioned that children were trained at the loom after they returned from school in the afternoon before the age of 12 (*Enquete*, Tilburg, question 11479). In his article on the Tilburg domestic weavers Ton Wagemakers concludes that domestic weaving 'was inextricably bound up with family labour' and therefore with child labour, this situation, in his opinion, still existed in 1887 (Wagemakers, 'Over buitenwevers', p. 119).

[33] For examples see *Onderzoekingen* III, p. 33.

7.3   Extended family relations and the family economy

We now need to consider whether the economic differentiation and involvement with industrial wage labour led to a collapse of extended family relations and a relative decline in the incidence of extended family households, as indeed a number of writers on the subject would have us believe. Was the factory worker's family really torn apart by the factory bell? In this section we will again employ the by now familiar techniques to assess the strength of extended family relations along the family cycle in the households of domestic weavers and factory workers.[34]

From the point in time at which the domestic weavers and factory workers embarked upon the history of their own household I traced the composition of the family through all of the successive stages of its cycle. As we have already seen, almost all of the weavers and factory workers set up their own households upon marriage. Very few indeed of the weavers and factory workers continued to co-reside with parents after their marriage, and, if they did, it was only for a very limited number of years. If, from that moment onwards, we survey the entire family cycle and tally the number of households in which extended kin were ever present, the similarity of the pattern between the two groups is striking. Of the domestic weavers 62.9% of the households co-resided with kin at least once during the whole of its history, while this was so for 61.2% of the factory workers.[35] In addition, the overall mean household size along the life cycle of 5.3 for both groups only strengthens the idea of more or less complete symmetry.[36]

There are, however, differences to be detected in the structural evolution of these households which are relevant to the analytical aims pursued in this chapter. If the proportion of extended households in both groups is charted by family cycle year, the result of which is presented in figure 7.1, it becomes clear that during the first twenty-five years of the family cycle the domestic weavers had extended kin present in the household considerably less often than did the factory workers.[37] In this period of the family cycle between

---

[34] For most parts of the analysis the uncorrected sample of factory workers is used, if, however, this is not the case, it is indicated in the text.

[35] These latter percentages are only marginally higher than for working-class families of the 1880–1920 cohort, see chapter 5, on account of the fact that total cycles were examined for factory workers and domestic weavers. It would seem that the experience in factory workers' and domestic weavers' families corresponded to general working-class patterns.

[36] These figures were based on the corrected sample of factory workers.

[37] For absolute numbers of households present for some years of the family cycle see appendix 46.

about 5% to 10% of the households of domestic weavers were extended at any one point. The proportion of extended households among factory workers on the other hand rises slowly but steadily to a maximum of about 18%. During the first half of the family cycle, therefore, the households headed by factory workers appear to have been more complex than those headed by domestic weavers. The pattern for the domestic weavers at this stage of the cycle appears to correspond more or less to the level found for all working-class households in Tilburg, both for the 1849 and the 1880 cohort.[38] The factory workers, however, clearly exceed these levels.

During the final fifteen years of the family cycle the proportion of extended households increases rapidly in both groups. This rise occurs firstly and most steeply among the households of the domestic weavers. The domestic weavers, after their steep ascent, stabilize the level of extensions at around 20% during a ten-year period, while over the same time span the proportion of extended households among factory workers gradually climbs towards a peak of 38% in the forty-seventh year of their cycle. After the fiftieth year the level of extensions among the domestic weavers rises sharply again before falling to zero during the final three years. We should not attach too much value to the curve during these final few years of the family cycle considering the small number of observations available for these years.[39]

Figure 7.1 indicates that household extension in the households of domestic weavers mainly occurred during the final phase of the household as the head and his wife began to reach old age. The extent of the differences in the early stages of the household between the two groups is further illustrated by table 7.2 which shows the proportion of extended households by decade.[40] Within the group of factory workers about one-quarter of the households received extended kin into their homes during each of the first three decades. For the domestic weavers it never rises higher than 16% per decade. Then, during the fourth and fifth decades the percentages jump to 32% and 37%, respectively, thereby effectively marking the dichotomy in the structural develoment of the households of domestic weavers. Although the differences are less pronounced within the group of factory workers, extended kin co-residence was also more frequent during the final stages of the family cycle than during the initial ones. In the fourth decade the proportion of extensions falls to 18% before

---

[38] See figures 5.1 and 5.2 on pp. 125–26.
[39] See also appendix 46.
[40] Corrected sample of factory workers was used for this table.

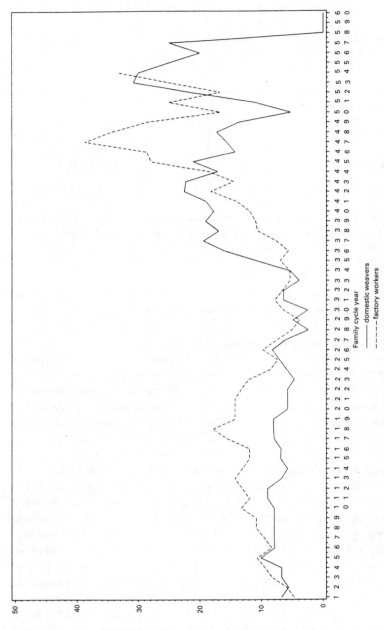

Figure 7.1. Proportion of extended family households by family cycle year for domestic weavers and factory workers (corrected sample for factory workers)

Family and social change

Table 7.2 *Extension by kin along the family cycle for domestic weavers and factory workers by decade*[a]

	Decade				
	1	2	3	4	5
Domestic weavers					
%					
Extended	14.6	16.9	16.1	32.1	37.9
N	89	89	87	78	58
Factory workers					
%					
Extended	22.4	25.0	25.0	18.2	36.8
N	85	84	84	77	57

[a] The point in time at which the histories of these households begin varies from 1860–70 to e.g. 1900–10.

rising during the final ten years to a level comparable to that of the domestic weavers. Of all fifty-seven households of factory workers present at the start of the fifth decade 36% came to reside with extended kin during this period.

It is interesting to note that the frequency with which domestic weavers in the countryside of Noord-Brabant co-resided with kin was very similar to the frequency with which the Tilburg domestic weavers did so. Whilst the proportion of households ever extended among the latter group was 62.9%, it was 64% among domestic weavers in the village of Nuenen.[41] Of the four decades following their marriage these rural weavers were particularly likely to experience extension during the first and fourth decades of the family cycle: when 35% and 56% respectively of all households were extended. However, in the study of Nuenen no distinction was made between the weaver's parental household, his own or perhaps the household headed by his married children in which the weaver came to reside during old age. This may have greatly inflated the number of extended households at either end of the cycle and the number of households ever extended, but to what extent this was so is unclear.

It would seem, therefore, that the phenomenon of extension over the family cycle between the two groups of households differed in two respects. First, households of factory workers were more likely to

[41] van der Heijden, 'Gezin', p. 137.

be extended in their initial years, and secondly, extension towards the end of the cycle occurred much earlier among the households of domestic weavers. In order to throw more light on the reasons behind these differences we need to consider in detail the type of kin who brought about these extensions.

Figure 7.2 indicates that in both groups widowed parents and unmarried siblings were the most common co-residents during the first twenty years. But, clearly, factory workers co-resided more often with these relatives, in particular with siblings, than did domestic weavers. (Figures on this are presented in appendix 47.) Had the domestic weavers' parents all died by that time? This is plausible considering the higher ages at which the weavers began their household. We do not know. Besides, age at marriage is not the only critical variable; also relevant is the individual's birth order within the sibling group. A first or second-born child who marries relatively late does not reduce the opportunities for co-residence with parents to the same extent as does a last-born child who also marries late. Moreover, the main difference between the two groups arises from the larger number of co-residing siblings. Noteworthy differences involving the types of co-residing relatives were not found except for the fact that in the factory workers' households a higher proportion of siblings, and even of widowed parents, out-migrated when compared with the domestic weaver's household.

The higher proportion of extensions in the households of the factory workers in the first half of the family cycle may have been the effect of the geographical origin of some of these families. A large part of the factory workers sample was drawn from the 1880–1920 cohort group which contains a certain number of migrant households. From the previous chapter we know that at least some migrant households were highly attractive to kin and were more often extended than native households. Indeed some of the factory workers were migrants, in all, fourteen cases. However, of these only two were extended at some time during the first twenty years of the cycle.[42] The higher level of extensions in the households of the factory workers during the first half of the cycle, therefore, cannot be attributed to the migrants in this group receiving a disproportionate number of extended kin.

Finally, cohort effects may have distorted our observation. The group of domestic weavers belonged to a much wider range of marriage cohorts in comparison with the factory workers. The latter

---

[42] In addition, one of these two was excluded from the corrected sample of factory workers.

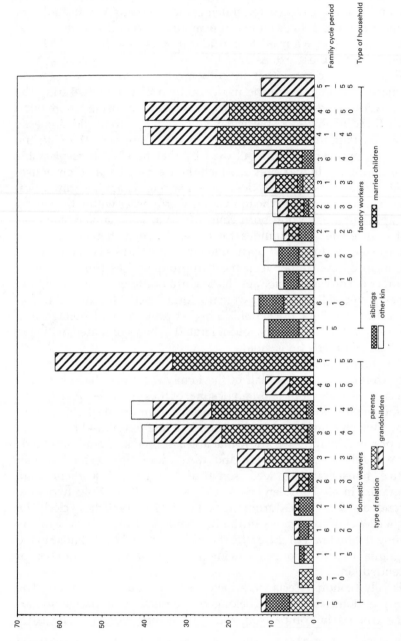

Figure 7.2. Proportion of households with entries by kin by family cycle period for domestic weavers and factory workers (corrected sample for factory workers)

group by contrast was more heavily concentrated in the marriage cohorts belonging to the period 1870–80. Appendix 43 may be consulted for figures on this. However, examination of those families which began their household's history between 1860 and 1880 still revealed a higher level of extensions for the households headed by factory workers (see appendix 48).

There is no obvious reason why the productive unit of the hand-loom weaver's household should have set limits to the number of relatives who could be present at any one time. Even if additional workers could not be used to assist in the household's productive work, relatives could always have been sent out to work for wages or to enable the wife to do some (more) productive work of her own. Moreover, the domestic weavers may even have had more room in their cottages to accommodate relatives, compared with the factory workers who were less likely to live in the more spacious houses on the outskirts of town. If work was slack, co-residing relatives working for wages would have been very welcome; but, also, when ample opportunities in domestic textiles existed this could have been a reason to attract kin in order to raise production. Consequently, the economic trend offers little hold in this issue.

In comparison with the factory workers, the domestic weavers might be expected to have had larger proportions of other household members present, that is, boarders or lodgers and adolescent children. These could have assisted the weaver and his wife, not only in weaving or burling but also in working the plot of land or in other productive tasks. This, however, was not the case. Neither the average number of children present, nor the number of lodgers or boarders co-residing in the weavers' households exceeded the level found for the factory workers' households. (Appendix 49 and 50 present figures on this.) Instead, extended kin, boarders and lodgers taken together were even less frequent in the households of domestic weavers during the first twenty years. It would be unreasonable to assume, therefore, that the diverging pattern of kin co-residence in the initial stages was related to diverging structural characteristics of the households themselves. Later on in this chapter we will return to this issue and suggest a possible explanation.

A second feature of the domestic weavers household which came out in figure 7.2 needs explaining; the much earlier entry into the parental household of married children. This could be the effect of a greater material attractiveness of the household of the domestic weaver to his married children. Did the domestic weaver have more to offer to the next generation? It could equally well be that the households of domestic weavers experienced greater hardship on account of the decline in domestic weaving after 1890, which the weavers subsequently tried to counter by attracting more workers. First of all, we need to remember that on average the domestic weavers were a little older when they set out on their family cycle (see appendix 44). This may have resulted in more compact household histories and the presence of married children earlier in the parental life course. However, one might also argue for the pre-1890 period that, when these extensions occurred, they were an expression of the greater economic assets of the productive unit of the domestic weaver in comparison with the households of the industrial wage labourer. The domestic weaving economy may still have had easily available employment to offer to the next generation and in addition there would be the loom and the house which may have attracted married children. I will argue below, however, that this is not likely to have been the case.

First of all, table 7.3 shows that the structural characteristics of the household of the domestic weaver and the factory worker at the time of entry of a married child and spouse corresponded very closely. For both groups of households it appeared that about two-thirds of married daughters, who constituted by far the largest group of co-residing married children, entered when both parents were still alive. Sons in both groups mainly entered when one of the parents had already died. It seems as if sons were only asked in when the household needed a replacement for a lost breadwinner. Daughters apparently did not rush to lend co-residential assistance to lone parents in old age. A comparable appeal will also have been made to them, and about one-third of these married daughters likewise entered the household of a widowed parent. However, most of the married daughters resided, perhaps we should say were allowed to reside, in the household of their parents for other reasons which, we may assume, can only have been connected to the daughters' own needs. More importantly for our present argument is that this pattern was the same for both groups of households. In addition, the ages of the parent(s) at the time when married children entered were also very close. Three-quarters of the fathers present at the entry of a married child were above the age of 60 and 63 respectively for factory workers and domestic weavers. The mothers still present in both groups were on average a few years younger.

Moreover, no differences were found in relation to co-residence by married children. In both groups married children entered in half of all cases because they married and brought their spouses into the

Table 7.3 *Structure of household at time of entry of married children for domestic weavers and factory workers*[a]

	domestic weavers		factory workers	
	sons	daughters	sons	daughters
1 parent only	7.7	7.1	0.0	9.1
1 parent + sibling(s)	53.9	28.6	62.5	27.3
2 parents only	0.0	0.0	12.5	4.6
2 parents + sibling(s)	38.5	64.3	25.0	59.1
N	13	28	8	26

[a] All single entries by married children were counted. Uncorrected sample of factory workers was used.

household, whereas the other half migrated into the household after having resided in other households, mostly their own, subsequent to their marriage. This situation applied to both sons and daughters in each group. In general married children remained just a few years in the households of their parents before leaving again. Again, in both groups, only a minority stayed on in order to take over the headship of the household shortly before or after the death of their parents.[43] In addition, only minor differences occurred between the two groups as to the place of residence of married children after their marriage. For almost all of them marriage coincided with exit from the parental household and the establishment of a new one. For sons only 5.2% and 3.8% of domestic weavers and factory workers respectively continued to reside in the parental household after their marriage; for daughters these percentages were also low but conspicuously higher than for sons: 10.2% and 9.8% of all first marriages were followed by continued residence in the parental household.

Finally, when we relate the timing of entry of married children into the households of their parents to historical time it is obvious why these co-residential arrangements arose. Almost all married children in both groups of households were present sometime during the

[43] The following number of co-residing married sons and daughters of domestic weavers eventually took over their parental households: 25% and 18.2%; for sons and daughters of factory workers the comparable percentages were: 57.1% and 20%. Not too much importance should be attached to the high percentage of factory workers' sons taking over the parental household as the total number of observation in this group was only seven.

period 1910–20: 83% of the married children in the group of domestic weavers and 81% of those in the group of factory workers. All remaining married children entered their parental households in the decade prior to 1910. The combined effect of the parents being slightly older as well as a greater range over marriage cohorts, which is shown in appendix 43 and 44, resulted in more domestic weavers experiencing the entry of married children at an earlier stage in the family cycle. For instance, a domestic weaver and his wife marrying at relatively late ages, say between age 35–39, and beginning their household's history around 1890, would encounter old age, as well as the problems associated with the period 1910–20, sooner than the factory worker who married at age 24 sometime between 1880 and 1890. If we exclude part of these effects and limit analysis to the cohorts of couples beginning their family cycle between 1860 and 1880, it is clear that both patterns come to resemble each other closely over the final half of the family cycle. Results of this exercise are shown in appendix 48. It seems likely, therefore, that the household extension of married children for domestic weavers as well as factory workers principally came about as a result of the higher mobility levels and shortages in the housing market which were characteristic of the 1910–20 decade.[44]

The figures presented above already may have created the idea that on balance many more domestic weavers and their wives co-resided with their married children when compared with factory workers. And this indeed proves to have been the case. For the domestic weavers 38% of the couples who had ever had children born to them came to co-reside with their married children in their own households at some point in time, as opposed to 26% of the couples in the sample of factory workers.[45] In the following section we will see that the domestic weavers were not more likely to have been abandoned by their unmarried children which would have necessitated them to attract married children instead. Economic conditions were undoubtedly harsh for the elderly domestic weavers who by 1910 belonged to a seriously outdated and perhaps also impoverished occupational group. On the other hand, the domestic weavers and their wives may still have managed to squeeze meagre incomes from some occasional domestic weaving, burling or darning. In addition, most of them had their plots of land and cattle providing them at the very least with

---

[44] For a discussion of labour mobility and the housing market and their potential effects on household structure see chapter 4, pp. 92–93.

[45] These percentages apply to households whose developmental cycles commenced prior to 1880.

some basic foodstuffs. They may well have been better able to support themselves in old age, despite the collapse of domestic weaving, than factory workers of comparable age.

What then brought about the higher level of co-residence by married children in the households of domestic weavers? It is perhaps reasonable to suggest that the domestic weavers, with their more spacious houses on the outskirts of town, had more and better accommodation to offer to married children who were having difficulties in obtaining appropriate housing after 1910.[46] The weavers may even have used the house and land that was theirs as a reward to the married child for the period of co-residential assistance. On the other hand, that should have lead to more children taking over the parental house and household eventually, and that did not happen as we shall see in the following section. Perhaps domestic weavers' children married in larger numbers, and if they also migrated out of town less often, this could have created a larger reservoir of young families confronted by the housing problem of the 1910s. However, the domestic weavers were less likely to marry early, and migration, as we know, frequently led to more rather than less kin co-residence. We have to conclude discussion of this issue by stating that similar circumstances probably promoted co-residence of married children in the households of domestic weavers and factory workers, but that in the former group this was more frequent as a result of better facilities.

This conclusion is strengthened by the overall figures on the numbers of working-class parents with co-resident married children in the 1880–1920 cohort, for which figures were presented in table 5.6. A strong overlap exists between the various groups. Many of the skilled labourers shared the family experiences of the domestic weavers, while many of the unskilled workers shared those of the factory workers. Moreover, the domestic weavers co-resided with married children only slightly more often than did the middle classes of the second cohort group of households, who certainly should not be regarded as families in distress.

On the basis of the figures presented so far one might suggest that the most important conclusion is that, while acknowledging the structural differences along the family cycle between the two samples studied in this chapter, ultimately the pattern of kin co-residence was very similar regardless of the type of family economy. This conclusion, however, would obscure the fact that the households of factory workers experienced far greater complexity than did households

[46] Average family size of domestic weavers in this period differed little from that of factory workers.

headed by domestic weavers. After all, table 7.2 also implies that household extension was more likely to have occurred at least twice along the family cycle of the factory workers. Of all factory workers who had ever lived with extended kin, 44.2% had done so on more than one occasion, as against only 28.6% for the domestic weavers. Unlike the households of domestic weavers, extended kin more often resided in the households of factory labourers in both the initial and the final stages of the family cycle. The total period of extension was also longer: 6.3 years as opposed to 4.4 years for the households of domestic weavers. Strikingly enough, a similar situation was found by Leboutte in nineteenth-century Belgium; although differences were small, households headed by proto-industrial gunsmiths co-resided with kin less often and for a smaller time span than did households of coalminers.[47] In mid-nineteenth-century Preston, however, self-employed hand-loom weavers were apparently no less likely to be taking kin into their homes than were factory workers.[48]

To sum up, it is certainly unjustified to regard factory workers' households as characterized by an absence of strong and intensive extended kinship relations, given the frequency with which they took extended kin into their households. It appears that extended kin were even more frequent during the early stages of the family cycle in the households of factory workers than in those headed by domestic weavers. Compared with working-class households in general, factory workers also had a higher level of extensions during the first half of the family cycle. Domestic weavers rarely co-resided with parents or siblings, but their households appeared to have had a far stronger attraction to married children. Kin co-residence in the households of domestic weavers was clearly a phenomenon confined to the final stages of the family cycle when married children with spouses and grandchildren were temporarily added to the household. In both groups married children entered the household partly to assist widowed parents and partly for reasons of their own. An entirely satisfactory explanation as to why co-residence by married children was more frequent in the households of domestic weavers was not easily found, but it was suggested that this was related to the better housing facilities the domestic weaver could offer.

7.4   Parents and children

In this section I shall explore in detail the strength of the ties between parents and children in both the domestic weaving economy and the

[47] Leboutte, 'Household dynamics', p. 9.
[48] Anderson, *Family structure*, p. 123.

wage economy of factory labourers. The occupational discontinuity between the generations observed in the households of factory workers may have broken the bonds between parents and children and in particular between the father and his sons. In these households the unity of family, property and labour had completely vanished, although a few of these families may still have been in possession of their own homes as well as a small plot of land.[49] However, the family clearly no longer possessed the means to function as an economic unit and educate the next generation in the trade of their fathers and grandfathers. This may have led to a growing independence on the side of the younger generation, or, at the very least, it may have reduced opportunities for fathers and sons to assist each other in the sphere of work, which in turn may have prompted earlier independence. Admittedly, economic differentiation was not wholly absent from the households of the domestic weavers; not all sons will have been called upon to remain at home to assist their fathers on the loom. However, the household did in principle offer opportunities for both adolescent boys and girls to be set to work, and indeed the family will have been in need of the labour of some of its children. This and the property belonging to the family economy of the domestic weaver may have caused individual life-course patterns to vary to some extent. On the other hand, the moral obligations between parents and children may have overruled the economic aspects of their relationship.[50]

Contemporaries were often somewhat critical of the influence of industrial wage labour on the relationships between parents and children. In their attempts to postpone children's early autonomy, working-class parents were sometimes offered assistance where it was not wanted. With the intention of helping their workers to preserve parental authority, some of the cotton mills in Hengelo, in the east of The Netherlands, began paying part of the wages of their adolescent workers to the fathers.[51] Parents rightly protested against this violation of their authority over their own children following which most regulations were abolished. Naturally, the parents' most anxious concerns focused on the possibility that the child would leave home at an early age, thereby severely reducing the family's standard of living. This section, therefore, explores the extent to which parents in the

---

[49] In *Sozialer und kultureller Wandel*, R. Braun assumes that those families with no property and characterized by weak family ties would be the first to enter the factories. Consequently, those to enter last were the ones whose material ties had been strongest and who had been most skilled in their trade. In other words the transition to factory labour involved a negative process of selection (pp. 26–36).

[50] This is suggested by Alter, *Family*, p. 160.

[51] de Regt, *Arbeidersgezinnen*, p. 131.

two samples of households were trying to restrict their children's autonomy and keep them from leaving home.

Families headed by factory workers were blessed with many children, even more so than were families headed by domestic weavers. Factory labourers and their wives had a median number of eight live-born children as opposed to seven for the weavers' families. A considerable number of these children died before they reached the age at which they could start contributing to the family purse; and child mortality was particularly high for the daughters of families of factory workers.[52] Then, shortly after children had reached working age, they began to leave the parental household for the first time.[53]

Figure 7.3 clearly shows that for the majority of weavers' sons this life-course transition occurred between the ages of 20 and 29: 66% of sons whose fathers were domestic weavers left home for the first time within this age group. Sons whose fathers were engaged in factory labour started to leave home earlier; whereas only 10% of the domestic weavers' sons left home within the age group of 15–19, as against 18% of factory workers' sons. The same issue may be stated differently, perhaps in a more concise way: 41% of all first departures from home of factory workers' sons took place after the age of 24, whereas 54% of the sons of domestic weavers left this late. The different distribution of the timing of first departure from home for sons also comes out in a lower mean age for this event: 21.9 years for factory workers' sons as opposed to 24.0 for weavers' sons. As figure 7.4 makes clear, broadly the same may be said for the daughters of both groups of families. Differences, however, are less marked. Girls left home much earlier than their brothers, and this applies to both groups. A noticeable proportion, 15% and 20% of the daughters of domestic weavers and factory workers respectively, left home between the ages of 15 and 19. For factory workers' daughters a further 10% left even earlier than that. But again, differences are small: 32.5% of the exits of factory workers' daughters occurred after the age of 25. This is not far short of the figure found for daughters of domestic weavers: 39.5%.

While sons in both groups of families could be retained more easily

[52] Of all daughters of factory workers 13.1% died before their first birthday, compared with 10.1% of the boys; for domestic weavers these figures were 10.5% and 11.5% respectively. The proportions of children dying before the age of 10 for the same categories of children were 22.7% and 17.9%, 19.3% and 18.8%.

[53] All following data on the timing of break away from the parental home relate to departures from the household occurring before the end of the household's history. In this way only 'free' moves were selected at the exclusion of those departures that were forced on the child, for instance by the death of his or her parents.

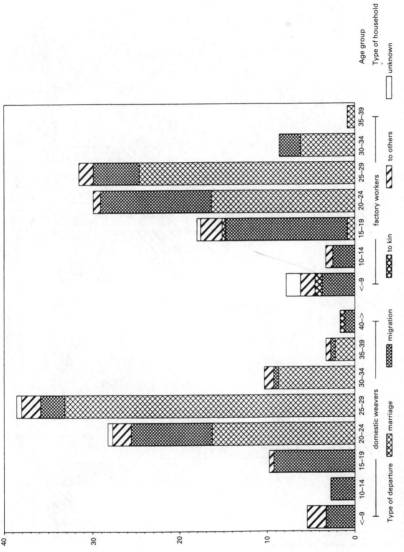

Figure 7.3. Timing and type of departure from parental household for sons by age group of son and type of household

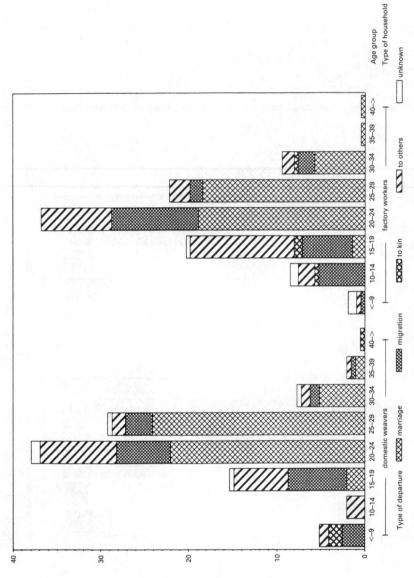

Figure 7.4. Timing and type of departure from parental household for daughters by age group of daughter and type of household

in the household until their early twenties, due to the fact that preferred occupations for sons did not militate against continued
residence at home, this was not the case for girls. In general, employment opportunities for girls were heavily concentrated in textiles and
domestic service. If the family failed to procure domestic textile work,
which in this period was in decline, it could either decide to send its
daughters to work in the factories or into domestic service. For 18% of
domestic weavers' daughters and 28% of factory workers' daughters
the parents decided in favour of domestic service, involving the
daughter's early departure from the parental household.[54] It is clear
that families could not resist the strong pull exercised by the textile
factories on adolescent labour because the largest proportion of
daughters remained at home until well into their twenties. We must
assume that girls of that age were either employed within the home
or engaged in factory work. Working-class parents can hardly be
expected to have been forgoing the additional income these
daughters could potentially bring in. The proportion remaining at
home at least until their twentieth birthday was slightly larger for
domestic weavers which may have been the result of the greater
employment opportunities for teenage girls within the domestic
weaving economy. The mean age for first departure from home,
however, shows little difference: 22.0 and 21.9 years for daughters of
factory workers and domestic weavers respectively.

At this stage it is appropriate to make a comparison between the
nineteenth-century urban experience with data on rural families in
pre-industrial Noord-Brabant. The mean age at which children
started to leave home in the late eighteenth century in Alphen, a
small agricultural community, was only 1.58 for boys and 15.2 for
girls.[55] These boys and girls left home to become what Peter Laslett
has termed life-cycle servants, which marked such a distinctive stage
in the individual life course before the nineteenth century.[56] The early
departure from home in Alphen was most likely related to the lack of
employment opportunities for young people in or near the parental
home in these eighteenth-century rural communities.[57] Towards the
end of the nineteenth century, however, this aspect of the life-course
pattern had apparently changed considerably in the countryside.[58] It

---

[54] These percentages include those leaving before the age of 20 because of 'migration',
 'to kin' and 'to others' (other households in Tilburg) minus the few who left for
 marriage. See figure 7.4.
[55] Lindner, 'De dynamische analyse', p. 69.
[56] Laslett, *Family life*, p. 34. In some preindustrial European communities the age at
 leaving home was markedly lower even than that, see e.g. Wall, 'The age'.
[57] Wall, 'The age', p. 195.
[58] See also Klep, 'Het huishouden', p. 58.

is reported that in the later part of the nineteenth century 41% to 44% of all lower-class children in the eastern part of Noord-Brabant stayed at home until at least the age of 25. This proportion is little higher than the figures presented above for Tilburg working-class sons in the same period.[59]

In nineteenth-century Tilburg both sons and daughters with fathers engaged in factory labour departed from their parental homes at earlier ages than the children of domestic weavers. However, these youngsters did return, sometimes after only a short period away from home, in order to experience in the end a final break at comparable ages to sons and daughters in the domestic weaving economy. The final departure from the parental household for sons and daughters of domestic weavers took place at the advanced mean ages of 26.9 and 25.0 respectively, while parents in the group of factory workers saw their children finally leave the household at slightly younger ages: 25.0 for sons and 24.2 for daughters. Clearly, differences in the timing of the final break away from home had become negligible. Of all final departures of domestic weavers' sons 66.5% took place after the age of 24, compared with 59.6% of sons of factory workers; for girls these percentages were 54.1 and 47.2 respectively.[60]

All this implies that sons and daughters of factory workers were a lot more mobile than their counterparts in the domestic weaving economy. The former came and went more often, and they did so more often for migratory reasons; children of domestic weavers, especially sons, continued to reside in their parental homes longer and more often until their marriage. This can be judged from the fact that 60.3% of the domestic weavers' sons exited from the parental household for a first time when they married, whilst only 29.3% did so for reasons of migration. In contrast, 48.8% of the sons of factory workers only left the parental houshold for the first time at marriage, while 40.6% left because they migrated out of Tilburg. For girls the same pattern was found in the reasons for first departure, though the difference was a little less clear cut: 54.4% and 45.3% of domestic weavers' and factory workers' daughters respectively left for a first time in order to marry and set up a household of their own. Although compared with differences between the two groups at first departure those for final departure from home were bound to be smaller, the same pattern is nevertheless visible, in particular for girls.[61]

So far, the data indicate that in the domestic weaving economy

---

[59] Meurkens, *Bevolking*, p. 160.
[60] Detailed figures are presented in appendix 51.
[61] Relevant figures are given in appendix 52.

boys were retained in the parental home a little longer in comparison with those whose father was employed in industrial wage labour. However, these data concern only those youngsters whom we have actually seen leaving, those who continued to reside in the parental household until its dissolution were excluded. Figure 7.5 therefore charts the percentage of sons and daughters who had not yet left permanently including those children staying on until the household ended or those dying. In this graph the proportion indicated to be still at home at a certain age may include some offspring who had been away for some time prior to that moment, or indeed were away at precisely that very moment, since, if the child returned to the parental nest he or she is counted as not yet having left permanently.[62] The graph confirms our earlier assessment that in the age range of 25 to 35 a somewhat larger proportion of the domestic weavers' sons were still residing with their parents than were sons whose fathers were in factory work. At the age of 35, 13.6% of the domestic workers' sons had not yet left permanently, as opposed to 5.9% for sons from factory workers' families.[63] Figure 7.5 also confirms our earlier conclusion that occupational influences on the life-course pattern of girls, at least concerning the final break with parents, appear to have been non-existent.

The differences in timing in the break from home between the two samples had no consequences at all for the timing of marriage. In earlier chapters it was established that the age at which working-class men and women married, as well as those from higher social classes, was relatively stable throughout the second half of the nineteenth

---

[62] See appendix 53 for percentages concerning those who had resided in the parental home continuously at different times.

[63] It is possible, however, that these differences are occasioned by cohort effects rather than through the effect of the two different family economies. Households of domestic weavers were slightly older and their children accordingly were more likely to belong to older cohort groups. The age at first departure and the proportion not yet away from home permanently was computed again, this time excluding sons born before 1870. This showed that sons of domestic weavers left home for a first time at the mean age of 23.4, 0.6 years earlier than for the entire group of such sons. This is still later than the age found for sons of factory workers who left home for a first time at the average age of 21.9. The age at which domestic weavers' sons born after 1870 made their final departure from the parental household was also still higher compared with sons of factory workers: 26.3 and 25.0 respectively. Moreover, the proportion of sons still residing at home in certain age groups remained higher for domestic weavers than for factory workers. At the age of 35 there was still a considerable difference in the proportion who had not yet left: twice as many sons of domestic weavers were still at home as were sons of factory workers of the same age (see for full table appendix 55). The effect therefore can not be attributed to cohort patterns only.

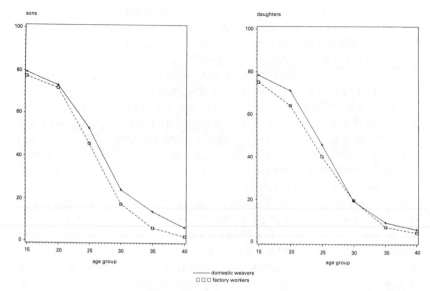

Figure 7.5. Proportion of children still at home by age group for domestic
weavers and factory workers

century. The same may be said for the sons and daughters of
domestic weavers and factory workers; these timed their marriages in
very similar ways to the working-class sons and daughters overall in
the two cohorts. In both cohorts sons married at the median age of 26
and daughters at the age of 25. Age at marriage for these sons and
daughters came early when compared with age at marriage in the
rural areas of the province. Domestic weavers in the countryside in
the same period, for instance, were marrying at mean ages of 29.8 for
men and 28.2 for women.[64]

However, not all of the sons of domestic weavers actually married,
nor did all of the daughters. More importantly, for sons of domestic
weavers in particular, the proportions unmarried at various ages
were higher than was the case for sons of factory workers. Whilst, at
the age of 39, 15.9% of the weavers' sons were still unmarried, this
was so for only 7.7% of the sons with fathers in factory work. The
pattern for daughters again differs only slightly: the frequency of
marriage for working-class women was not influenced by the occupational background of their families of origin.[65]

[64] van der Heijden, 'Gezin', p. 139.
[65] For full table see appendix 54.

Before we are able to reach a conclusion on the strength of inter-generational ties in the respective families of domestic weavers and factory workers, however, there is still the fate of parents to consider. What did the final stages of their households look like, and if their households were dissolved, in what ways did this come about? The above figures might mean that parents heading families engaged in industrial employment would more often end their lives without the assistance of at least one of their children. Of all couples who had ever had children born to them and whose households had com-menced before 1880, about one-third ended up on their own at the end of their household's history: 30.6% for domestic weavers and 33.8% for factory workers. These percentages correspond with those found for all working-class households of the second age-cohort of married couples.[66] Similar proportions of domestic weavers and fac-tory workers had married children present: 20.9% and 20.3%. The main difference between the two groups existed in the number of households in which parents had already died before the last of their children had left the household. In 16.1% of the households of domestic weavers, unmarried children were still present at the final break-up of the household without either of the parents. For house-holds headed by factory workers this was so for only 8.1% of all households created before 1880.

There was thus a slightly higher proportion of factory workers and their wives who lived to see all of their children leave the household. However, not all of these lone parents were actually being abandoned in the face of old age and death. In general, it may be said that as long as both parents were still alive they preferred to continue to head their own households; moves to other households were mainly con-templated by widows and widowers. All nine couples in the group of factory workers whose households had started before 1880 and who found themselves on their own, continued to head their own house-hold until the end of the period of observation; none of them was observed moving to other households.[67] Of the sixteen cases involv-ing a widowed parent only five were observed to be still heading their own household in 1920, but most of them had been on their own mainly for one to three years. Of the remaining eleven parents who were seen to move out, this was in one case as a result of death, seven

[66] For parents who had ever had children and who had at least one of these children still residing in town only 25.6% and 27.5% respectively lived without any children.

[67] For the group of domestic weavers there were only two cases available in which both parents were still alive and on their own at the end of their household's history, making comparison impossible.

decided to move to the household of a married child, two out-migrated and the last moved into one of the institutions for elderly people. A similar pattern existed in the households of domestic weavers: of fourteen widowed parents departing from the household six moved to a married child while three exited through death. It therefore seems fair to say that most of the ageing parents who came to reside on their own frequently decided to move into the household of one of their married children. The pattern appeared to be the same in both groups of households.

However, not all parents came to reside on their own in old age. Some parents chose or were forced to move out shortly before all of their children had left them. If that moment arrived, where did parents go, and could parents in both groups make an equal appeal for assistance to their married children? Table 7.4 presents data on the reasons for the departure of parents from the household. The table excludes those parents who were still heading their own households at the end of 1920, and were consequently not observed to depart at all, as well as those who died early. From table 7.4 it is clear that most parents of 60 and over resided in their households until death, and we again note that this was more frequent for men than for women, but it was also more frequent for domestic weavers than for factory workers. Most of the couples in the households of factory workers, in contrast to those in the domestic weaving economy, were forced to move out of their households. Factory workers, so to say, more often survived the end of the history of their own household. This is undoubtedly related to the fact that unmarried children departed from these households somewhat earlier. Moreover, the younger ages at which these factory workers had begun their family cycle will have increased the likelihood of the final 'empty-nest phase' occurring during their life time. In both groups, of those that actually decided to give up headship of the household, the largest proportion moved into households of married offspring. Some parents invited married children to come to live with them, after which the headship of the household was passed on to the next generation. This type of event is indicated in the table by the 'change head' category. This type of household continuity was more frequent for men than for women, and it was surprisingly also more frequent for factory workers than for domestic weavers. If anything, we would expect the family economy of the weavers, and their modest family property, to have generated more family continuity over generations rather than less in comparison with factory workers. However, in both groups household continuity between generations is a marginal phenom-

Table 7.4 *Type of departure from household of parents for domestic weavers and factory workers, those aged 60 and over*

Type of departure	Domestic weavers		Factory workers	
	Husbands	Wives	Husbands	Wives
death	72.6	64.3	61.1	54.6
change head	3.9	2.4	11.1	6.1
to household of child	11.8	23.8	19.4	24.2
to household of kin	—	4.8	2.8	—
to household of others	7.8	—	—	3.0
to institution	2.0	—	5.6	9.1
migration	2.0	4.8	—	3.0
N	51	42	36	33

enon; in general, parents continued heading their own households as long as possible, and if they could no longer sustain an independent household their first choice would be to move in with their married children.

In conclusion we may say that there were strong intergenerational ties between parents and children on the behavioural level in the factory workers' families, despite their involvement in industrial wage labour and despite the high levels of economic differentiation of these households. Children maintained strong connections to their parental households well into adulthood in both groups of households. At the moment at which children finally departed from the household, most of them were well into their twenties. In addition, the age at marriage did not appear to change at all as a consequence of the different types of labour in which the family was involved.

However, some noteworthy differences in relations between parents and children did occur between the two family economies. Daughters, and more especially sons, of fathers engaged in factory work left home for the first time somewhat earlier than did children in the domestic weaving economy. Children of factory workers were rather more mobile, migrating more often, while children of domestic weavers continued to live with parents in larger numbers, mostly until marriage, just as they were also more likely to remain unmarried. The families engaged in factory work had more children to take care of, so that perhaps they could afford to let more of their children leave, and at earlier ages. Alternatively, these parents may well have been forced to send more of their children out to contribute to the family budget away from the home. Whatever the precise motivation may have been for young people to move out of the parental household at early ages, it did increase chances of parents being left on their own in old age. This in turn led to a situation in which elderly parents in the group of factory workers more often arranged to move into the households of their married children.

7.5　Conclusion

Clearly, the factory bells did not toll for the disintegration of family life in late-nineteenth and early-twentieth-century Tilburg. Although industrialization and the processes which accompanied it may have worked to change some of the structural aspects of the family cycle, these changes in all probability only served to increase the incidence of extended households rather than stimulate a more 'modern' development towards individualism and household nuclearization. This development occurred, it must be stressed, despite the fact that industrialization had clearly altered the economic basis supporting the family economy of the industrial wage labourer. The factory workers' families in this study undoubtedly demonstrate that economic specialization, and the separation between work and family, did not immediately bring about the destruction of the bonds uniting parents and children, brothers and sisters. Not only in the domestic weaving economy, but also in the households of factory workers, family values continued to shape family patterns. Results confirm the high degree of continuity between the family economy and the family wage economy proposed by Tilly and Scott.

An investigation into the sources of income available to families revealed the fact that the households headed by factory workers, power-loom weavers apart, were characterized by an enormous amount of occupational discontinuity. None of these factory workers had sons employed in the same occupation; none of them could consequently have experienced a situation of working side by side with the generation succeeding them. None of these fathers, apparently, was in control of employment opportunities to the extent that employment could be secured in favour of their sons.

Occupational discontinuity is assumed to have a negative effect on family relations, reducing the ability of the family to find employment for relations, and thereby the attractiveness of kin relations and the willingness on the part of the individual to submit to family interests. In other words, economic differentiation is believed to dissolve family ties. But it did not. In fact, in the initial stages of the family cycle, when the household was still expanding through the regular addition of another new-born infant, extended family members were relatively common in the households of those engaged in industrial wage labour; more common than in either the households of domestic weavers or the households of working-class families in general.

In accordance with extension patterns for working-class households established in chapter 5, extension in the initial stages only came about through co-residence with widowed parents and unmarried siblings. This was the same for both domestic weavers and factory labourers. But why should extension of this type be more frequent in the households of the latter as opposed to the former? It is impossible to provide a conclusive answer here, but the following explanation seems plausible. Widowed parents and unmarried brothers and sisters would in general only appeal to their married children and siblings when they found it impossible to reside in their own households. If the differences in mobility and departure from the home of sons and daughters between the two groups were greater in the generation preceding the households studied here, it would have resulted in the relatively early dissolution of the paternal households of the factory workers themselves. As a consequence these factory workers would be more likely to be asked to provide a home for widowed parents and unmarried siblings on the move.

During the final stages of the family cycle, when the household gradually decreased in size, differences in extension patterns between the two samples became less pronounced. In both groups the level of extensions rose as married children came to co-reside with their elderly parents. For both groups it is assumed that similar factors were responsible for these extended family arrangements with married children: the old age of the parents, and assistance to children with mobility and housing problems. Extension of this type, however, was more typical of domestic weavers, in whose households this pattern was also visible at a much earlier stage as a result of more compact family cycles. As argued before, it would seem that the domestic weaving economy possessed a somewhat stronger pull on the families of married children as a result of their greater material assets. In this respect they clearly resembled other skilled workers and the middle classes who attracted equal proportions of co-resident married children in the decade following 1910. This supports the proposition that the depression in domestic weaving did not leave these parents deprived and destitute; they still had something to offer to their children.

In general, the domestic weaving economy seemed to exercise a somewhat stronger hold over their children. This was apparent in the late age at which sons, especially, were leaving the household as well as the higher proportions of sons still unmarried and still residing in the parental home. It seems likely that the domestic weaving economy could retain its children until later ages due to the continued ability of the father to provide employment opportunities within textiles, either at the mill or at home for the members of his family.[68] The question remains as to what extent these family patterns are related to differences in family property, in the sense that domestic weavers more often will have owned the family home and a patch of land.[69] By comparison, sons and daughters of factory workers were more mobile: they departed from home more often and at earlier ages. Combined with their higher marriage frequency this would appear to suggest that factory workers' children had acquired more and earlier autonomy. We should take care not to exaggerate this given the fact that their parents were not left alone any more than in the case of the domestic weavers. Admittedly, factory workers more often found themselves living on their own in the final stages of their life course and they more often saw the last of their children leave the household. However, the data indicate that many more of them as a result were eventually either taken into the households of their married children or arranged for the latter to come and live with them.

To conclude, economic specialization and differentiation in the nineteenth century did not foster a spirit of individualism as strongly as some theorists would have us believe. Theories stressing the disruptive effects on the family of the shift from home to the factory do not sufficiently recognize the continued importance of family relations for nineteenth-century working-class families. If indeed industrialization had diminished the importance of the father and the family economy for obtaining employment, so that children were forced to look elsewhere, this does not preclude the possibility that family relations could be beneficial or even crucial in many cases. Widowed parents could find domestic support in the families of their married children, brothers and sisters could find a place to live between jobs or as a substitute for their family of origin, and young married couples, unable to find a family home, could find at least a temporary shelter in the parental home. In short, family historians and sociologists should take care not to attach too great value to the impact of the loss of productive functions on nineteenth-century family life.

[68] Compare e.g. Wall, 'Work', p. 272, who indicates such patterns existed in Colyton, England.

[69] See also note 49 above.

Conclusion

In this study I have attempted to trace the impact of the process of industrialization on family life in nineteenth-century Tilburg. In the mid-nineteenth century the town still consisted of a group of small hamlets whose population for the greatest part lived off the returns of small-scale domestic production and some small-scale farming. The textile mills and smoking chimneys that were already scattered throughout the town's spacious landscape had not yet decisively affected the rural outlook of a large part of its population. By the beginning of the twentieth century, however, major changes had occurred. Domestic textile production had almost completely disappeared or was at best relegated to the margins of the family economy; industrial production had assumed its dominant place. Labour had been removed from the household and centralized in the mills. In 1910 the town had become the tenth most populous city of The Netherlands, accounting for the major share of the national production of woollen textiles. These were certainly big changes, and may have removed the structural forces underpinning the community's traditional family system.

In the analysis of the impact of these changes on the strength of kinship ties I was led by structuralist family theories stressing a necessary development towards a nuclear family system in industrial society. Industrialization, these theories claim, would not only lead to a dissolution of extended kinship relations; the nuclear family, being best adapted to the mobility demands of industrial society, would also be the socially superior family form when compared with more 'traditional' types such as the extended family. Unencumbered by restricting family ties the individualistic nuclear family would be best able to launch its members upwards on to higher places on the social scale. The removal of the central role of the family group in produc-

233

tion and the shift towards individual mobility in industrial society had created the nuclear family and weakened family ties in general, or so these theories claimed.

Basically, the structuralist perspective assumes that family behaviour and attitudes may be adapted easily and immediately to fit any new economic roles people have assumed. Recent social historical writings have suggested the incorrectness of such a direct causal relationship between economic structures, behaviour and attitudes. A strong emphasis on family values would not be shaken off instantly as though one were changing clothes, it is argued. Individuals perceive the structural changes surrounding them from the perspective of values they already hold and they continue to act according to these values. Patterns of behaviour arising in changing circumstances are then the result of individuals relying on old values to formulate answers to completely new problems. Of course, attitudes and values do change, they are not rigid entities, but the process of change is slow and creates complicated transitional patterns of behaviour. In the course of this process 'old' values may lead to a temporary intensification of 'traditional' behavioural patterns as a result of reactions to entirely new problems.

These competing perspectives on family behaviour in periods of structural change have informed the present study. Through an analysis of the family cycles of two age-cohorts of married couples I have attempted to measure the extent to which family ties were affected or relinquished. The strength of kinship bonds was first assessed by looking at the extent to which families were co-residing with their extended kin. In addition I looked at relations between parents and children; the readiness with which children abandoned their parents or their willingness to postpone independence for the sake of lending domestic support to elderly parents.

One may argue about the appropriateness of these indicators of the strength of kinship ties. After all, kinship does not stop at the front door. If families did not co-reside with ageing grandparents but preferred to live next door to them so that they could assist them in domestic matters they could hardly be accused of relinquishing family ties.[1] Unfortunately, the Tilburg population registers do not permit the study of the geographical propinquity of kin prior to 1910. On the other hand, if families did co-reside with their extended kin and continued to do so for whatever reason we must assume that the

---

[1] In twentieth-century British working-class families many young married couples did not want to live with parents but they preferred to live near them, see: Young and Willmott, *Family*, p. 20.

presence of kin in the home on a daily basis inevitably brought with it a strong involvement in family affairs. Kin co-residence remains the most unambiguous manifestation of family cohesion that the family historian is able to pursue and therefore best suited to fit my research purposes.

The issue of the relationship between parents and children appears to be more straightforward. If it is clear that despite increased opportunities for early independence, adolescents and most young adults did not abandon middle-aged and elderly parents, this can only mean that family values continued to be strong. However, it should also be stressed that this study can only offer insight into behavioural patterns, it cannot by definition lead to conclusions concerning the way these families actually felt about their kin. The fact that a grandmother was taken in as a co-residing relative does not necessarily indicate that she was welcomed and cared for as a much respected member of the household. Equally, the son who remained with his parents until they died may have done so as a result of a bargaining process rather than from a disinterested wish to take care of the elder generation. Nevertheless, I believe that kin co-residence and co-residential support of elderly parents by their children do express a continued adherence to the idea that kin should take care of each other, and as such it indicates a sense of duty and responsibility towards kin. Taken together I believe that these indicators are sufficiently reliable as a basis for an analysis of the strength of kinship ties.

The longitudinal perspective adopted in this study has proved of great importance. It has enabled us to outline the tremendous importance of kin relations in general and kin co-residence in particular in a coherent and systematic way. It has been crucial in establishing the great significance of kin co-residence for some social groups, and most notably in the lives of migrant families in nineteenth-century Tilburg. The results of this study indicate that statistics describing family structure at isolated points in time, even those which include the age of the household head, may be totally inadequate as measures of certain household structures. Moreover, the longitudinal perspective allows more precise consideration of the mechanisms bringing about specific patterns of kin co-residence because it is possible to determine who moved in with whom, in what way, and at what time, and what the other structural characteristics of the household looked like. Moreover, the dynamic approach has enabled me to reveal the strong bonds between parents and children over the parental life course. It was possible to describe in detail the process by which children broke away from home and to trace important discontinuities in the lives of parents. Finally, the population registers not only facilitated a rigorous and consistent implementation of the principle that the family should be considered as a process; they also allowed us to collect additional socio-economic information on the families concerned. Families could therefore be located more precisely in the local social hierarchy.

How strong then were kinship ties in Tilburg, and to what extent were they affected by the process of transformation of this community? Did individualism rise to destroy cohesive family bonds? Quite the contrary, the results of this study indicate that the experience of nineteenth-century family life in Tilburg was totally at odds with the themes of individualism and the decline of family cohesion. Kinship ties remained of considerable importance to families and individuals in the industrializing context. My conclusion, therefore, is that it is incorrect to assume an immediate and imperative causal relationship between industrialization in its emerging stages and the weakening of family relations. Extended kin were not increasingly excluded from the inner circle of the family, and quite clearly the bonds between parents and children were not severely weakened to the detriment of the older generation.

Of course, family patterns did change, under the influence of concomitant processes such as a rise in life expectancy, the community's connection to larger networks of geographical mobility, and the increasing pressures on the housing market. However, the exigencies created by these processes in fact tended to promote more complex or so-called traditional family patterns rather than the simple pattern of the nuclear family. Individuals reacted to the problems created by these changes in such a way that would seem to indicate continued adherence to family commitments and obligations. My conclusion then is that family bonds retained a considerable durability and were used actively and in an overall rational way in an attempt to overcome some of the problems facing nineteenth-century families. Moreover, extended family arrangements, rather than being disrupted, appeared to have been promoted in some instances by the social and geographic mobility engendered by industrial society. I shall now elaborate more specifically on the general conclusion offered here and relate its elements to some of the more important results of this study. In addition, I will attempt to provide an explanation for the continuities and discontinuities that were found.

First of all, the analysis of family structure over time, of which the results were presented in chapter 4, made clear that kin co-residence over the history of the household did not become less frequent between 1849 and 1920. Many families did receive an extended kin member at some point along their developmental cycle. During the first ten or twenty years of this cycle the extended kin who were present in these Tilburg families consisted of the nearest relatives of the couple, widowed parents and unmarried brothers and sisters. The latter half of the family cycle saw the entry of married children and grandchildren. The frequency with which families co-resided with kin rose significantly between the two cohorts that were analysed. In the second cohort the number of families that had ever received extended kin into their homes increased to such an extent that a large majority, at least once, went through a phase of extended family living. This rise in kin co-residence was caused by a growing number of parents receiving married children into their homes.

The extended family arrangements that arose through the addition to the household of widowed parents and unmarried siblings most likely served to offer domestic support to those who had lost their own families. It appears implausible to argue that these arrangements came about in order to enable the mother to work for wages outside the home, nor did these extended kin appear to be added to the household to redress the balance between the number of producers and consumers. These may have been advantages included in the bargain for the receiving family, but they did not constitute the primary cause in bringing them about. Between the two cohorts of families, no differences were detected in this regard.

The mechanisms underlying the entrance of married children in the later stages of the family cycle, however, did change. In the earlier cohort, married children primarily entered their parental household after the death of one of their parents, quite clearly to assist the remaining parent in his or her final years. Married children in the second cohort also came to co-reside with their parents for their own reasons. Housing at the time was in short supply, while in addition some of these children were taking part in migratory flows within regional, national, also even international networks. The parental household was used by these married children as a place from which to venture out into the world, a safe place to retreat to, or as a temporary accommodation until an appropriate family dwelling had been acquired. Thus, specific local or regional historical circumstances were responsible for the rise in the number of extended families occurring in the households of the second cohort of married couples.

Other processes, quite surpassing the local level, were also underway. Parents in the second cohort generally lived longer, which increased their chances of experiencing the entry of married offspring into their household. However, their longer life expectancy also had the effect that more parents might eventually end up on their own, not only without the assistance of a spouse, but also without co-resident children. For many parents this would mark the time when they moved into the households of their married children. The experience of having to give up independent living and headship of the household constituted a break in the historical patterning of the parental life course; the majority of the parents in the previous cohort died before their co-residential situation would have forced them to give up their independent position.

The fact that these elderly parents eventually ended up living alone at the beginning of the twentieth century was not the result of children moving out of their households at earlier ages. The children of the second cohort of married couples did indeed start leaving home earlier, but many returned in order to marry or leave permanently at much the same age as had previous generations of children. The children of the second cohort continued to meet familial obligations. This was demonstrated in one way by the fact that they did not marry at younger ages and thereby shift their financial support away from parents, although this had definitely become feasible economically for the younger birth-cohorts. Moreover, we have also seen that when necessary they took parents into their homes. Clearly, elderly, widowed parents were rarely abandoned.

Thus the general direction of family change in this emerging industrial community did not at all point towards the loss of family cohesion and the drifting apart of family members. This conclusion applies *a fortiori* to the Tilburg middle classes who were in all respects the champions of family life. A large majority of the Tilburg middle classes did at one time or another co-reside with their kin; of all social groups they had the highest likelihood of co-residence with kin in both the initial and the final stages of the family cycle. However, the linchpin of middle-class family life was formed by a remarkably strong connection between parents and children. Middle-class parents were those most able to postpone the timing of departure of their children from the household and to delay the anxieties of solitary old age. Daughters in particular were persuaded to remain single and co-reside with their families until quite advanced ages.

Some of the results for both the unskilled labourers and the local elite seemed to indicate that families on either end of the social scale were surrounded by considerably less-tight-knit family networks. For the elite, however, this was only a matter of outward appearances, they were simply better able to live up to the cultural norm of simple family households. Fewer upper-class families co-resided with extended kin, but the type of kin found in these households indicated that upper-class families recognized and felt responsibility to a far wider circle of kinship than did other social groups. Their material assets had the further effect that they could exercise a considerable influence over the timing of marriage and departure from home of their children.

It is particularly significant that in the first cohort of married couples all upper-class parents still had single children at home at the end of their family cycle. This enabled them to avoid having to move into the households of their married children, and explains the relative absence of co-residing grandparents in the families of the elite. The upper classes, however, could not totally escape developments which increasingly stimulated the occurrence of the empty-nest phase at the end of the history of the household. But when solitary old age did arrive for upper-class parents in the second cohort, they were still less likely than parents from other social classes to move in with their married children. Instead they preferred to continue living on their own or to ask married children to come and live with them. This indicates that elderly parents generally valued domestic autonomy but that the lack of resources forced some working and middle-class parents eventually to sacrifice their independent position in exchange for domestic support.

These results confirm earlier suggestions by those scholars who assume a positive relationship between social class and family cohesion, with the latter increasing with a family's position in society. To this I should add the crucial remark that it was precisely the greater cohesiveness of family relations at the top of the social hierarchy, in addition to their greater resources, that enabled families to avoid frequent occurrences of extended family living arrangements. By contrast, the skilled labouring and middle classes due to their lesser financial resources were more dependent upon kin, for instance, in old age or in pursuit of employment, but their material assets were still adequate enough to be able to attract kin for the purpose of domestic support.

The fact that extended families in nineteenth-century Tilburg did not arise only amongst those occupying a marginal economic position would seem to discredit Parsonian theory and its proposition of the social superiority of the nuclear family in industrial society. However, the functionalist position was further and much more seriously undermined by the finding that families who actually co-resided with kin were not at all hampered in their efforts to improve their position within the social hierarchy. Various measurements of social mobility indicated that there was no ground at all for the Parsonian proposition of a structural fit between the nuclear family and society during the initial phases of the process of industrialization. Neither fathers nor sons from nuclear families showed themselves better able to operate successfully in industrial society.

The analysis of migrant families in Tilburg further revealed that social success, or its promise, might in some cases only serve to attract co-residing kin. Migrant families who had been living with extended kin at some time during the first twenty years of their family cycle experienced high rates of social mobility. They proved to be extremely successful in life. For native families this effect was totally absent. I suggested that, in contrast to kin who were taking the far less drastic step of moving in with locally available related households, kin who in addition had to change their social environment were more inclined to pick upon their more promising relatives. This is obvious if we further assume that most of the relatives residing in migrant households had migrated in order to try to improve their situation. Migrant families principally provided accommodation and assistance for young migrating brothers and elderly widowed grandmothers. The brothers were most likely to have been searching for more favourable employment opportunities. In such a situation it is surely logical to take into account the economic position of the relative who will provide aid and support. Quite likely the co-residing grandmother would act along similar lines except that her motivation was directed towards a well-cared-for old age.

The migrant families in this study effectively undermined the functionalist idea of the disruptive effects of geographical mobility on extended kin relations. Compared with native families many more migrant couples took in their parents and siblings, but it required a longitudinal perspective to discover this relationship. Cross-sectional analysis is clearly most inadequate when we are trying to capture patterns of the fastest changing and most dynamic families within a certain population. These migrants also indicated that it would be a mistake to reject the association between what is usually considered to be the more dynamic urban scene and extended family contacts and living arrangements. Extended family households were not pre-eminently found among rural migrants, of whom perhaps a still strong normative orientation on extended family relations might be expected. On the contrary, a more frequent exchange of co-residing relatives between urban areas appeared to be in operation than between rural–urban areas. The urban milieu may perhaps also have promoted, through having stimulated greater geographical mobility, the formation of extended family households as kinship constituted one of the major support mechanisms for nineteenth-century migration.

Family cohesion among the Tilburg working classes was rather less in evidence on the behavioural level when compared with that in the middle-class family. This may be attributed, as is suggested by many scholars, to the fact that, among the middle classes, work and the family still overlapped in the form of the artisan's workshop or the small-scale commercial enterprise. The significance of this overlap within the family economy for the working classes was analysed in this study by a comparative examination of the households of factory workers and domestic weavers. Domestic weavers' families were generally not only much less diversified in their sources of income in comparison with factory workers, but were also characterized by having a productive unit as the core of their family economy.

However, despite the occupational discontinuity, the probable absence of family property and the greater specialization of the factory worker's family, differences between the two groups of households were only minimal. The departure rate of children and their marital patterns did not exhibit any marked dissimilarity. Yet, two diverging patterns of behaviour could be detected between the two groups. First of all, the factory worker's household was characterized by a higher level of extensions in its initial stages while, secondly, the domestic weaving economy experienced a larger number of co-residential arrangements involving married children in the later stages of the household. This, however, was quite similar to the pattern found among skilled workers in general. These married children were entering the households of domestic weavers at the time of the housing shortages of 1910–20. Despite the total decline of the domestic weaving economy in this period the parental household of the ageing domestic weaver still had something to offer to the younger generation: a family home. I suggested that domestic weavers and their wives more often experienced the entry of a married child in this period because they had more and better accommodation to offer in their homes. The domestic weavers often occupied and owned the more spacious homes situated on the outskirts of town.

The two different patterns described above balanced each other out; considered along the entire family cycle kin co-residence was as frequent in the households of factory workers as in the households of domestic weavers. It would thus seem that the greater specialization of the family, the loss of economic functions and the absence of real property did not create greatly diverging family patterns among the Tilburg working classes, at least not to the extent that it is justified to speak of the loss of family bonds. The factory workers and their children demonstrate that family behaviour is not merely and passively formed as a response to changing economic conditions. The different economic basis of the factory worker's household did not lead to a disintegration of family life, basic family values informed the behaviour of the members of the factory worker's family just as much as it did in the case of the domestic weavers.

If continuity can be seen as the prevailing theme of this study, what was its source? Was it a manifestation of inertia as a result of the partiality of the structural changes of the local economy? Why did developments not lead to a weakening of kinship ties during the last four decades of the period under study? Why did working-class sons and daughters of the second cohort remain with their families for so long? They could have married and thereby achieved individual autonomy at earlier ages than before. And what made them after marriage take in and provide services to elderly parents and unmarried siblings? The same questions may apply to the middle-class families in the second cohort, who were exercising an extremely strong hold over their daughters and were frequently co-residing with relatives. Moreover, what provided the cohesion in the families of the factory workers? How could strong family relations and values survive in this community in the face of structural changes in its economy? In other words, what produced the time lag in family change? Or is family change by definition slower than social structural change, irrespective of the context, so that a time lag will always occur?

In his study of life-course patterns of women in nineteenth-century Verviers, George Alter concluded that the bond between parents and children remained strong because parents 'maintained a moral authority rooted in culture and supported by the urban community'.[2] However, without reducing family relations to purely economic relations of exchange, it is clear that economic factors can have a considerable effect on the family, affecting its bargaining power and attractiveness to children and extra-nuclear kin. Indeed the strength of family bonds increased with the family's resources; this was so both in Tilburg and in Verviers where elite daughters generally remained at home much longer than other girls. We might therefore

---

[2] Alter, *Family*, p. 202.

also expect some influence on family patterns when economic processes started to remove the structural factors underpinning familial interdependency.

Several factors might be put forward as potentially having retarded the undermining effect of the industrializing context on family patterns in nineteenth-century Tilburg. First of all, the town retained a somewhat isolated position until the end of the nineteenth century despite its connection to the railway network in the 1860s. The influence of the larger industrial centres in the west of the Netherlands or the Ruhr area in Germany were filtered, as it were, by the towns on either side of Tilburg. To the north it was closed off by the natural boundaries of important waterways while to the south the Belgian border provided a social and economic discontinuity. This geographically marginal position also expressed itself in the marked homogeneity of the community even at the beginning of the twentieth century. The overwhelming majority of the Tilburg population had been born and raised within the city. The absence of continuous and substantial flows of migrants left untouched the social fabric of the community with its tight-knit network of highly intertwined neighbourhood and family relations and the values and attitudes on which people based their lives.

In these circumstances the community may still have been able to enforce observance of family obligations which, and this is important to realize, were clearly still of interest to most people and in particular to parents and elderly persons in general.[3] In addition, the influence of the clergy in this homogeneous Catholic community may have provided a great deal of continuity in family patterns irrespective of whether they were propagating family obligations explicitly. Recent research has already outlined the role of Catholicism in retarding the acceptance of modern patterns of fertility restriction.[4] It is certainly clear that the clergy did not shy away from far-reaching interference with private and family affairs wherever this was deemed necessary and that they could initiate sanctions against those who did not abide by still commonly accepted rules of family and morality. Individuals grossly neglecting certain duties to parents and siblings may have found their reputation seriously damaged within this tight-knit community and this could affect their opportunities for favourable employment and various types of community assistance.

[3] Similar factors were indicated by Michael Anderson as helping maintain strong commitments to family obligations in Ireland and the countryside of Lancashire. See: *Family structure*, pp. 86–90.
[4] Engelen, *Fertiliteit*.

Other elements also specific to the community's historical development may have played a considerable role in the continuation of
parental and familial authority during the community's transition to
modern industrial society. Even at the turn of the century, the town
had only recently succeeded in definitely shaking off its rural past
based on small-scale domestic production. Until the final decade of
the nineteenth century traditional forms of textile production continued to exist side by side with centralized mechanical production.
Many families in the labouring and lower middle classes may have
preserved from this recent past a somewhat rural and propertied
outlook. They may have owned a small plot of land, perhaps a family
home, and have been involved in some marginal domestic production and petty commerce. It seems highly likely that even the factory
workers' households I examined managed to preserve some of these
characteristics. A thorough and early proletarianization of the Tilburg
working and middle classes had evidently not been one of the
ingredients of nineteenth-century development. In addition, most
married women, because they were not allowed to enter the mill,
continued to be engaged in household-based production, most likely
together with the family's younger children. However weak the element of continuity, and however modest its material basis may have
been, it can still have afforded a sense of continued obligation to the
family economy of parents and children in this sheltered community.
Together these factors may successfully have counteracted the disruptive forces of the factory bells.

Following this line of reasoning, it might be argued that these
special characteristics disqualify Tilburg as a suitable case to examine
the Parsonian perspective on the relationship between industrialization and the family. Indeed, most historical research in this particular
field of family history has focused on places that conform more
closely to the classical idea of what a nineteenth-century industrial
city was like: characterized by dramatic and all-pervading change as a
result of large-scale industrialization, proletarianization and high
rates of population turnover. However, this type of classical
industrial development may now safely be considered as the exception in historical reality. The great mass of the population in the
nineteenth century, even if we only consider the urban population,
experienced social and economic change of a much more gradual and
limited nature. Tilburg is such a case. Even though the specific
characteristics producing continuity may be unique to this particular
town, the principle of continuity within change is not. I believe it is
there that we have to study theories of family change. Consequently,

I believe the results of this study may be generalized to cover large parts of the north-western European family experience.

Finally, I think it is important to stress that processes of industrialization, whatever their scale or impact, did not take place in a void. In the case of Tilburg we should rather think of it as slowly and unevenly transforming a society which attached great value to family bonds and obligations. This strong family orientation had been shaped in a preindustrial past in which family members worked together in collective dependency in the family economy. This sense of the importance of family solidarity continued to shape the lives of the families studied here. Industrialization in its early stages did not destroy these values, rather people made use of them in various ways to address circumstances viewed as problematic or otherwise unacceptable.

Many of the considerations and conclusions presented above and in other parts of the book do not exceed the level of what I regard as the most likely explanation for the patterns that were established. Their value and explanatory power must be assessed through comparative analysis with other Dutch and west-European nineteenth-century communities. It would be of particular interest for Dutch family history to compare the family patterns established in this Brabantine urban community with similar communities in the north or west of the country. This would enable us first of all to outline the extent of the regional variation in household and family patterns commonly believed to have continued well into the twentieth century. Comparative analysis might perhaps reveal that urban family patterns did not differ as much as is sometimes assumed. Alternatively, it might reveal that in different communities people were formulating different answers to similar problems, but which were all similarly products of a large degree of continuity between generations. Further research along this line should also concentrate on the role of property and home ownership in determining family dynamics and the link between cohorts among the working classes in the urban setting.

In addition, systematic comparative analysis would increase our understanding of the factors which direct or retard changes in the behaviour of individuals and families. The range of conclusions resulting from this type of research would far exceed the immediate boundaries of family history and could be brought to bear upon other aspects of human behaviour, undergoing or resisting processes of change. Comparative analysis, then, in my view would have to be carried out on a limited number of communities differing in strategic respects from the one studied here: undergoing more thorough processes of proletarianization, faced by larger levels of population turnover and less isolated from 'foreign' influence. This study has indicated, however, that it is imperative that such attempts at comparison, whenever possible, adopt a longitudinal perspective on individuals and families.

Finally, I would like to remark that quantitative family studies such as the present one are all limited to the extent that they can only offer conclusions on behavioural levels without passing judgement on the quality of family relations or the way people themselves felt about them. These limitations can only be surpassed in qualitative research on family relations. Quantitative and qualitative family research should therefore be viewed as being complementary rather than mutually exclusive. However, quantitative research into the family finds its attractiveness and justification in its ability to encompass all social groups within society and to present a behavioural framework within which more qualitative manifestations and expressions of family and kinship may be assessed.

Appendices

Appendix 1 *Certainty of dates of events in the population register in percentage of all events* [a]

Samples	Date certain	Day uncertain	Year uncertain	N
1840–1890 cohort	83.5	—	16.5	5753
1880–1920 cohort	94.2	—	5.9	9547
domestic weavers	94.7	—	5.3	2224
factory workers	94.3	—	5.7	2441

[a] Events: migratory moves, births, deaths and marriages.

Appendix 2 *Unregistered births in the population registers in the two samples of domestic weavers and factory workers*

Population register	Registered births	Unregistered births
1849–1859	11	—
1860–1869	72	7
1870–1879	446	1
1880–1889	498	1
1890–1899	219	—

Appendix 3 *Example of data-entry files for longitudinal household data*

Static file

Hhid	Ppid	Famname	Christian name	Yrbirth	Plcbirth	Fid	Mid
267	3125	driessen	martinus bern	18450214	deventer	0	0
267	3126	oostendorp	maria	18481124	deventer	0	0
267	3127	driessen	gerardus bern	18730519	tiburg	3125	3126
267	3128	driessen	theodorus herm	18760614	tilburg	3125	3126
267	3129	driessen	wilhelmus mart	18781111	tilburg	3125	3126
267	3130	driessen	johannes mart	18810927	tilburg	3125	3126
267	3131	driessen	johanna ma	18831028	tilburg	3125	3126
267	3132	driessen	hermanus mart	18850410	tilburg	3125	3126
267	3133	driessen	antonia ma	18860928	tilburg	3125	3126
267	3134	driessen	gerarda joh	18880620	tilburg	3125	3126
267	4267	driessen	dina sus	19000408	tilburg	3125	3126
267	4530	v lieshout	henricus jos lamb	18870917	tilburg	0	0
267	4531	v lieshout	maximinus mart ma	19170720	tilburg	4530	3131
267	4532	v lieshout	maria cath ant	19180809	tilburg	4530	3131
267	4533	v lieshout	catharina jos ma	19191004	tilburg	4530	3131

Dynamic file

Hhid	Ppid	Type	Date	Comment
267	3131	demo	18831028	entry birth
267	3131	rel	18831028	daughter
267	3131	occup	19000000	seamstress
267	3131	demo	19120705	exit migr helmond
267	3131	demo	19130514	entry migr helmond
267	3131	demo	19160912	marriage in
267	3131	rel	19160912	daughter m
267	3131	spouse	19160912	4530
267	3131	demo	19201231	exit observation

Appendix 4

Computer-based storage of household histories

For the purposes of this study a methodology was developed which enables computer-based storage and processing of population register data while using the principle of 'direct-entry'.[1] This concept refers to the fact that data are fed directly from the source into a micro-computer without any intermediate processing by hand. This enables the historian to visit the archives, carrying a portable pc. The methodology is of course highly influenced by the specific questions informing this project, however, with slight adaptations the basic principles may be applied successfully in other longitudinal studies based on the same source.[2]

When storing data from continuous population registers one encounters a number of methodological problems. First of all there are the various, intertwining analytical levels in the register. The register not only divides the entire population into households, one page per household, but within each household it also lists a collection of separately registered individuals. Naturally, both units have to be retained in computer files as we will want to ask questions on both the level of the household and the individual. Then we must also take into consideration that events at the level of one individual may affect the entire household as well as other individuals present in the household. The death of one person for instance changes the marital status of a possible partner, while it also has a certain influence on the structure of the household. Or, in a much more complex situation, when the parents die, an important change occurs in the status of co-

---

[1] A more detailed explanation of the computer methodology used in this research is found in: Janssens, 'Een "direct-entry" methodology' and also in: Janssens, 'Managing longitudinal historical data'.

[2] It in fact has already been used by two other researchers who both focused on the co-residential experience of elderly people, see Bulder, *Household structures* and Gordon, *The bevolkingsregisters*.

resident married and single children who may still be present in the household, next to other relatives of the original heads. This complex, interrelated jumble of events and relationships should ideally have to be kept intact in the database in all its complexity.

The element of time constitutes the most important complicating factor in the population registers. Through time the household consists of continually changing combinations of individuals. Households do not all follow the same course or display the same number of structural changes. That is why the history of one household may amount to a mass of information whereas the history of another household is told in only one or two lines. At the level of the individual a similar problem occurs. In the registers the arrivals and departures of each individual are recorded as well as his movement through various households. With every move we gather a mass of ever changing personal information on the individual concerned, mostly regarding occupation and marital status. This results in data sets which are different in size as well as character for each individual. While one person enters a household at birth in order to exit after a short while through death, another person can be observed for a long period of time and hence add an enormous amount of information to the system. One person may have five different entries concerning his occupation and no information on marital status, for a second person on the other hand a marriage is recorded twice but no information is available on occupation. Population registers create problems not so much by a shortage of historical data but rather more by an irregular surplus of information.

In order to cope with these problems I have made use of an event-based storage of information at the level of the individual.[3] The core of the system was formed by two separate data-entry files which enabled a distinction to be made between two different types of information offered by the population register. On the one hand there is fixed information which only needs to be entered once, and on the other hand, variable information whose size cannot be properly established beforehand. The data are entered from the perspective of the individual, giving each household and each individual a unique identification number.[4]

The first file contains all fixed, or in other words, all static information on household members: household and person identification codes, date and place of birth, and the person codes of both parents.

[3] The dBase III database management programme was used for data-entry.
[4] This household and person code is decided upon by the order in which they appear in the database.

All persons who at any given time were present in the household are listed once in this static file. The second, dynamic file can best be described as an 'event file', everything that happened to a person in the course of the life cycle of the household is entered here. These can be real events, such as a person's death or birth, but also pseudo-events, for example becoming a widow, or changes in the relationship to the head. The file therefore contains information as to the type of event which is recorded.

The most important type of event in the dynamic file records a person's entrance into and departure from the household. These so-called demo-events also contain a reference as to the cause of the entry or exit concerned, for example 'exit marriage' indicates that the person is leaving the household on the occasion of his or her marriage. Another important event indicates the person's relationship to the head, which of course may change over time as well. Apart from such categories as servants and lodgers, all members of the household are recorded in terms of the genealogical relationship to the male household head. Remaining event types relate to a person's marital status, the address of the household,[5] a person's occupation, and to the person code of spouses. This latter type of event may be used to connect spouses residing in the household other than the head and his wife.[6] All events are recorded under reference of the household and person code, and of course the date at which the event occurred. For an illustration of the two data-entry files see appendix 3.

With the use of the household and person codes both files could be linked to bring together all the information pertaining to one individual or one household. Linkages during the data-entry stage were necessary in order to work through successive population registers[7] and to process other sources such as the municipal income tax and the military enrollment registers. Information on incomes and occupation from these sources was stored in separate files together with the appropriate household and person codes.

As was indicated earlier a number of considerations necessitated

---

[5] Of course, this is not really individually related information. However, in order to avoid unnecessary complications the address of the entire household is recorded under registration of the head's individual and household codes.

[6] Mostly used for co-residing married children and their spouses.

[7] The use of sample groups in a study of this scope entails by definition, and most certainly in a town of moderate size such as Tilburg, that linkage between different registers is most easily done by hand, by means of the indexes on the population register. Automatic record linkage makes data storage even more complex and requires more elaborate programming. Therefore no facilities were created for automatic record linkage in this methodology.

registration of various members of the family after their exit from the parental household, in so far as they remained living in Tilburg. First of all, the research into the intergenerational mobility of sons required the registration of all of the sons' addresses. The addresses were needed to access the municipal tax registers. Secondly, registering children outside the conjugal unit keeps us informed about the locally available kinship system of the parents. Finally, in this way it is possible to overcome the constraints on the registration of parents as set by the definition of the household. It is of course always possible to incorporate these other, new households (of departing children and parents) into the research. This, however, would expand the research group enormously, which is the reason why a limited type of registration was chosen. As soon as a child or a parent left the household, the household code was dropped. From that moment onwards, registration would take place under household code O, and would only be linked to the person code. In this way all addresses were recorded together with the type of household in which he or she was living.

After all the data had been entered a number of programs were run to check the files on missing data and internal logic. The data-entry files were then transferred onto a mainframe to be processed and analysed by means of programs written in SAS.

Appendix 5 *Household structure in 1849 and 1880: all married couples and research cohorts*

Age group	Nuclear families	Extended families
All married couples in 1849		
<30	131 – 92.9	10 – 7.1
30–35	447 – 87.0	67 – 13.0
>35	1235 – 90.9	124 – 9.1
All	1813 – 90.0	201 – 10.0
All married couples in 1880		
<30	363 – 91.4	34 – 8.6
30–35	971 – 88.7	124 – 11.3
>35	2629 – 90.7	269 – 9.3
All	3963 – 90.3	427 – 9.7
Research cohorts in 1849 and 1880a structure	1849	1880
nuclear	310 – 85.9	661 – 88.5
extended	51 – 14.1	86 – 11.5

[a] Consisting of households headed by 30–35-year-old married couples of either migrant or native origin only.

Appendix 6 *Number of households present for specific family cycle years for two age-cohorts of married couples*

Cycle year	Total	Extended
Cohort 1849–1890		
1	361	51
11	332	35
21	313	35
31	266	30
41	200	29
Cohort 1880–1920 (corrected sample)		
1	343	49
11	330	34
21	320	29
31	256	32
41	164	38

Appendix 7 *Relationship of co-resident kin to head of household by decade*
for two age-cohorts of married couples

Relation	Decade 1	Decade 2	Decade 3	Decade 4
Cohort 1849–1890				
parents	34.2	21.1	4.7	0.0
siblings	56.6	34.2	11.1	2.0
married children	0.0	5.3	28.6	25.5
grandchildren	0.0	7.9	30.2	62.2
uncles/aunts	4.0	5.3	0.0	0.0
cousins	1.3	2.6	7.9	4.1
other kin	4.0	23.7	17.5	6.1
N	76	38	63	98
Cohort 1880–1920				
parents	38.9	7.8	0.0	0.4
siblings	45.1	27.5	3.7	1.9
married children	0.0	5.9	34.6	39.4
grandchildren	0.0	11.8	48.2	55.4
uncles/aunts	3.4	3.9	2.5	0.0
cousins	4.6	2.0	2.5	0.7
other kin	8.0	41.2	8.6	2.2
N	175	51	81	269

Appendix 8 *Proportion of female co-resident kin*
members by type of kin for two age-cohorts of married
couples

Type of kin	1849–1890	1880–1920
parents	56.8	68.5
siblings	36.9	43.6
married children	40.0	51.1
grandchildren	47.0	53.1
uncles/aunts	60.0	70.0
cousins	54.6	38.5
other kin	51.7	50.0
total	45.8	52.6
N	275	576

Appendix 9 *Marital status of co-resident ever-married children at time of entry for two age-cohorts of married couples*

Marital status	1849–1890		1880–1920	
	Sons	Daughters	Sons	Daughters
married	66.7	92.9	81.7	98.8
widowed	33.3	7.1	15.9	1.3
divorced	—	—	2.4	—
N	18	28	82	80

Appendix 10 *Age at first departure from parental household for offspring of two age-cohorts of married couples*

Age group	1849–1890		1880–1920	
	Sons	Daughters	Sons	Daughters
<–9 year-old	2.7	4.2	5.0	3.6
10–14 year-old	6.1	4.3	11.6	11.9
15–19 year-old	8.5	11.5	17.5	22.8
20–24 year-old	29.2	34.2	28.9	32.7
25–29 year-old	40.6	31.7	27.7	21.7
30–34 year-old	9.7	10.6	7.2	6.2
35–39 year-old	2.9	2.7	1.7	0.9
40–> year-old	0.3	0.9	0.4	0.2
mean age	24.1	23.5	21.6	21.0
median	25	24	22	21
N	626	556	946	872

Appendix 11 *Frequency of departures from parental household for offspring of two age-cohorts of married couples*

Frequency	1849–1890		1880–1920	
	Sons	Daughters	Sons	Daughters
1	83.4	90.3	65.4	70.0
2	15.2	9.2	23.0	21.6
3	1.1	0.5	7.5	6.0
4	0.3	—	2.2	1.5
5	—	—	0.9	0.7
6	—	—	0.6	0.1
7	—	—	0.2	0.2
8	—	—	0.1	—
N	626	556	948	872

Appendix 12.   Mean number of children present in the household by family cycle year for two age-cohorts of married couples (corrected sample for 1880–1920 cohort)

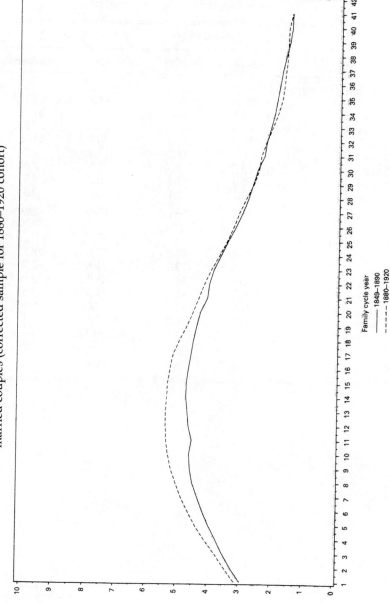

Family cycle year
——— 1849–1890
– – – 1880–1920

Appendix 13 *Proportion of sons and daughters still at home by age group for two age-cohorts of married couples*

Age group	1849–1890		1880–1920	
	Sons	Daughters	Sons	Daughters
Before first departure				
15 year-old	78.9	77.9	68.8	69.7
20 year-old	71.7	68.4	54.7	51.8
25 year-old	45.9	42.1	31.4	27.8
30 year-old	17.5	20.5	10.1	11.9
35 year-old	8.6	11.2	3.9	4.7
40 year-old	3.7	5.0	1.5	2.6
45 year-old	1.0	1.2	0.3	0.7
50 year-old	0.1	0.1	0.0	0.0
N	954	955	1349	1269
Before final departure				
15 year-old	84.0	81.3	77.8	78.7
20 year-old	78.6	73.9	71.6	67.7
25 year-old	55.6	46.6	48.4	42.0
30 year-old	24.1	23.2	19.5	21.3
35 year-old	12.0	12.7	9.0	9.5
40 year-old	5.2	6.0	3.4	5.1
45 year-old	1.4	1.3	0.9	1.1
50 year-old	0.3	0.1	0.0	0.0
N	954	955	1349	1269

Appendix 14 *Median age at first marriage by birth-cohort for offspring of two age-cohorts of married couples*

Birth cohort	1849–1890		1880–1920	
	Age	N	Age	N
Sons				
1830–1839	27	35	—	—
1840–1849	26	244	—	—
1850–1859	26	204	—	—
1860–1869	25	28	28	15
1870–1879	—	—	26	340
1880–1889	—	—	26	314
1890–1899	—	—	26	31
All	26	511	26	700
Daughters				
1830–1839	25	21	—	—
1840–1849	26	222	—	—
1850–1859	25	206	—	—
1860–1869	24	30	26	20
1870–1879	—	—	25	279
1880–1889	—	—	26	290
1890–1899	—	—	25	36
All	25	479	25	625

Appendix 15 *Proportion unmarried by age group for offspring of two age-cohorts of married couples*

	1849–1890		1880–1920	
Age	%	N	%	N
Sons				
19 year-old	99.9	784	99.6	1028
24 year-old	80.9	723	79.3	943
29 year-old	39.2	635	38.9	821
34 year-old	25.1	503	21.0	661
39 year-old	15.1	345	13.9	438
44 year-old	10.9	173	9.8	205
49 year-old	6.7	45	8.3	36
54 year-old	0.0	5	0.0	2
59> year-old	—	—	—	—
Daughters				
19 year-old	98.8	765	98.1	968
24 year-old	72.6	693	71.1	866
29 year-old	40.8	588	38.4	745
34 year-old	27.8	472	22.8	566
39 year-old	20.3	306	19.5	379
44 year-old	16.0	125	13.0	161
49 year-old	9.7	31	0.0	29
54 year-old	0.0	2	0.0	2
59> year-old	—	—	—	—

Appendix 16

Social stratification: sources and methods

For the social stratification of household heads and their sons we made use of two different sources: the municipal income tax registers, the so-called *kohieren van de hoofdelijke omslag*, and the military enrollment registers, the *militieregisters*. The municipal income tax (*hoofdelijke omslag*) was established in 1851 as a follow-up to its predecessor, the *personele belasting*, both being used by the municipal authorities to meet local budgets.[1] In Tilburg registers were available for our entire research period. The registers were drawn up on a yearly basis, listing all male or female household heads residing in the community by neighbourhood and address, specifying occupation and yearly income. Income was, unfortunately, left unmentioned if it did not exceed the tax-free minimum. In 1865 the tax allowance was f1.175, rising to f1.400 in 1874, f1.500 in 1898 and f1.800 in 1917. Apart from the household head, co-residing adult relatives were frequently listed as well, as they were considered to be providing for their own upkeep. Taxation was based on presumed incomes resulting from rents, interest on capital, occupation or any other source. The municipal regulations stated that incomes were estimated, but as in most other communities it remains unclear how this was done. If estimating the household's income proved difficult, its external circumstances and consumption would be taken into account. After initial recording, the registers were available for inspection by the public in the town hall and complaints could be lodged in case of disagreement concerning the estimated income. This was frequently done, leading to many upward as well as downward corrections in the registers.

The tax registers are generally believed to yield information on occupation which is reasonably reliable. The frequent corrections con-

[1] For further information see the first issue in the series of source commentaries: Klep, Lansink and van Mulken, 'De kohieren'.

cerning income indicate that both the individual citizen and the municipal authorities were watching closely to see that the correct amount was being established. The registers also contained many corrections concerning migration within Tilburg or out-migration. This suggests that each year a new register was drafted on the basis of the previous one after which people who later appeared to have moved were crossed out and transferred to their new address. References concerning the old and new address made it possible, in most cases, to follow people throughout the town thereby providing a check of the population registers.

Problems in the use of the Tilburg tax registers turned up on the following occasions.

Prior to 1874 the registers recorded the number of apportionments on which the person was assessed for taxation instead of listing his or her income. The amount of tax that was due was mentioned but the level of income remained unclear. Through comparison of the amount of tax paid by a number of particular persons according to the 1873 and 1874 registers a satisfactory connection could be made between the incomes in 1874 and the apportionments of 1873.[2] A similar procedure for the registers between 1850 and 1873 was conducted so as to ensure a correct assessment of the apportionments over the period.

In 1898 a tax allowance was introduced based on the number of children in the household under the age of 16, and from 1916 onwards the income recorded had already been reduced by the appropriate allowance. However, the basis for allowance, the number of children, and the rates used were mentioned as well so that real incomes could easily be computed.

A more serious problem was created by the fact that after 1907 the authorities stopped recording those heads of household who did not exceed their personal tax allowance, so that in some cases occupational information had to be found elsewhere. However, after 1900 the level of income had risen substantially so that only a few households were exempted from taxation. If the registers immediately prior to or following the year for which occupation and income were required, also did not mention the person concerned, I resorted to the occupational information in population registers or city directories. In this period the recording of

---

[2] This was done with the help of the separate collector's registers following a lay-out similar to the taxation listings.

occupations in the population registers seemed to have improved somewhat; for instance, from 1900 onwards the occupational status of the head, self-employed or wage earner, was consistently and quite correctly mentioned.

The registers for the period 1910–13 were inaccessible due to the loss of the alphabetical indexes that were required after 1910. In these cases the registers of 1909 and 1914 were used. The same problem applied to the 1917 register in lieu of which the 1918 register was used.

In addition to the tax registers the militia registers were used in order to obtain occupational information on the sons at the start of their careers. The population registers do not usually provide occupations for adolescents or young adults as long as they are not the head of the household and the family's breadwinner. Therefore, we made use of the military enrollment registers which yearly and alphabetically listed all 19 year-old male inhabitants. The registers record a considerable amount of personal information, including the young man's occupation.[3] In addition, both parents' names were recorded enabling a correct and swift identification procedure. Given the elaborate regulations to which the registers were subject, they are considered very reliable. But of course, the entry on occupation is based on information provided by the individual himself, thereby introducing a subjective element. However, considering the circumstances under which this information was provided, there is no reason to assume that information was frequently and greatly distorted. The only problem encountered in the use of the militia registers concerned those following the year 1901; all registers after this date were confiscated in 1940 by the German military authorities. For a number of sons reaching the age of 19 after 1901 occupational information in the population register was used.

The militia registers were used for only one allocation of social position: that of the sons at age 19. (See main text for explanation of the various allocations (p. 119).) Categorization could, therefore, proceed only on the basis of occupation. The tax registers were used for all remaining allocations of social class which enabled stratification on the basis of both occupation and income. The listing below should give some indication of the categorization procedure.

Class I: Upper upper class
This contained the local elite: big industrialists and commercial

---

[3] See Koerhuis and van Mulken, 'De militieregisters'.

entrepreneurs. The minimum income required for this category was fl.2200 or 20 apportionments. In practice the main difference between class I and II was the level of income.

Class II: Lower upper class

In this class we find the larger independent producers, professionals, for instance, a physician or a technical engineer, industrial manufacturers or merchants. Income should exceed fl.1200 or 10 apportionments and could range up to fl.2200.

Class III: Middle class

This contained master craftsman, butcher and baker, clerical worker, salesman, schoolteacher, café proprietor, mill overseer, chief bench worker, chief train conductor and shopkeeper. Placement in this category was conditional upon being assessed for taxation for at least an income of fl.500 or, prior to 1874, for three apportionments. The only exception was made for schoolteachers whose income was sometimes below the margin for this class. Incomes ranged within this class from fl.500 to fl.1200.

Class IV: Skilled labourers

Those categorized as skilled workers were: various artisanal workers, skilled textile occupations such as weaver, spinner, loom-fixer, mechanic and all factory workers assessed for taxation. Traders, shopkeepers and other minor commercial occupations if not assessed for taxation. Some of the occupations in this class were earning wages over and above the tax-free minimum level but most did not.

Class V: Unskilled labourers

This group contained the following occupations: factory worker, day labourer, worker, servant, watchman, piecer, woolsorter, spooler, soldier, porter, farmhand, errand-boy etc. Incomes were always below the tax-free threshold so that not one of the persons categorized into class V was able to pay the tax.

Most occupations could be placed quite satisfactorily within the scheme outlined above. However, those factory workers who were not assessed for taxation may not always have been correctly categorized in class V. It was quite possible for a skilled mill worker to remain under the level of the tax threshold. In all such cases we checked with the occupational entries in the population register, making corrections when necessary. For the period after 1910 extensive corrections were necessary in the income range required for classes I, II and III. Incomes started to rise rapidly, as a result of

World War I, while some sectors of the local economy (metallurgical sector) were more affected by this rise than others (textiles). This had the effect that the range of incomes within classes began to diverge further, while considerable overlap developed between classes. Minimal income levels in this period required for class I, II and III were respectively fl.4000, fl.3000 and fl.1500.

Appendix 17 *Type of first departure for sons by initial social class for two age-cohorts of married couples*

Departure	Lower class	Skilled labour	Middle class	Upper class
Cohort 1849–1890				
marriage	67.5	67.4	38.9	14.6
migration	18.1	18.8	40.3	46.9
to others	2.5	4.1	1.4	8.3
to kin	1.3	1.2	5.6	2.1
unknown	10.6	8.5	13.9	27.1
N	160	340	72	48
Cohort 1880–1920				
marriage	47.1	47.2	25.3	10.4
migration	41.9	37.5	60.3	85.4
to others	7.8	10.2	6.9	2.1
to kin	2.9	2.7	5.5	—
unknown	0.3	2.5	2.1	2.1
N	308	443	146	48

Appendix 18 *Type of first departure for daughters by initial social class for two age-cohorts of married couples*

Departure	Lower class	Skilled labour	Middle class	Upper class
Cohort 1849–1890				
marriage	70.2	69.8	54.0	27.6
migration	14.2	12.4	20.6	48.3
to others	3.5	8.6	14.3	1.7
to kin	4.3	1.7	6.4	1.7
unknown	7.8	7.6	4.8	20.7
N	141	291	63	58
Cohort 1880–1920				
marriage	46.0	38.6	22.0	16.3
migration	29.3	33.7	62.6	79.6
to others	20.6	22.8	12.9	—
to kin	1.0	3.1	1.6	2.0
unknown	3.2	1.8	1.6	2.0
N	311	386	123	49

Appendix 19 *Type of final departure for sons by initial social class for two age-cohorts of married couples*

Departure	Lower class	Skilled labour	Middle class	Upper class
Cohort 1849–1890				
marriage	76.4	76.9	52.1	27.7
migration	14.0	12.8	31.0	44.7
to others	1.3	3.9	—	6.4
to kin	—	0.9	4.2	2.1
unknown	8.3	5.6	12.7	19.2
N	157	337	71	47
Cohort 1880–1920				
marriage	59.9	59.8	41.1	45.5
migration	26.4	24.5	40.4	50.0
to others	11.0	10.3	12.8	2.3
to kin	2.3	3.7	5.0	—
unknown	0.3	1.6	0.7	2.3
N	299	428	141	44

Appendix 20 *Type of final departure for daughters by initial social class for two age-cohorts of married couples*

Departure	Lower class	Skilled labour	Middle class	Upper class
Cohort 1849–1890				
marriage	77.9	74.1	58.7	40.4
migration	8.8	10.7	20.6	40.4
to others	3.7	6.9	9.5	1.8
to kin	3.7	1.0	6.4	1.8
unknown	5.9	7.2	4.8	15.8
N	136	290	63	57
Cohort 1880–1920				
marriage	55.9	48.0	38.3	32.6
migration	24.0	22.8	46.7	65.1
to others	16.5	24.7	12.5	—
to kin	0.7	2.9	1.7	2.3
unknown	3.0	1.6	0.8	—
N	304	377	120	43

Appendix 21 *Proportion of sons still at home before final departure from parental household by initial social class for two age-cohorts of married couples*

Age group	Labour class	Middle class	Upper class
Cohort 1849–1890			
15 year-old	84.3	82.6	82.2
20 year-old	78.7	81.4	72.6
25 year-old	53.5	67.6	57.8
30 year-old	20.3	39.8	38.2
35 year-old	10.1	19.8	20.6
40 year-old	4.1	11.6	7.1
45 year-old	1.1	3.4	1.9
50 year-old	0.2	1.2	0.0
N	766	115	73
Cohort 1880–1920			
15 year-old	78.8	74.6	72.5
20 year-old	72.8	66.2	68.7
25 year-old	47.7	51.3	51.6
30 year-old	18.3	26.3	17.0
35 year-old	8.7	11.5	6.3
40 year-old	3.4	3.4	3.5
45 year-old	0.9	0.6	1.8
50 year-old	0.0	0.0	0.0
N	1078	201	69

Appendix 22 *Proportion of daughters still at home before final departure from parental household by initial social class for two age-cohorts of married couples*

Age group	Labour class	Middle class	Upper class
Cohort 1849–1890			
15 year-old	81.4	79.4	82.2
20 year-old	74.3	73.3	71.6
25 year-old	45.2	57.3	43.5
30 year-old	21.0	35.8	24.4
35 year-old	12.0	17.8	11.8
40 year-old	5.7	7.6	6.9
45 year-old	1.2	1.1	2.9
50 year-old	0.2	0.0	0.0
N	744	121	90
Cohort 1880–1920			
15 year-old	78.5	78.3	82.9
20 year-old	66.7	72.5	70.8
25 year-old	39.8	54.2	42.6
30 year-old	18.3	37.1	23.7
35 year-old	7.5	21.3	8.8
40 year-old	4.0	10.4	8.8
45 year-old	1.0	0.8	3.7
50 year-old	0.0	0.0	0.0
N	1020	180	70

Appendix 23 *Mobility of heads of first-phase nuclear families, 1849–1890*
age-cohort of married couples

	I	II	III	IV	V	total
I	3 75.0	1 25.0				4 1.9
II	5 55.6	4 44.4				9 4.2
III	2 11.8	1 5.9	10 58.8	3 17.7	1 5.9	17 8.0
IV		2 1.6	6 4.7	87 68.5	32 25.2	127 59.6
V			1 1.8	23 41.1	32 57.1	56 26.3
total	10 4.7	8 3.8	17 8.0	113 53.1	65 30.5	N=213

Total upward mobility	18.8%
Unchanged	63.8%
Total downward mobility	17.4%
Mobility of labourers into class III–I	4.9%

Appendix 24 *Mobility of heads of first-phase extended families,*
1849–1890 age-cohort of married couples

	I	II	III	IV	V	total
I	3 75.0		1 25.0			4 5.2
II		2 100.0				2 2.6
III		9 45.0	10 50.0	1 5.0		20 26.0
IV			2 6.2	24 75.0	6 18.8	32 41.6
V				4 21.0	15 79.0	19 24.7
total	3 3.9	11 14.3	13 16.9	29 37.7	21 27.3	N=77

Total upward mobility	19.5%
Unchanged	70.1%
Total downward mobility	10.4%
Mobility of labourers into class III–I	3.9%

Appendix 25 *Mobility of heads of first-phase nuclear families, 1880–1920 age-cohort of married couples*

	I	II	III	IV	V	total
I	4 100.0					4 1.8
II	4 57.1	2 72.4	1 14.3			7 3.2
III	4 16.0	3 12.0	12 48.0	5 20.0	1 4.0	25 11.4
IV			16 15.2	76 72.4	13 12.4	105 47.7
V			4 12.1	36 45.6	39 49.4	79 35.9
total	12 5.5	5 2.3	33 15.0	117 53.2	53 24.1	N=220

Total upward mobility	30.5%
Unchanged	60.5%
Total downward mobility	9.1%
Mobility of labourers into class III–I	10.9%

Appendix 26 *Mobility of heads of first-phase extended families,*
1880–1920 age-cohort of married couples

	I	II	III	IV	V	total
I	4 100.0					4 2.8
II	5 71.4	1 14.3	1 14.3			7 5.0
III	6 19.4	6 19.4	16 51.6	2 6.5	1 3.2	31 22.0
IV			8 12.9	42 67.7	12 19.4	62 44.0
V			3 8.1	18 48.7	16 43.2	37 26.1
total	15 10.6	7 5.0	28 19.9	62 44.0	29 20.6	N=141

Total upward mobility	32.6%
Unchanged	56.0%
Total downward mobility	11.3%
Mobility of labourers into class III–I	11.1%

Appendix 27 *Mobility of heads of first-phase extended families, extended for 5 years or more, 1849–1890 age-cohort of married couples*

	I	II	III	IV	V	total
I	2 100.0					2 3.9
II		1 100.0				1 1.9
III		6 40.0	8 53.3	1 6.7		15 28.9
IV		1 4.4	2 8.7	16 69.6	4 17.4	23 44.2
V				2 18.2	9 81.8	11 21.2
total	2 3.9	8 15.4	10 19.2	19 36.5	13 25.0	N=52

Total upward mobility   21.2%
Unchanged   69.2%
Total downward mobility   9.6%

Mobility of labourers   8.8%
into class III–I

Appendix 28 *Mobility of heads of first-phase extended families, extended for 5 years or more, 1880–1920 age-cohort of married couples*

	I	II	III	IV	V	total
I	2 100.0					2 2.7
II	4 80.0	1 20.0				5 6.9
III	3 21.4	4 28.6	5 35.7	2 14.3		14 19.2
IV			3 9.1	22 66.7	8 24.2	33 45.2
V			2 10.5	10 52.6	7 36.8	19 26.0
total	9 12.3	5 6.9	10 13.7	34 46.6	15 20.5	N=73

Total upward mobility	35.6%
Unchanged	50.7%
Total downward mobility	13.7%
Mobility of labourers into class III–I	9.6%

Appendix 29 *Intergenerational mobility of sons under the age of 30 by social class and total mobility scores by first-phase household structure for two age-cohorts of married couples*

Class	Nuclear families	Extended families	Extended 5–> years
Cohort 1849–1890			
I	—	—	—
II	0.0	0.0	0.0
III	0.0	0.0	0.0
IV	1.1	4.9	6.8
V	56.2	59.3	57.9
total upward mobility	13.3	19.9	20.0
unchanged	57.2	43.9	41.5
total downward mobility	29.5	36.2	38.5
from class IV–V to III–I	0.8	2.9	4.1
N	610	196	130
Cohort 1880–1920			
I	—	—	—
II	0.0	0.0	0.0
III	1.6	8.3	13.9
IV	2.8	3.5	2.3
V	66.8	81.3	77.4
total upward mobility	26.8	25.7	25.0
unchanged	50.9	43.4	50.0
total downward mobility	22.3	30.9	25.0
from class IV–V to III–I	1.8	2.9	2.1
N	638	389	192

Appendix 30 *Intergenerational mobility of sons at the age of 30–35 by social class and total mobility scores by first phase household-structure for two age-cohorts of married couples*

Class	Nuclear families	Extended families	Extended 5–> years
Cohort 1849–1890			
I	—	—	—
II	21.4	0.0	0.0
III	3.9	5.4	9.5
IV	6.3	10.1	8.3
V	59.0	48.9	42.9
total upward mobility	18.2	19.6	17.7
unchanged	59.0	51.5	48.0
total downward mobility	22.8	28.8	34.3
from class IV–V to III–I	6.4	6.0	5.3
N	539	163	102
Cohort 1880–1920			
I	—	—	—
II	62.5	11.8	14.3
III	6.8	10.1	6.3
IV	11.5	13.5	8.2
V	80.4	84.6	82.4
total upward mobility	37.6	32.1	28.8
unchanged	48.9	48.5	54.4
total downward mobility	13.5	19.4	16.9
from class IV–V to III–I	9.1	13.5	9.6
N	622	377	184

Appendix 31 *Intergenerational mobility of sons at the age of 40 or above by social class and total mobility scores by first-phase household structure for two age-cohorts of married couples*

Class	Nuclear families	Extended families	Extended 5–> years
Cohort 1849–1890			
I	—	—	—
II	12.5	0.0	0.0
III	25.5	0.0	0.0
IV	12.2	13.3	13.0
V	73.8	58.5	36.4
total upward mobility	27.8	24.8	17.7
unchanged	51.8	56.6	56.1
total downward mobility	20.4	18.6	26.8
from class IV–V to III–I	11.5	7.9	8.8
N	446	129	82
Cohort 1880–1920			
I	—	—	—
II	83.3	35.7	35.7
III	19.5	41.3	77.3
IV	18.2	18.1	16.5
V	93.2	95.1	90.9
total upward mobility	47.5	44.0	46.6
unchanged	42.5	40.7	41.0
total downward mobility	10.0	15.3	12.4
from class IV–V to III–I	16.1	21.2	12.2
N	501	307	161

Appendix 32 *Number of households present and extended for specified family cycle years by initial social class of the head for two age-cohorts of married couples*

	Working class		Middle class		Upper class	
Year	Total	Extended	Total	Extended	Total	Extended
Cohort 1849–1890						
1	288	31	49	16	24	4
11	271	22	40	9	21	4
21	253	25	40	10	20	0
31	212	23	36	6	18	1
41	157	23	27	4	16	2
Cohort 1880–1920 (corrected sample)						
1	270	33	54	15	19	1
11	261	25	52	8	17	1
21	255	17	51	8	14	4
31	206	25	41	7	9	0
41	132	33	27	4	5	1

Appendix 33 *Number of households and persons involved in total population by age group and migration status of couple heading the household, Tilburg 1849 and 1880*

Age group	Non-migrant couples		Migrant couples		Mixed couples		Solitary heads[a]	
	hh	pp	hh	pp	hh	pp	hh	pp
1849[b]								
< 30	103	348	5	19	33	114	37	82
30–35	310	1521	51	266	153	747	53	155
35 >	707	4198	200	1111	452	2373	944	3125
total	1120	6067	256	1396	638	3234	1034	3362
1880[c]								
< 30	176	618	92	341	129	451	27	83
30–35	466	2370	281	1365	348	1674	47	113
35 >	1315	8033	794	4463	789	4491	1261	3991
total	1957	11021	1167	6169	1266	6616	1335	4187

[a] Included in this category are households headed by unmarried or widowed men and women
[b] Total persons: 14059
  Total households: 3048
  Not included: 161 persons in religious institutions
[c] Total persons: 27993
  Total households: 5725
  Not included: 613 persons in religious institutions

Appendix 34 *Proportion of households headed by migrant and non-migrant couples in 1849 and 1880 of all households headed by couples, in total research cohort and sample*[a]

Households headed by couples in 1849	
All households headed by couples	1376
of which migrant	256
All households in 1814–1819 cohort	361
of which migrant	51
All households in sample	361
of which migrant	51
Households headed by couples in 1880	
All households headed by couples	3124
of which migrant	1167
All households in 1845–1850 cohort	747
of which migrant	281
All households in sample	389
of which migrant	169

[a] Excluded in this survey are households headed by couples of mixed migration status. The figures for the 1880–1920 sample concern the uncorrected sample; the corrected sample contains 343 households of which 156 are households headed by migrants.

Appendix 35 *Proportion of extended households during second phase of family cycle for migrant and non-migrant families for two age-cohorts of married couples*[a]

Cohort	Non-migrant %	Migrant %
1849–1890	29.3	30.0
1880–1920	45.3	43.2

[a] Corrected sample was used for the 1880–1920 cohort.

Appendix 36 *Mean length of co-residence in years for different types of kin by migration status of household for two age-cohorts of married couples*[a]

Type of kin	Non-migrant	Migrant
Cohort 1849–1890		
fathers (in-law)	5.3	4.5
mothers (in-law)	6.6	5.6
brothers (in-law)	8.8	7.2
sisters (in-law)	11.0	8.1
married children	4.0	5.1
grandchildren	4.0	3.6
other kin	7.2	3.0
all	5.8	5.8
N	272	39
Cohort 1880–1920		
fathers (in-law)	5.2	5.5
mothers (in-law)	6.8	4.6
brothers (in-law)	4.1	3.0
sisters (in-law)	7.1	2.5
married children	1.4	1.5
grandchildren	2.1	1.5
other kin	5.1	3.8
all	2.9	2.4
N	469	287

[a] Uncorrected sample was used for the 1880–1920 cohort

Appendix 37 *Class-specific upward social mobility of heads by first-phase household structure and migration status for two age-cohorts of married couples*[a]

	Non-migrants		Migrants	
	Nuclear	Extended	Nuclear	Extended
Cohort 1849–1890				
upper upper class	0.0	0.0	0.0	0.0
lower upper class	55.6	0.0	—	—
middle class	13.3	50.0	50.0	33.3
skilled labour	6.0	3.3	10.0	50.0
unskilled labour	42.0	21.1	50.0	—
N	194	68	19	9
Cohorts 1880–1920				
upper upper class	—	0.0	0.0	—
lower upper class	100.0	100.0	50.0	50.0
middle class	26.7	28.6	30.0	47.1
skilled labour	14.7	10.0	16.2	18.2
unskilled labour	47.5	52.2	54.1	64.3
N	126	84	94	57

[a] Uncorrected sample was used for the 1880–1920 cohort

Appendix 38 *Initial social position of heads by first-phase household structure and migration status for two age-cohorts of married couples*[a]

	Non-migrant		Migrants	
	Nuclear	Extended	Nuclear	Extended
Cohort 1849–1890				
upper classes	6.2	7.4	5.3	11.1
middle class	7.7	20.6	10.5	66.7
skilled labour	60.3	44.1	52.6	22.2
unskilled labour	25.8	27.9	31.6	0.0
N	194	68	19	9
Cohort 1880–1920				
upper classes	0.8	8.3	10.6	7.0
middle class	11.9	16.7	10.6	29.8
skilled labour	54.0	47.6	39.4	38.6
unskilled labour	33.3	27.4	39.4	24.6
N	126	84	94	57

[a] Corrected sample was used for the 1880–1920 cohort

Appendix 39 *Total upward intergenerational mobility by age group of sons and migration status for two age-cohorts of married couples*[a]

Age group sons	Non-migrant	Migrant
Cohort 1849–1890		
< 30	15.6 (733)	8.2 (73)
30–35	18.9 (641)	14.8 (61)
40 >	27.5 (534)	22.0 (41)
Cohort 1880–1920		
< 30	23.5 (663)	31.6 (364)
30–35	32.3 (650)	41.6 (349)
40 >	43.6 (566)	52.1 (242)

[a] Absolute numbers of observation given in parentheses

Appendix 40 *Social stratification and class-specific upward mobility of migrant sons by first-phase household structure, 1880–1920 age-cohort of married couples*[a]

Sons	Stratification		Upward mobility	
	Nuclear	Extended	Nuclear	Extended
Age 30–35				
upper upper class	3.2	0.8	0.0	—
lower upper class	0.5	6.3	50.0	0.0
middle class	13.6	32.0	4.4	10.8
skilled labour	67.4	49.2	16.9	24.0
unskilled labour	15.4	11.7	85.4	82.4
N	221	128	221	128
Age 40 >				
upper upper class	3.2	7.1	0.0	—
lower upper class	0.6	7.1	75.0	0.0
middle class	24.7	31.0	23.1	26.1
skilled labour	52.5	53.6	26.6	20.6
unskilled labour	19.0	1.2	87.0	100.0
N	158	84	158	84

[a] Uncorrected sample was used for the 1880–1920 cohort

Appendix 41 *Effect of social class on the relationship urbanity of background and first-phase family structure for migrant households, 1880–1920 age-cohort of married couples*

Class	% extended families	
	Rural	Urban
middle upper class	44.8	70.0
labour class	30.4	39.3

Nineteenth-century weavers' books and the identification of domestic weavers and factory workers

Chapter 7 makes use of the nineteenth-century weavers' books, or weavers' registers, of the textile factories of 'Diepen', 'Brouwers' and 'Van Dooren en Dams'. The purpose was to identify unambiguously a number of domestic weavers and factory weavers who would subsequently be traced in the population registration of the town. Other sources fail to make the distinction between different types of weavers. For the nineteenth-century period the companies mentioned above were the only ones with weavers' registers available. The following series were processed:

> The company of Brouwers: a complete series covering the period 1892–1900 (Municipal Archive Tilburg, depot inventory numbers 189 up to and including 197).
> The company of Diepen: covering three single years 1887, 1892, 1897 (Municipal Archive Tilburg, inventory numbers 282, 283, 284, all deposited with the Catholic University of Brabant in Tilburg).
> The company of Van Dooren en Dams: books covering four separate years 1875, 1880, 1887, 1893 (Municipal Archive Tilburg, inventory numbers 1–4).

Of the three the company of Brouwers was the only one which registered its domestic weavers separately from the weavers within the factory walls. A remark to this extent was recorded in one of the books on the inside of the cover: one half of the register was said to pertain to the so-called *buitenwevers*, the domestic weavers, whilst the other side recorded the power-loom weavers, the *binnenwevers*. A check of the weavers' book over the year 1892 confirmed this division. The weavers recorded as factory weavers clearly displayed a number of characteristics typical of power-loom weavers. They were paid much lower wages for each ply of wool compared to the domestic weavers while their production exceeded the productive capacity of the hand loom. A comparison of the names on each side of this register further revealed that the same names did not appear on both sides. Unfortunately, however, the registers of this company were sometimes barely legible due to sloppy writing. Moreover, registration of the weavers' names was often too poor for easy and unambiguous identification in the population registration of the town. As a result only a small number of weavers could ultimately be extracted from the registers of the company of Brouwers.

The weavers' registers of the other two companies, Diepen and Van Dooren en Dams, provided no direct clue as to the question of what type of weavers they contained. In his thesis on Armand Diepen, owner of the Diepen mill in the second half of the nineteenth century, the economist Van den Dam assumed that the Diepen registers recorded only those weavers working within the factory walls.[1] A comparison of some of the figures provided by Van den Dam himself in his book and a thorough examination of the registers themselves, however, revealed the registers to contain both domestic and factory weavers. It appeared that the total number of woollen cloths produced in the period 1883–4 by the weavers Van den Dam had handled for his study, corresponded almost exactly to the number mentioned elsewhere concerning total production for the same period.[2] The obvious conclusion, therefore, must be that the registers contained all of the weavers working for the Diepen mill. This could then also explain the enormous variation in the numbers of active weavers per month as well as the few recorded female weavers who were most certainly domestic weavers. Finally, this conclusion is more consistent with the small number of looms reported in the factory's stock inventory. For the registers of Van Dooren en Dams the situation appeared to be the same. Here too, female weavers were occasionally recorded in the weavers' books, while there was a tremendous amount of fluctuation in the numbers of active weavers which constantly and amply exceeded the number of looms mentioned in the stock inventories. Thus, for the registers of the companies of Van Dooren en Dams, and Diepen, which were otherwise high-quality material with clear and full name references, I next tried to develop a method separating both types of weavers on the basis of the information provided by the books themselves. It proved impossible to decide unequivocally for all weavers concerned. In the end only a

---

[1] van den Dam, *Arnold Leon Armand Diepen*.
[2] Compare ibid., pp. 223, 227.

small number of weavers whose status was clear and unambiguous could be extracted from the weavers' registers according to the following process of selection.

The weavers' books recorded every single cloth produced by the weaving mill together with the name of the weaver, date of production and the technical specification of the yarn that was used. This information was listed by order of date of production. Automated processing of the registers facilitated the arrangement of the material according to a large number of different criteria. Among others, total production listings were made for the two mills, by month as well as for every individual weaver separately. This information was next supplemented with figures concerning the number of looms placed in the mill to determine the maximum number of weavers which could be employed by the mill at any one moment.[3] Both mills employed a large number of weavers which could only mean, considering the small number of looms operated in the mills, that the large majority of them were actually domestic weavers. A simple and straightforward identification of the power-loom weavers on the basis of the volume of their production, however, was not possible in all cases. Full-scale mechanization of the weaving mills was at that time still very much in its infancy, especially in the Diepen mill, so that a considerable proportion of the few looms were outdated or second-hand, and could attain only modest production levels. Only towards the beginning of the 1890s did most of the mills undertake a thorough modernization of the weaving process. Therefore, judging solely by their production capacity most of the weavers could well have been either domestic weavers or factory weavers.

The next step was to conduct an identification process of all 458 names of weavers extracted from the weavers' books in the population registers of the town and the civil registers on births, deaths and marriages.[4] Positive identification was assumed if, first, both Christian and last names corresponded and, second, the person was stated to be a weaver. Potential candidates for identification could only be males above the age of 18. When more than one candidate was available meeting all of the requirements, positive identification was considered impossible.

[3] This was recorded in the factory inventories. For the Diepen mill see: Municipal Archive Tilburg, inventory numbers 406–7, likewise deposited with the Catholic University of Brabant in Tilburg. For the Van Dooren en Dams mill see: Municipal Archive Tilburg, depot inventory numbers 13 and 16.
[4] This number included double-counts due to names appearing in the weavers' books of more than one of the three companies.

For every successfully identified weaver all occupational entries to be found in the population registers, the civil registers as well as in the yearly taxation listings for the entire period 1880–1900 were collected. Thus, occupational and demographic histories emerged on the basis of which a decision had to be taken concerning the question on which side of the factory walls each weaver was employed. For a limited number of names this decision was easy enough: they can only have been power-loom weavers considering the level of production that was reached in the 1890s.[5] For some of the Diepen weavers the correctness of the decision was confirmed by the fact that these weavers were referred to as working on 'mechanical looms' in two alphabetical registers listing all of the company's weavers.[6] Other indications provided further justification. After about 1890 these weavers started to receive a lower wage rate due to large increases in the productivity of the looms they were operating. In addition, a few were recorded in the population register of 1890 as a 'mechanical weaver'. This part of the procedure resulted in a limited number of names who were both positively identified as power-loom weavers and also successfully identified in the population registration.

Most of the remaining weavers were of two types. One group comprised those with a very marginal production, only two or three 'pieces' per month during the two or three months in which production peaked each year. The other group consisted of regular but average producers throughout the year. Among these later weavers there were still some who must have been factory weavers because those who had already been identified as power-loom weavers did not occupy all of the looms in the two mills. Nevertheless, even from this latter group a number of weavers could be identified to have been domestic weavers. In the first place it appeared that some had been working for both mills, which were actually situated in the same neighbourhood, at the same time. In that case the weaver in question was assumed to be a domestic weaver at work for both employers, which practice was not infrequent at busy times. In addition, a number of the Diepen or Van Dooren en Dams weavers also appeared in the registration of the Brouwers company, and these were then also

---

[5] In the assessment of the productive capacity of the looms reported in the factory inventories I received the invaluable help of J. Esman, the master-weaver of the Netherlands Textile Museum in Tilburg, and P.J.M. van Gorp, well known for his many writings on technical aspects of the history of Dutch textiles. To determine the monthly production a power-loom weaver could possibly attain, given the working hours of the time, use was made of the technical information available in the museum on the looms these weavers were operating.

[6] See Diepen Archive: Municipal Archive Tilburg, inventory number 289–90.

accepted as domestic weavers. Finally, all identified weavers of Diepen and Van Dooren en Dams who were marginal and part-time producers were accepted into the sample of domestic weavers. The weavers thus collected all had to meet with one other requirement: they had to be registered consistently as 'weaver' in every single year in the taxation listings and the population registers of the period. Even the occasional entry of 'factory worker' would disqualify them as domestic weaver. In this way we hope to have excluded all weavers who combined factory labour with home production.

After this laborious and time-consuming process of selection the two samples, of domestic weavers and factory weavers, proved too small for meaningful analysis: the samples counted seventy-three and twenty-three weavers respectively. The two samples therefore needed to be supplemented in a number of ways. To begin with, seventy-two factory workers could be drawn from the 1880–1920 cohort and, quite unexpectedly, another two households of domestic weavers were found in this group as well. Next, a number of domestic weavers could be obtained from two other research projects. The first concerned a project on the employees of the textile company of J.A.A. Kerstens, conducted by T. Wagemakers, while the second involved an oral history research into the conditions in the Tilburg domestic industry carried out by De Bruijn, Ruiter and Strouken.[7] This finally resulted in a sample containing ninety-five factory workers and another one consisting of eighty-nine domestic weavers. For all of them the entire history of the household they headed was reconstructed with the help of the population registers and, whenever necessary, the civil registers on births, deaths and marriages.

---

[7] Wagemakers, 'Een levensgeschiedenis'; de Bruijn, Ruiter and Strouken, *Drapiers en buitenwevers*. Both studies were able to construct a short list of domestic weavers who were still active in the period 1900–10.

Appendix 43 *Date of beginning of the history of the household for domestic weavers and factory workers*[a]

Decade	Domestic weavers	Factory workers	
1840–1849	1.1	—	
1850–1859	5.6	—	
1860–1869	28.1	12.9	(13.7)
1870–1879	38.2	67.1	(68.4)
1880–1889	15.7	11.8	(10.5)
1890–1899	10.1	5.9	(5.3)
1900–1910	1.1	2.4	(2.1)
N	89	85	(95)

[a] Figures in between brackets concern the uncorrected sample of factory workers. Note: date of beginning of household need not necessarily coincide with date of marriage of husband and wife. See main text, page 119.

Appendix 44 *Age of head at start of the history of the household for domestic weavers and factory workers*

Age	Domestic weavers	Factory workers
20–24 year old	25.8	24.7
25–29 year old	44.9	60.0
30–39 year old	28.1	14.1
40– > year old	1.1	1.2
N	89	85

Appendix 45 *Occupational diversification in households of domestic weavers and factory workers: wives, fathers, and fathers-in-law with same occupation as head*

	Domestic weavers	Factory workers
Wife with		
same occupation	4.3	1.1
textile occupation	18.1	17.2
textiles, including factory workers	30.9	56.9
seamstresses	16.0	6.4
domestic servants	13.8	11.8
other occupations	5.3	4.3
without occupation	31.9	18.2
N	94	93
Father with		
same occupation	57.1	23.5
textile occupation	57.1	23.5
textiles, including factory workers	64.3	56.8
artisanal occupation	16.1	17.6
other occupations	10.1	15.6
without occupation	8.9	5.8
N	56	51
Father-in-law with		
same occupation	37.5	18.5
textile occupation	37.5	16.6
textiles, including factory workers	45.8	46.2
artisanal occupation	8.3	27.7
other occupations	37.5	14.8
without occupation	8.3	7.4
N	48	54

Appendix 46 *Number of households present for specified family cycle years for households of domestic weavers and factory workers*

Year	Domestic weavers	Factory workers
1	89	85
11	89	84
21	87	84
31	78	77
41	58	57
46	35	35
47	32	31
48	29	29
49	22	21
50	19	12
51	18	8
52	14	6
53	13	4
54	10	3
55	8	—
56	5	—
57	4	—
58	3	—
59	3	—
60	3	—
61	3	—
62	2	—
63	1	—
64	1	—

Appendix 47 *Relationship to head of co-resident kin in the households of domestic weavers and factory workers[a]*

Relation	Domestic weavers	Factory workers
parents	7.4	17.1
siblings	9.4	26.4
married children	29.5	21.4
grandchildren	47.6	26.4
uncles/aunts	—	1.4
cousins	0.7	2.1
other kin	5.4	5.0
N	149	140

[a] Corrected sample of factory workers was used.

Appendix 48. Proportion of extended family households by family cycle year for domestic weavers and factory workers, households starting between 1860–1880 (corrected sample for factory workers)

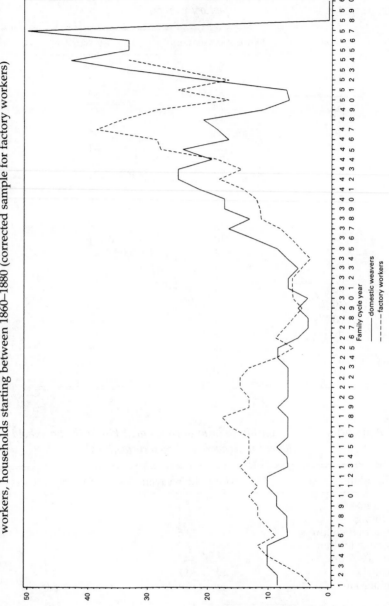

Appendix 49.   Mean number of children present in the household by family cycle year for domestic weavers and factory workers (corrected sample for factory workers)

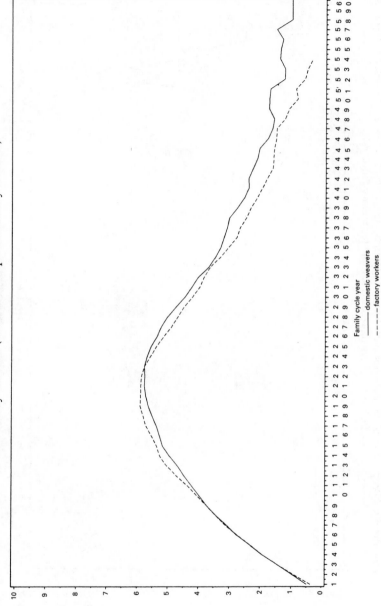

Family cycle year
—— domestic weavers
- - - - factory workers

Appendix 50. Proportion of households with kin or lodgers by family cycle year for domestic weavers and factory workers (corrected sample for factory workers)

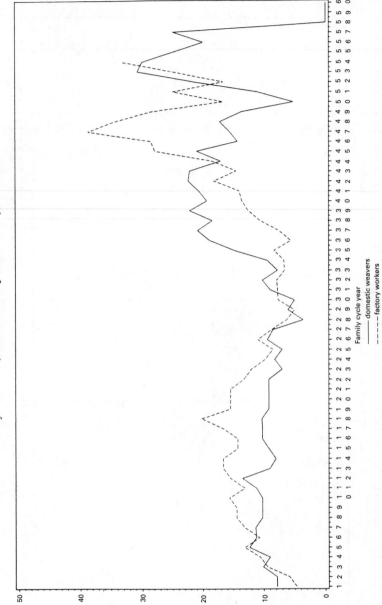

Appendix 51 *Age at final departure from parental household for sons and daughters of domestic weavers and factory workers*[a]

Age	Domestic weavers		Factory workers	
	Sons	Daughters	Sons	Daughters
< 10 year-old	0.0	2.1	3.3	1.4
10–14 year-old	0.5	2.1	0.8	3.8
15–19 year-old	4.4	7.7	7.5	14.6
20–24 year-old	28.6	34.0	28.8	33.0
25–29 year-old	41.2	36.1	42.5	30.7
30–34 year-old	15.4	13.4	12.5	12.7
35–39 year-old	7.1	3.1	2.9	1.4
40 > year-old	2.7	1.5	1.7	2.4
mean age	26.9	25.0	25.0	24.2
N	182	194	240	212

[a] Departures not coinciding with the end of the history of the household. Uncorrected sample of factory workers was used.

Appendix 52 *Type of final departure from parental household for sons and daughters of domestic weavers and factory workers*[a]

Type of departure	Domestic weavers		Factory workers	
	Sons	Daughters	Sons	Daughters
marriage	64.3	60.8	64.2	52.8
migration	20.9	13.4	25.0	21.7
to hh of kin	1.1	3.1	0.8	1.4
to hh of others	12.6	21.1	8.3	22.2
unknown	1.1	1.5	1.7	1.9
N	182	194	240	212

[a] Excluding departures by death and those coinciding with the end of the history of the household. Uncorrected sample of factory workers.
hh = household

Appendix 53 *Proportion of sons and daughters still at home by age group for domestic weavers and factory workers[a]*

Age	Domestic weavers		Factory workers	
	Sons	Daughters	Sons	Daughters
15 year-old	74.1	75.0	72.1	69.9
20 year-old	64.8	61.7	59.2	54.2
25 year-old	44.2	33.8	32.8	29.1
30 year-old	16.5	12.7	10.1	11.9
35 year-old	9.0	6.1	3.0	2.3
40 year-old	4.6	3.6	0.3	1.7
45 year-old	1.2	1.5	0.3	0.7
50 year-old	0.4	0.7	0.0	0.0

[a] Uninterrupted residence within the home is measured. Sample of factory workers is uncorrected.

Appendix 54 *Proportion unmarried by age group for sons and daughters of domestic weavers and factory workers[a]*

Age	Domestic weavers		Factory workers	
	%	N	%	N
Sons				
19 year-old	100.0	236	98.0	273
24 year-old	82.4	213	79.6	245
29 year-old	42.0	181	33.2	205
34 year-old	25.5	157	16.4	159
39 year-old	15.9	113	7.7	104
44 year-old	8.8	68	3.9	52
49 year-old	5.9	34	0.0	11
54 year-old	13.3	15	0.0	2
59 > year-old	0.0	7	—	—
Daughters				
19 year-old	98.0	246	98.4	246
24 year-old	71.3	216	68.7	217
29 year-old	36.1	180	39.3	186
34 year-old	20.0	135	18.3	131
39 year-old	17.2	99	15.5	84
44 year-old	14.9	67	5.1	39
49 year-old	18.2	33	0.0	7
54 year-old	18.2	11	0.0	1
59 > year-old	40.0	5	—	—

[a] Sample of factory workers is uncorrected.

Appendix 55 *Proportion sons and daughters still at home by age group for domestic weavers and factory workers, only those born after 1870[a]*

Age	Domestic weavers		Factory workers	
	Sons	Daughters	Sons	Daughters
15 year-old	78.4	77.3	77.0	75.3
20 year-old	71.3	70.2	71.3	64.0
25 year-old	51.2	46.4	45.4	40.3
30 year-old	23.8	19.7	17.3	19.9
35 year-old	12.7	8.9	6.1	6.9
40 year-old	5.4	5.4	2.0	4.2
45 year-old	0.9	3.2	0.7	1.1
50 year-old	0.0	0.5	0.0	0.0
N	273	277	352	336

[a] Those who have not yet departed from the parental home permanently. Uncorrected sample of factory workers.

Bibliography

Alter, G. *Family and the female life course: the women of Verviers, Belgium, 1849–1880*, Madison: University of Wisconsin Press, 1988.

Anderson, M. *Family structure in nineteenth-century Lancashire*, Cambridge: Cambridge University Press, 1971.

'The study of family structure', in: E.A. Wrigley (ed.), *Nineteenth-century society. Essays in the use of quantitative methods for the study of social data*, Cambridge: Cambridge University Press, 1972, pp. 47–81.

'Some problems in the use of census type material for the study of family and kinship systems', in: J. Sundin, E. Söderlund (eds.), *Time, space and man*, Atlantic Highlands: Humanities Press, 1979, pp. 69–81.

Approaches to the history of the western family 1500–1914, London: Macmillan, 1980.

Anderson, M. (ed.) *The sociology of the family*, Harmondsworth: Penguin Education, 1971.

Andorka, R., T. Faragó, 'Pre-industrial household structure in Hungary', in: R. Wall, J. Robin, P. Laslett (eds.), *Family forms in historic Europe*, Cambridge: Cambridge University Press, 1983, pp. 281–308.

Anshen, R.N. (ed.) *The family: its function and destiny*, New York: Harper and Row, 1949.

Ariès, Ph. *Centuries of childhood*, Harmondsworth: Penguin Books, 1973.

L'Enfant et la vie familiale sous l'Ancien Régime, Paris: Editions du Seuil, 1973.

Armstrong, W.A. 'The interpretation of the census enumerators books for Victorian towns', in: H.J. Dyos (ed.), *The study of urban history*, London: Edward Arnold, 1968, pp. 67–87.

Barentsen, P.A. 'Het gezinsleven in het oosten van Noord-Brabant', in: G.J.M. van den Brink, A.M.D. van der Veen, A.M. van der Woude (eds.), *Werk, kerk en bed in Brabant. Demografische ontwikkelingen in oostelijk Noord-Brabant 1700–1920*, 's-Hertogenbosch: Stichting Brabantse Regionale Geschiedbeoefening: Het Noordbrabants Genootschap, 1989, pp. 17–32.

de Belder, J. 'Beroep of bezit als criterium voor de sociale doorsnede. Een aanzet tot uniformiteit van reconstructie-methoden', *Tijdschrift voor Sociale Geschiedenis*, 6 (1976), pp. 257–79.

Berkner, L.K. 'The stem family and the developmental cycle of the peasant household: an eighteenth-century Austrian example', *American Historical Review*, 77 (1972), pp. 398–418.

'Recent research on the history of the family in western Europe', *Journal of Marriage and the Family*, 35 (1973), pp. 395–405.

'The use and misuse of census data for the historical analysis of family structure', *Journal of Interdisciplinary History*, 5 (1975), pp. 721–38.

'Inheritance, land tenure and peasant family structure: a German regional comparison', in: J. Goody, J. Thirsk, E.P. Thompson (eds.), *Family and inheritance: Rural society in Western Europe, 1200–1800*, Cambridge: Cambridge University Press, 1976, pp. 71–95.

Bodnar, J. *Workers' world: kinship, community, and protest in an industrial society, 1900–1940*, Baltimore: London: Johns Hopkins University Press, 1982.

Boeren, P.C. *Het hart van Brabant*, Tilburg: Henri Bergmans, 1942.

Bonfield, L., R. Smith, K. Wrightson (eds.) *The world we have gained*, Oxford: Blackwell, 1986.

Boonstra, O.W.A. 'De dynamiek van het agrarisch-ambachtelijke huwelijkspatroon. Huwelijksfrequentie en huwelijksleeftijd in Eindhoven, 1800–1900', in: G.J.M. van den Brink, A.M.D. van der Veen, A.M. van der Woude (eds.), *Werk, kerk en bed in Brabant. Demografische ontwikkelingen in oostelijk Noord-Brabant 1700–1920*, 's-Hertogenbosch: Stichting Brabantse Regionale Geschiedbeoefening: Het Noordbrabants Genootschap, 1989, pp. 83–100.

Bott, E. *Family and social network: roles, norms and external relationships in ordinary urban families*, London: Tavistock Publications, 1968.

Braun, R. *Industrialisierung und Volksleben: Die Veränderungen der Lebensformen in einem ländlichen Industriegebiet vor 1800*, Zürich/Stuttgart: Rentsch Verlag, 1960.

Sozialer und kultureller Wandel in einem ländlichen Industriegebiet, Zürich/Stuttgart: Rentsch Verlag, 1965.

'The impact of cottage industry on an agricultural population', in: D.S. Landes (ed.), *The rise of capitalism*, New York: Macmillan, 1966, pp. 53–64.

van den Brink, G.J.M. 'De structuur van het huishouden te Woensel, 1716–1738', in: G.J.M. van den Brink, A.M.D. van der Veen, A.M. van der Woude (eds.), *Werk, kerk en bed in Brabant. Demografische ontwikkelingen in oostelijk Noord Brabant 1700–1920*, 's-Hertogenbosch: Stichting Brabantse Regionale Geschiedbeoefening: Het Noordbrabants Genootschap, 1989, pp. 33–52.

van den Brink, G.J.M., A.M.D. van der Veen, A.M. van der Woude (eds.) *Werk, kerk en bed in Brabant. Demografische ontwikkelingen in oostelijk Noord-Brabant*, 's-Hertogenbosch: Stichting Brabantse Regionale Geschiedbeoefening: Het Noordbrabants Genootschap, 1989.

van den Brink, T. 'The Netherlands Population Registers', *Sociologia Neerlandica*, 3 (1966), pp. 32–53.

de Bruijn, M.W.J., H.Th.M. Ruiter, H.T.L.C. Strouken, *Drapiers en buitenwevers, Een onderzoek naar de huisnijverheid in de Tilburgse wollenstoffenindustrie*, Utrecht: Nederlands Centrum voor Volkscultuur, 1992.

Bulder, E.A.M. *Household structures of elderly in the past. A case study of two Dutch communities in the period 1920–1940*, NIDI-report no. 13, The Hague, 1990.

302 *Bibliography*

Cancian, F.M., L.W. Goodman, P.H. Smith, 'Capitalism, industrialization and kinship in Latin-America: major issues', *Journal of Family History*, 3 (1978), pp. 319–36.

Christensen, H.T. (ed.) *Handbook of marriage and the family*, Chicago: Rand McNally, 1964.

Conklin, G.H. 'The household in Urban India', *Journal of Marriage and the Family*, 38 (1976), pp. 771–9.

'Family modernization values and factory employment: an example from South India', *Journal of Comparative Family Studies*, 8 (1977), pp. 315–26.

Conze, W. (ed.) *Sozialgeschichte der Familie in der Neuzeit Europas*, Stuttgart: Klett, 1976.

Crozier, D. 'Kinship and occupational succession', *The Sociological Review*, new series, 13: 1 (1965), pp. 15–45.

Cross, G., P.R. Shergold, 'The family economy and the market: wages and residence of Pennsylvania women in the 1890s', *Journal of Family History*, 11 (1986), pp. 245–65.

Czap, P. 'The perennial multiple family household, Mishino, Russia, 1782–1858', *Journal of Family History*, 7 (1982), pp. 5–26.

van den Dam, J.P.A. *Arnold Leon Armand Diepen, 1846–1895*, Tilburg: Stichting Zuidelijk Historisch Contact, 1966.

Danhieux, L. 'The evolving household: the case of Lampernisse, West Flanders', in: R. Wall, J. Robin, P. Laslett (eds.), *Family forms in historic Europe*, Cambridge: Cambridge University Press, 1983, pp. 409–20.

Dasberg, L. et al. 'Het socioculturele leven in Nederland 1875–1895', in: *Algemene Geschiedenis der Nederlanden*, vol. 13, Haarlem: Fibula-Van Dishoeck, 1978, pp. 127–64.

'Het socioculturele leven in Nederland 1895–1914', in: *Algemene Geschiedenis der Nederlanden*, vol. 13, Haarlem: Fibula-Van Dishoeck, 1978, pp. 359–94.

Deere, C.D. 'The differentiation of the peasantry and family structure: a Peruvian case study', *Journal of Family History*, 3 (1978), pp. 422–39.

Degler, C.N. *At odds: women and the family in America from the revolution to the present*, Oxford: Oxford University Press, 1980.

Demos, J. *A little commonwealth: family life in Plymouth colony*, New York: Oxford University Press, 1970.

Demos, J., S. Spence Boocock (eds.), *Turning points: historical and sociological essays on the family*, American Journal of Sociology Supplement, vol. 84, Chicago 1978.

Derks, H.L.H. 'De bevolkingsontwikkeling vanaf 1809 tot 1940', in: H.F.J.M. van den Eerenbeemt, H.J.A.M. Schurink (eds.), *De opkomst van Tilburg als industriestad. Anderhalve eeuw economische en sociale ontwikkeling*, Nijmegen: Centrale Drukkerij, 1959, pp. 129–45.

Diederiks, H.A. 'Klassen en klasebewustzijn. Een commentaar', *Mededelingenblad, Orgaan van de Nederlandse Vereniging tot beoefening van de Sociale Geschiedenis*, 46 (1974), pp. 109–18.

van Dijk, H. *Rotterdam 1810–1880; aspecten van een stedelijke samenleving*, Schiedam: Interbook, 1976.

van Doremalen, H. 'Arbeid en arbeidsomstandigheden in Tilburg 1810–1870', unpublished MA thesis, Nijmegen University, 1982.

'Sociale onrust, aktie en vroege organisatievormen onder de arbeidende bevolking in Tilburg 1825–1875', *De Lindeboom*, 6 (1982), pp. 115–34.

'Tilburg en de arbeidsenquête van 1887, achtergronden en kant-tekeningen', *De Lindeboom*, 7 (1983), pp. 65–100.

Douglass, W.A. 'Cross-sectional and longitudinal analyses of extended family households in an eighteenth-century South Italian town', unpublished paper for the Conference on Family Structures and Relations in the Modern Era: The Italian Experience and European Comparisons, Trieste, Italy, 1983.

'The Basque stem family household: myth or reality?', *Journal of Family History*, 13 (1988), pp. 75–90.

Drake, M. *Historical demography: problems and projects*, Open University Press, London, 1974.

Dyos, H.J. (ed.) *The study of urban history*, London: Edward Arnold, 1968.

van den Eerenbeemt, H.F.J.M. (ed.) *Aspecten van het sociale leven in Breda na 1850*, Tilburg: Stichting Zuidelijk Historisch Contact, 1965.

van den Eerenbeemt, H.F.J.M., H.J.A.M. Schurink (eds.), *De opkomst van Tilburg als industriestad. Anderhalve eeuw economische en sociale ontwikkeling*, Nijmegen: Centrale Drukkerij, 1959.

van den Eerembeemt, H.J.F.M. *Ontwikkelingslijnen en scharnierpunten in het Brabants industrieel bedrijf 1777–1914*, Tilburg: Stichting Zuidelijk Historisch Contact, 1977.

Elder, G.H. Jr, 'Families and lives: some developments in life-course studies', *Journal of Family History*, 12 (1987), pp. 179–99.

Engelen, Th.L.M. *Fertiliteit, arbeid, mentaliteit. De vruchtbaarheidsdaling in Nederlands-Limburg, 1850–1960*, Assen: Van Gorcum, 1987.

Engelen, Th., J. Hillebrand, 'Vruchtbaarheid in verandering. Een gezinsreconstructie in Breda, 1850–1940', *Tijdschrift voor sociale geschiedenis*, 11 (1985), pp. 248–89.

Enquete betreffende de werking en uitbreiding der wet van 19 September 1874 (Staatsblad no. 180) en naar den toestand van fabrieken en werkplaatsen, Sneek, 1887.

Flandrin, J.-L. *Families in former times: kinship, household and sexuality*, Cambridge: Cambridge University Press, 1979.

Frinking, G.A.B. 'Demografische analyse van de huwelijkssluiting in Nederland', in: H.J. Heeren (ed.), *Huwelijksleeftijd in Nederland. Demografische en sociologische beschouwingen over de dalende huwelijksleeftijd in Nederland*, Meppel: Boom, 1973, pp. 23–39.

Frinking, G.A.B., F.W.A. van Poppel, *Nuptialiteit in Nederland*, Voorburg: NIDI, 1976.

Geschiedenis van de statistiek in het Koninkrijk der Nederlanden, 's-Gravenhage: Belinfante, 1902.

Giele, J., G.J. van Oenen, 'De sociale structuur van de Nederlandse samenleving rond 1850', *Mededelingenblad, Orgaan van de Nederlandse Vereniging tot beoefening van de Sociale Geschiedenis*, 45 (1974), pp. 2–33.

'Wel discussie, geen vooruitgang. Een antwoord op klassen en klassenbewustzijn van Herman A. Diederiks', *Tijdschrift voor Sociale Geschiedenis*, 1 (1975), pp. 147–50.

'Theorie en praktijk van het onderzoek naar de sociale structuur', *Tijdschrift voor Sociale Geschiedenis*, 5 (1976), pp. 167–86.

Glasco, L.A. 'The life cycles and household structure of American ethnic groups: Irish, Germans, and native-born whites in Buffalo, New York

1855', in: T.K. Hareven (ed.), *Family and kin in urban communities 1700–1930*, New York: Franklin Watts, 1977, pp. 122–43.

'Migration and adjustment in the nineteenth-century city: occupation, property and household structure of native-born whites, Buffalo, New York, 1855', in: T.K. Hareven, M.A. Vinovskis (eds.), *Family and population in nineteenth-century America*, Princeton: Princeton University Press, 1978, pp. 154–79.

Goode, W.J. *World revolution and family patterns*, New York: The Free Press, 1963.

'Industrialization and family change', in: B.F. Hoselitz, W.E. Moore (eds.), *Industrialization and society*, New York: Unesco, 1966, pp. 237–55.

Goody, J., J. Thirsk, E.P. Thompson (eds.) *Family and inheritance: rural society in Western Europe, 1200–1800*, Cambridge: Cambridge University Press, 1976.

Gordon, C. *The bevolkingsregisters and their use in analysing the co-residential behaviour of the elderly*, NIDI-report no. 9, The Hague, 1989.

Greenfield, S.M. 'Industrialization and the family in sociological theory', *American Journal of Sociology*, 27 (1961–2), pp. 312–22.

Grever, M. et al. (eds.) *Vrouwendomein. Woongeschiedenis van vrouwen in Nederland*, Amsterdam: SUA, 1986.

Grever, M., A. van der Veen (eds.) *Bij ons moeder en ons Jet. Brabantse vrouwen in de 19de en 20ste eeuw*, Zutphen: Walburg Pers, 1989.

Griffen, S., C. Griffen, 'Family and business in a small city: Poughkeepsie, New York, 1850–1880', in: T.K. Hareven (ed.), *Family and kin in urban communities 1700–1930*, New York: Franklin Watts, New Viewpoints, 1977, pp. 144–64.

Gutmann, M.P., E. Van de Walle, 'New sources for social and demographic history: the Belgian population registers', *Social Science History*, 2 (1978), pp. 121–43.

Haines, M.R. 'Industrial work and the family life cycle, 1889–1890', in *Research in Economic History*, (1979), pp. 289–356.

Haks, D. *Huwelijk en gezin in Holland in de 17de en 18de eeuw*, Assen: Van Gorcum, 1985.

Hareven, T.K. 'Family time and industrial time: family and work in a planned corporation town, 1900–1924', in: T.K. Hareven (ed.), *Family and kin in urban communities, 1700–1930*, New York: Franklin Watts, New Viewpoints, 1977, pp. 187–207.

Hareven, T.K. (ed.) *Family and kin in urban communities, 1700–1930*, New York: Franklin Watts, New Viewpoints, 1977.

'The dynamics of kin in an industrial community', J. Demos, S. Spence Boocock (eds.), *Turning points. Historical and sociological essays on the family*, American Journal of Sociology Supplement, vol. 84, Chicago 1978, pp. 151–83.

'Postscript: The Latin-American essays in the context of family history', *Journal of Family History*, 3 (1978), pp. 454–8.

Family time and industrial time. The relationship between the family and work in a New England industrial community, Cambridge: Cambridge University Press, 1982.

'Family history at the crossroads', *Journal of Family History*, 12 (1987), pp. ix–xxiii.

Harkx, W.A.J.M. *De Helmondse textielnijverheid in de loop der eeuwen. De grond-slag van de huidige textielindustrie 1794–1870*, Tilburg: Stichting Zuidelijk Historisch Contact, 1967.

Harris, C.C. *The family and industrial society*, London: Allen and Unwin, 1983.

Harris, C.C. (ed.) *Readings in kinship in urban society*, Oxford: Pergamon, 1970.

Heeren, H.J. (ed.) *Huwelijksleeftijd in Nederland. Demografische en sociologische beschouwingen over de dalende huwelijksleeftijd in Nederland*, Meppel: Boom, 1973.

van der Heijden, C.G.W.P. 'Gezin en huishouden in Oost-Brabant (1850–1900). Een aanzet tot beeldvorming', in: G.J.M. van den Brink, A.M.D. van der Veen, A.M. van der Woude (eds.), *Werk, kerk en bed in Brabant. Demografische ontwikkelingen in oostelijk Noord-Brabant 1700–1920*, 's-Herto-genbosch: Stichting Brabantse Regionale Geschiedbeoefening: Het Noordbrabants Genootschap, 1989, pp. 131–44.

Hill, R., R.H. Rodgers, 'The developmental approach', in: H.T. Christensen (ed.), *Handbook of marriage and the family*, Chicago: Rand McNally, 1964, pp. 171–211.

Hofstee, E.W. *De demografische ontwikkeling van Nederland in de eerste helft van de negentiende eeuw*, Deventer: Van Loghum Slaterus, 1978.

'Demografische ontwikkeling van de Noordelijke Nederlanden circa 1800 – circa 1975', in: *Algemene Geschiedenis der Nederlanden*, vol. 10, Haarlem: Fibula-Van Dishoeck, 1978, pp. 63–93.

Korte demografische geschiedenis van Nederland van 1800 tot heden, Haarlem 1981.

Hofstee, E.W., G.A. Kooy, 'Traditional household and neighbourhood group: survivals of the genealogical-territorial societal pattern in eastern parts of the Netherlands', *Transactions of the Third World Congress of Sociology*, 4 (1956), pp. 75–9.

Hoselitz, B.F., W. Moore, *Industrialization and society*, New York: Unesco, 1966.

Hubbard, W.H. 'Forschungen zur städtischen Haushaltsstruktur', in: W. Conze (ed.), *Sozialgeschichte der Familie in der Neuzeit Europas*, Stuttgart: Klett, 1976, pp. 283–92.

'Städtische Haushaltsstruktur um die Mitte des 19. Jahrhunderts', in: W.H. Schröder (ed.), *Moderne Stadtgeschichte*, Stuttgart: Klett, 1979, pp. 198–216.

Humphries, J. '"... The Most Free from Objection ...". The sexual division of labor and women's work in nineteenth-century England', *Journal of Economic History*, 87 (1987), pp. 929–50.

Idenburg, Ph.J. *Schets van het Nederlandse schoolwezen*, Groningen: Wolters, 1964.

Ishwaran, K. *Family Life in the Netherlands*, Den Haag: Van Keulen, 1959.

Jackson, J.H., Jr, 'Migration in Duisburg, 1867–1890: occupational and familial contexts', *Journal of Urban History*, 8 (1982), pp. 235–70.

Janssens, A.A.P.O. 'Industrialization without family change? The extended family and the life cycle in a Dutch industrial town, 1880–1920', *Journal of Family History*, 11 (1986), pp. 25–42.

'Een "direct-entry methodology" voor negentiende eeuwse bevolkingsre-gisters', *Cahiers voor Geschiedenis en Informatica*, 3 (1989), pp. 19–42.

'Managing longitudinal historical data; an example from nineteenth-century

Dutch population registers', *History and Computing*, 3 (1992) pp. 161–74.

de Jong, G.F.A. 'Enige sociale aspecten van de arbeid in de textielindustrie gedurende de 19e eeuw', in: H.F.J.M. van den Eerenbeemt, H.J.A.M. Schurink (eds.), *De opkomst van Tilburg als industriestad. Anderhalve eeuw economische en sociale ontwikkeling*, Nijmegen: Centrale Drukkerij, 1959, pp. 167–99.

'Industrial growth in the Netherlands (1850–1914)', in *Acta Historiae Neerlandica, Historical Studies in the Netherlands*, 5 (1971), pp. 159–212.

De industrialisatie in Nederland tussen 1850–1914, Nijmegen: SUN, 1976.

Katz, M.B. *The people of Hamilton, Canada West. Family and class in a mid-nineteenth-century city*, Cambridge Mass.: Harvard University Press, 1975.

Katz, M.B., I.E. Davey, 'Youth and early industrialization in a Canadian city', J. Demos, S. Spence Boocock (eds.), *Turning points. Historical and sociological essays on the family*, American Journal of Sociology Supplement, 84, Chicago 1978, pp. 81–120.

Katz, M.B., M.J. Doucet, M.J. Stern, *The social organization of early industrial capitalism*, Cambridge Mass.: Harvard University Press, 1982.

Keilman, N., N. Keyfitz, 'Recurrent issues in dynamic household modelling', in: Nico Keilman, Anton Kuijsten, Ad Vossen (eds.), *Modelling household formation and dissolution*, Oxford: Clarendon Press, 1980, pp. 254–85.

Kertzer, D.I. *Family life in Central Italy, 1880–1910*, New Brunswick: Rutgers University Press, 1984.

'Future directions in historical household studies', *Journal of Family History*, 10 (1985), pp. 98–107.

Kertzer, D.I., Andrea Schiaffino, 'Industrialization and coresidence: a life-course approach', in: P.B. Baltes and O.G. Brim, Jr (eds.), *Life span development and behavior*, vol. 5, New York: Academic, 1983, pp. 359–91.

Keune, A.W.M. 'De industriële ontwikkeling gedurende de 19e eeuw', in: H.F.J.M. van den Eerenbeemt, H.J.A.M. Schurink (eds.), *De opkomst van Tilburg als industriestad. Anderhalve eeuw economische en sociale ontwikkeling*, Nijmegen: Centrale Drukkerij, 1959, pp. 11–60.

Klep, P.M.M., 'Het huishouden in Westelijk Noord-Brabant; structuur en ontwikkeling, 1750–1849', *A.A.G. Bijdragen*, 18 (1973), pp. 23–94.

Bevolking en arbeid in transformatie. Een onderzoek in Brabant 1780–1900, Nijmegen: SUN, 1981.

'Over de achteruitgang van de Noordbrabantse huisnijverheid, 1810–1920', *Brabants Heem*, 39 (1987), pp. 29–44.

Klep, P.M.M., A. Lansink, W. van Mulken, *De kohieren van de gemeentelijke hoofdelijke omslag 1851–1922*, Broncommentaren, vol. 1 (1st revised edition), 's-Gravenhage, 1987.

Kloek, E. *Gezinshistorici over vrouwen*, Amsterdam: ASVA/SUA, 1981.

Kocka, J. 'Familie, Unternehmer und Kapitalismus. An Beispielen aus der frühen deutschen Industrialisierung', *Zeitschrift für Unternehmensgeschichte*, 24 (1979), pp. 99–135.

Koerhuis, B., W. van Mulken, *De militieregisters 1815–1922*, Broncommentaren, vol. 5, 's-Gravenhage 1986.

Kooij, P. *Groningen 1870–1914*, Assen: Van Gorcum, 1987.

Kumagai, F. 'Modernization and the family', *Journal of Family History*, 11 (1986), pp. 371–82.

Landes, D.S. (ed.) *The rise of capitalism*, New York: Macmillan, 1966.

Laslett, B. 'Social change and the family, Los Angeles, California, 1850–1870', *American Sociological Review*, 42 (1977), pp. 268–91.

Laslett, P. 'Mean household size in England since the sixteenth century', in: P. Laslett, R. Wall (ed.), *Household and family in past time*, Cambridge: Cambridge University Press, 1972, pp. 125–59.

Family life and illicit love in earlier generations, Cambridge: Cambridge University Press, 1977.

'Family and household as work group and kin group: areas of traditional Europe compared', in: R. Wall, J. Robin, P. Laslett (eds.), *Family forms in historic Europe*, Cambridge: Cambridge University Press, 1983, pp. 513–63.

Laslett, P., R. Wall (eds.) *Household and family in past time*, Cambridge: Cambridge University Press, 1972, pp. 1–25.

Leboutte, R. 'Household dynamics and industrialization: The Liégeoise Basse-Meuse in the second half of the nineteenth century', unpublished paper presented to the postgraduate workshop on 'Labour in transformation', Department of Social and Economic History, Nijmegen University, March 1989.

Lees, L.H. 'Patterns of lower-class life: Irish slum communities in nineteenth-century London', in: S. Thernstrom, R. Sennett (eds.), *Nineteenth-century cities*, New Haven, Conn.: Yale University Press, 1969, pp. 359–85.

Le Play, F. *L'Organisation de la famille selon le vrai modèle signalé par l'histoire de toutes les races et de tous les temps*, Tours: Alfred Mame et Fils, 1895.

Levine, D. 'Industrialization and the proletarian family in England', *Past and Present*, 107 (1985), pp. 168–203.

van Lieshout, J., B. Rikken, 'Geen lusten zonder lasten. Huwelijk, seksualiteit en geboorten op de Kempse zandgronden, 1850–1940', in: M. Grever, A. van der Veen (eds.), *Bij ons moeder en ons Jet. Brabantse vrouwen in de 19de en 20ste eeuw*, Zutphen: Walburg Pers, 1989, pp. 34–50.

Lindner, A. 'De dynamische analyse van huishoudens te Alphen, 1753–1803', in: G.J.M. van den Brink, A.M.D. van der Veen, A.M. van der Woude (eds.), *Werk, kerk en bed in Brabant. Demografische ontwikkelingen in oostelijk Noord-Brabant 1700–1920*, 's-Hertogenbosch: Stichting Brabantse Regionale Geschiedbeoefening: Het Noordbrabants Genootschap, 1989, pp. 53–82.

Litwak, E. 'Geographic mobility and extended family cohesion', *American Sociological Review*, 25 (1960), pp. 385–94.

'Occupational mobility and extended family cohesion', in *American Sociological Review*, 25 (1960), pp. 9–21.

van Loo, L.F. *Armelui, Armoede en bedeling te Alkmaar, 1850–1914*, Bergen: Octavo, 1986.

Lucassen, J., Th. van Tijn, 'Naschrift', *Tijdschrift voor Sociale Geschiedenis*, 5 (1976), pp. 187–9.

'Nogmaals: sociale stratificatie', *Tijdschrift voor Sociale Geschiedenis*, 4 (1976), pp. 74–91.

Medick, H. 'The proto-industrial family economy', *Social History*, 1 (1976), pp. 291–315.

Meurkens, P. *Bevolking, economie en cultuur van het oude Kempenland*, Bergeijk:

Stichting Eicha, 1985.

Mitterauer, M., R. Sieder, *The European family: patriarchy to partnership from the middle ages to the present*, Oxford: Blackwell, 1982.

Modell, J., F. Furstenberg, Th. Hershberg, 'Social change and transitions to adulthood in historical perspective', *Journal of Family History*, 1 (1976), pp. 7–32.

Morgan, P.H.J., *Social theory and the family*, London: Routledge and Kegan Paul, 1975.

Netting, R.Mc., R.R. Wilk, E.J. Arnould (eds.) *Households. Comparative and historical studies of the domestic group*, Berkeley: University of California Press, 1984.

Neuman, A.R. 'The influence of family and friends on German internal migration, 1880–1885', *Journal of Social History*, 13 (1979), pp. 277–88.

Nimkoff, M.F., R. Middleton, 'Types of family and types of economy', in: *American Journal of Sociology*, 66 (1960), pp. 215–25.

Onderzoekingen naar de toestanden in de Nederlandse huisindustrie, 3 vols., 's-Gravenhage: Algemeene Landsdrukkerij, 1914.

Park, R.E., E.W. Burgess, *The city*, Chicago: University of Chicago Press, 1925.

Parsons, T. 'The kinship system of the contemporary United States', *American Anthropologist*, 45 (1943), pp. 22–38.

'The social structure of the family', in: R.N. Anshen (ed.), *The family: its function and destiny*, New York: Harper and Row, 1949, pp. 173–201.

The social system, Glencoe, Ill.: The Free Press, 1952.

Essays in sociological theory, revised edition, Glencoe, Ill.: The Free Press, 1958.

'Reply to his critics', in: M. Anderson (ed.), *The sociology of the family*, Harmondsworth: Penguin Education, 1971, pp. 120–1.

Parsons, T., R.F. Bales, *The family: socialization and interaction process*, Glencoe, Ill.: The Free Press, 1955.

Peeters, H., L. Dresen-Coenders, T. Brandenbarg (eds.) *Vijf eeuwen gezinsleven. Liefde, huwelijk en opvoeding in Nederland*, Nijmegen: SUN, 1988.

Peters, J.P.M. 'De migratie naar Tilburg (1860–1870) en de Amerikaanse Secessie-oorlog', *Noordbrabants Historisch Jaarboek*, 1 (1984), pp. 143–77.

Pleck, E.H. 'Two worlds in one: work and family', in: *Journal of Social History*, 10 (1976–77), pp. 178–95.

van Poppel, F.W.A. *Stad en platteland in demografisch perspectief: De Nederlandse situatie in de periode 1850–1960*, NIDI-report 29, Voorburg 1984.

van de Put, C.A.M.M. *Volksleven in Tilburg rond 1900*, Assen: Van Gorcum, 1971.

Rabb, Th.K., R.I. Rotberg (eds.) *The family in history*, New York: Harper and Row, 1971.

Reddy, W.M. 'Family and factory: French linen weavers in the Belle Epoque', *Journal of Social History*, 8 (1974), pp. 102–12.

de Regt, A. *Arbeidersgezinnen en beschavingsarbeid. Ontwikkelingen in Nederland 1870–1940*, Meppel: Boom, 1984.

Riehl, W.H. *Die Naturgeschichte des Volkes als Grundlage einer deutschen Sozial-Politik*, Stuttgart: Cotta, 1873.

van Rijswijk-Clerkx, L.E. *Moeders, kinderen en kinderopvang*, Nijmegen: SUN, 1981.

Robin, J. 'Family care of the elderly in a nineteenth-century Devonshire parish', *Ageing and Society*, 4 (1984), pp. 505–16.

Rodman, H. 'Talcott Parsons' view of the changing American family', in: H. Rodman (ed.), *Marriage, family and society: a reader*, New York: Random House, 1969, pp. 262–87.

Rodman, H. (ed.) *Marriage, family and society: a reader*, New York: Random House, 1969.

Rossen, M.J.J.G. 'Het Tilburgse volkshuisvestingsbeleid 1902–1919', *Noord-brabants Historisch Jaarboek*, 3 (1986), pp. 183–206.

'Huize Lydia. Alleenstaande vrouwen in het begin van deze eeuw', in: M. Grever et al. (eds.), *Vrouwendomein. Woongeschiedenis van vrouwen in Nederland*, Amsterdam: SUA, 1986, pp. 97–108.

Het gemeentelijk volkshuisvestingsbeleid in Nederland. Een comparatief onderzoek in Tilburg en Enschede (1900–1925), Tilburg: Stichting Zuidelijk Historisch Contact, 1988.

Ruggles, S. *Prolonged connections: The rise of the extended family in nineteenth-century England and America*, Madison: University of Wisconsin Press, 1987.

Salaff, J. *Working daughters of Hong Kong: filial piety or power in the family?*, Cambridge, Cambridge University Press, 1981.

Sassen, A. *Een blik op de nijverheid en de toestand der arbeiders te Tilburg. Staatkundig en staathuishoudkundig Jaarboekje*, Amsterdam: Muller, 1871.

Schilstra, W.N. *Vrouwenarbeid in landbouw en industrie in Nederland in de tweede helft der negentiende eeuw*, Nijmegen: SUN, 1976.

Schröder, W.H. (ed.) *Moderne Stadtgeschichte*, Stuttgart: Klett, 1979.

Schurink, H.J.A.M., J.H. van Mosselveld (eds.) *Van heidorp tot industriestad*, Tilburg: Henri Bergmans, 1955.

Scott, J.W., L.A. Tilly, 'Women's work and the family in nineteenth-century Europe', *Comparative Studies in Society and History*, 17 (1975), pp. 36–64.

Segalen, M. 'The family cycle and household structure: five generations in a French village', *Journal of Family History*, 2 (1977), pp. 223–36.

'Life course patterns and peasant culture in France: a critical assessment', *Journal of Family History*, 12 (1987), pp. 213–24.

Sennett, R. *Families against the city. Middle class homes of industrial Chicago 1872–1890*, Cambridge, Mass.: Harvard University Press, 1970.

Seward, R.R. *The American family. A demographic history*, Beverly Hills: Sage, 1978.

Sheridan, G.J. Jr, 'Family and enterprise in the silk shops of Lyon: the place of labor in the domestic weaving economy, 1840–1870', *Research in Economic History*, supplement 3 (1984), pp. 33–60.

Shorter, E. 'Illegitimacy, sexual revolution, and social change in modern Europe', *Journal of Interdisciplinary History*, 2 (1971), pp. 237–73.

The making of the modern family, New York: Basic Books, 1975.

Sieder, R., M. Mitterauer, 'The reconstruction of the family life course: theoretical problems and empirical results', in: R. Wall, J. Robin, P. Laslett (eds.), *Family forms in historic Europe*, Cambridge: Cambridge University Press, 1983, pp. 309–45.

Silver, C.B. (ed.) *Frédéric Le Play on family, work and social change*, Chicago: University of Chicago Press, 1982.

Simons, M.D. 'De armoede in Tilburg ruim een eeuw geleden', in: H.J.A.M.

Schurink, J.H. van Mosselveld (eds.), *Van heidorp tot industriestad*, Tilburg: Henri Bergmans, 1955, pp. 192–206.

Smelser, N.J. *Social change in the industrial revolution. An application of theory to the Lancashire cotton industry 1770–1840*, London: Routledge and Kegan Paul, 1959.

'The modernization of social relations', in: M. Weiner (ed.), *Modernization: The dynamics of growth*, New York: Basic Books, 1966, pp. 119–48.

Smelser, N.J., S. Halpern, 'The historical triangulation of family, economy, and education', in: J. Demos, S. Spence Boocock (eds.), *Turning points. Historical and sociological essays on the family*, American Journal of Sociology Supplement, vol. 84, Chicago, 1978, pp. 288–315.

Smith, R.J. 'Early Victorian household structure', *International Review of Social History*, 15 (1970), pp. 68–84.

Sterkens, J.C.M. 'De zorg voor de vrouwelijke jeugd in de fabriek na 1850', in: H.F.J.M. van den Eerenbeemt, H.J.A.M. Schurink (eds.), *De opkomst van Tilburg als industriestad. Anderhalve eeuw economische en sociale ontwikkeling*, Nijmegen: Centrale Drukkerij, 1959, pp. 214–38.

Stone, L. *The family, sex and marriage in England 1500–1800*, London: Weidenfeld and Nicolson, 1977.

Strumingher, L.S. 'The artisan family: traditions and transition in nineteenth-century Lyon', in *Journal of Family History*, 2 (1977), pp. 211–22.

Sundin, J., E. Söderlund (eds.) *Time, space and man*, Atlantic Highlands: Humanities Press, 1979.

Sussman, M.B. 'The isolated nuclear family: fact or fiction', *Social Problems*, 64 (1959), pp. 333–39.

Sussman, M.B., L.G. Burchinal, 'The kin family network in urban-industrial America', in: M. Anderson (ed.), *Sociology of the family*, Harmondsworth: Penguin Education, 1971, pp. 99–112.

Taietz, P. 'The extended family in transition: a study of family life of old people in the Netherlands', in: C.C. Harris (ed.), *Readings in kinship in urban society*, Oxford: Pergamon, 1970, pp. 321–37.

Thernstrom, S., R. Sennett (eds.), *Nineteenth-century cities*, New Haven, Conn.: Yale University Press, 1969.

Thompson, E.P. *The making of the English working class*, London: Gollancz, 1963.

van Tijn, Th. 'Voorlopige notities over het ontstaan van het moderne klassebewustzijn in Nederland', *Mededelingenblad, Orgaan van de Nederlandse Vereniging tot beoefening van de Sociale Geschiedenis*, 45 (1974), pp. 34–37.

'Het sociale leven in Nederland', in: *Algemene Geschiedenis der Nederlanden*, vol. 13, Haarlem: Fibula-Van Dischoeck, 1978, pp. 295–326.

Tilly, Ch. (ed.) *An urban world*, Boston: Little, Brown, 1974.

Tilly, Ch., C. Harold Brown, 'On uprooting, kinship and the auspices of migration', in: C. Tilly (ed.), *An urban world*, Boston: Little, Brown, 1974, pp. 108–33.

Tilly, L.A. 'Occupational structure, women's work, and demographic change in two French industrial cities, Anzin and Roubaix, 1872–1906', in: J. Sundin, E. Söderlund (eds.), *Time, space and man*, Atlantic Highlands: Humanities Press, 1979.

Tilly, L.A., J.W. Scott, *Women, work, and family*, New York: Holt, Rinehart and Winston, 1978.

Uitkomsten der derde tienjarige volkstelling in het Koninkrijk der Nederlanden op den negentiende november 1849, 's-Gravenhage: Algemeene Landsdrukkerij, 1852.

Uitkomsten der zesde tienjarige volkstelling in het Koninkrijk der Nederlanden op den een en dertigste december 1879, 's-Gravenhage: Van Weelden en Mingelen, 1881.

van der Veen, A. *Zij telt voor twee. Vrouwenarbeid in Noord-Brabant, 1889–1940*, Zutphen: Walburg Pers, 1989.

van de Ven, W. 'Geloof, werk en liefde in Oost-Brabant. Over leef- en ervaringswereld van de Oostbrabantse plattelandsbevolking', *Brabants Heem*, 36 (1984), pp. 160–77.

Vermunt, K.J.G.M. 'Buitenechtelijke geboorten; een sociaal statistische be-schrijving van het verschijnsel te Breda gedurende de negentiende eeuw', in: H.F.J.M. van den Eerenbeemt (ed.), *Aspecten van het sociale leven in Breda na 1850*, Tilburg: Stichting Zuidelijk Historisch Contact, 1965, pp. 166–76.

Wachter, K.W., E.A. Hammel, P. Laslett, *Statistical studies of historical social structure*, New York: Academic, 1978.

Wagemakers, T. 'Over Buitenwevers, kinderarbeid, lonen en hun woningen naar enquete 1887', *Actum Tilliburgis*, 12 (1981), pp. 114–23.

'Een levensgeschiedenis in onderzoek', in: M. du Bois-Reijmond, T. Wagemakers (eds.), *Mondelinge geschiedenis*, Amsterdam: SUA, 1983, pp. 115–26.

'Excellente arbeiderscultuur; nr. 80 over C. Mommers & Co. 1907–1914', *Textielhistorische Bijdragen*, 25 (1985), pp. 59–69.

Wall, R. 'The age at leaving home', *Journal of Family History*, 3 (1978), pp. 181–202.

'Introduction', in: R. Wall, J. Robin, P. Laslett (eds.), *Family forms in historic Europe*, Cambridge: Cambridge University Press, 1983, pp. 1–63.

'Work, welfare and family: an illustration of the adaptive family economy', in: L. Bonfield, R. Smith, K. Wrightson (eds.), *The world we have gained*, Oxford: Blackwell, 1986, pp. 261–94.

'Relationships between the generations in British families past and present', unpublished paper of the Cambridge Group for the History of Population and Social Structure.

Wall, R., J. Robin, P. Laslett (eds.), *Family forms in historic Europe*, Cambridge: Cambridge University Press, 1983.

van de Walle, E. 'Household dynamics in a Belgian village, 1846–1866', *Journal of Family History*, 1 (1976), pp. 80–94.

van de Weijer, A. *De religieuse practijk in een Brabantse industriestad*, Assen: Van Gorcum, 1955.

Weiner, M. (ed.) *Modernization: the dynamics of growth*, New York: Basic Books, 1966.

Wolf, A.P. 'Family life and the life cycle in rural China', in: R. McC. Netting, R.R. Wilk, E.J. Arnoud (eds.), *Households. Comparative and historical studies of the domestic group*, Berkeley: University of California Press, 1984, pp. 279–98.

van der Woude, A.M. 'De trek van alleenlopenden naar Eindhoven tussen 1865 en 1920', in: G.J.M. van den Brink, A.M.D. van der Veen, A.M. van der Woude (eds.), *Werk, kerk en bed in Brabant. Demografische ontwik-*

kelingen in oostelijk Noord-Brabant 1700–1920, 's-Hertogenbosch: Stichting Brabantse Regionale Geschiedbeoefening: Het Noordbrabants Genoot-schap, 1989, pp. 167–83.

van der Woude, A.M. 'De omvang en samenstelling van de huishouding in Nederland in het verleden', *A.A.G. Bijdragen,* 15 (1970), pp. 202–40.

'Variations in the size and structure of the household in the United Provinces of the Netherlands in the seventeenth and eighteenth centuries', in: P. Laslett, R. Wall (eds.), *Household and family in past time,* Cambridge: Cambridge University Press, 1972, pp. 299–319.

Wrigley, E.A. 'Reflections on the history of the family', *Daedalus,* 106 (1977), pp. 71–85.

Wrigley, E.A. (ed.) *Nineteenth-century society. Essays in the use of quantitative methods for the study of social data,* Cambridge: Cambridge University Press, 1972.

Yans-McLaughlin, V. 'Patterns of work and family organization: Buffalo's Italians', in: Th.K. Rabb, R.I. Rotberg (eds.), *The family in history,* New York: Harper and Row, 1971, pp. 111–27.

Family and Community: Italian immigrants in Buffalo, 1880–1930, Ithaca, NY: Cornell University Press, 1977.

Young, M., P. Willmott, *Family and kinship in East London,* London: Routledge and Kegan Paul, 1959.

Index

Cambridge Studies in Population, Economy and Society in Past Time

Titles available in paperback are marked with an asterisk